北大高等教育文库
·学术规范与研究方法丛书·

How to Write and Submit an Academic Paper in 18 Weeks

如何成为学术论文写作高手
针对华人作者的18周技能强化训练

[美]史帝夫·华乐丝(Steve Wallace)著

著作权合同登记号　图字：01-2015-1048

图书在版编目(CIP)数据

如何成为学术论文写作高手：针对华人作者的18周技能强化训练：英文/（美）华乐丝（Wallace, S.）著.—北京：北京大学出版社，2015.10
（北大高等教育文库·学术规范与研究方法丛书）
ISBN 978-7-301-26378-5

Ⅰ.①如…　Ⅱ.①华…　Ⅲ.①英语—论文—写作　Ⅳ.①H315

中国版本图书馆CIP数据核字（2015）第241973号

本书由华乐丝语文顾问有限公司授权北京大学出版社有限公司出版。

书　　名	如何成为学术论文写作高手：针对华人作者的18周技能强化训练 Ruhe Chengwei Xueshu Lunwen Xiezuo Gaoshou
著作责任者	[美]史帝夫·华乐丝　著
责任编辑	泮颖雯
标准书号	ISBN 978-7-301-26378-5
出版发行	北京大学出版社
地　　址	北京市海淀区成府路205号　100871
网　　址	http://www.pup.cn　　新浪微博：@北京大学出版社
电子信箱	zyl@pup.cn
电　　话	邮购部62752015　发行部62750672　编辑部62767857
印　刷　者	三河市北燕印装有限公司
经　销　者	新华书店
	650毫米×980毫米　16开本　22印张　310千字 2015年10月第1版　2021年12月第8次印刷
定　　价	69.00元

未经许可，不得以任何方式复制或抄袭本书之部分或全部内容。
版权所有，侵权必究
举报电话：010-62752024　电子信箱：fd@pup.pku.edu.cn
图书如有印装质量问题，请与出版部联系，电话：010-62756370

前　言

　　这些年来，我所能接触到的、关于专业性写作指导的教学材料一直让我感到沮丧和担忧。这些关于专业性写作的教材很难被学生理解。

　　写作本书的想法，源于我在台湾交通大学教授技术性写作课程的经验，以及一直萦绕我心的华人研究者的需要。本人在本书中所使用的概念和语言都是被尽可能地简化了的，目的是为了减少读者在学习技术性写作的过程中遇到的障碍。本书包含十六章，涵盖了写作、修改以及在国际性期刊上提交学术论文等内容。每一章都包括了以下的小节：

● 如何撰写……（How to...）

　　这一小节通过在开头提出一系列问题来说明一篇标准的研究论文中包含的每个部分。通过回答这些问题，学生能够收集起那些他们撰写论文所需要的信息。这本书提供了针对摘要、引言、研究方法、研究结果、讨论、参考文献以及推荐信等内容的版式设计指导。

● 常见的写作错误以及改正方式（Common Writing Errors and Their Corrections）

　　此小节介绍常见的写作错误，并给出改正后的例句。

● 标点符号（Punctuation Point）

　　这一小节通过具体例子来介绍最基础的一些英语语法规则。

● 写作进程（The Writing Process）

　　这一小节提供了一些关于如何通过培养良好的写作习惯来保持积极和高效的写作状态的小建议。

- **向学术期刊投稿的建议（Tips for Journal Submission）**

　　这一小节教授利用编辑回应、审读人评论以及期刊投稿指导等内容来掌握关键的发表论文策略。善用这些指南，学习者能够避免犯常见的投稿错误，譬如：攻击潜在的评论者，或是暗示论文此前被拒过。

- **不恰当的词汇以及改进建议（Inappropriate Vocabulary and Improvement）**

　　针对学生在技术性写作中常用的一些易被误解的单词和短语，这个小节将教给学生一些表述更有力的、可用于替换的单词或短语。

- **学术词汇（Academic Vocabulary）**

　　这个部分列举了每个学生都需要了解的一些重要词汇。

目　录

第一编　撰写引言

第一章	研究的问题是什么？	1
第二章	这个问题为什么重要？	35
第三章	研究所要指出的是什么矛盾或尚未被解答的问题？	59
第四章	研究正在挑战或拓展哪些先前得出的研究结果？	77
第五章	有什么解决方案？	94

第二编　撰写研究方法部分

| 第六章 | 如何研究这个问题？ | 116 |
| 第七章 | 如何着手？ | 136 |

第三编　撰写研究结果部分

| 第八章 | 观察到了什么？ | 155 |
| 第九章 | 如何描述数据？ | 174 |

第四编　撰写讨论部分

第十章	观察意味着什么？	196
第十一章	你的研究结果怎样才能引起更广泛的兴趣？	216
第十二章	如何清楚地描述因果关系？	233

第五编　修改论文

第十三章　如何运用例子?　　　　　　　　256

第六编　撰写摘要

第十四章　简而言之,你的报告阐述了什么?　　267

第七编　参考文献部分

第十五章　如何介绍帮助过我们的人?　　　　291

第八编　撰写给编辑的推荐信

第十六章　如何撰写给编辑的推荐信?　　　　317

参考文献　　　　　　　　　　　　　　　　　338

Table of Contents

I WRITING THE INTRODUCTION

Chapter 1 What Is the Problem? 1

Chapter 2 Why Is the Problem Important? 35

Chapter 3 What Conflicts or Unanswered Questions Does Your Research Address? 59

Chapter 4 What Previous Findings Are You Challenging or Extending? 77

Chapter 5 What Solution Do You Propose? 94

II WRITING THE METHODS SECTION

Chapter 6 How Did You Study the Problem? 116

Chapter 7 How Did You Proceed? 136

III WRITING THE RESULTS SECTION

Chapter 8 What Did You Observe? 155

Chapter 9 How Can You Describe Quantities? 174

IV WRITING THE DISCUSSION SECTION

Chapter 10 What Do Your Observations Mean? 196

Chapter 11 How Do Your Results Fit into the Broader Context? 216

Chapter 12 How Can You Describe Causes and
            Effects?   233

V REVISING

Chapter 13 How Can You Use Examples?   256

VI WRITING THE ABSTRACT

Chapter 14 What Is the Report About in Short?   267

VII CITATIONS

Chapter 15 How Can We Write About Others Who Have
            Helped Us?   291

VIII WRITING THE COVER LETTER TO THE EDITOR

Chapter 16 How Can We Write a Cover Letter to the
            Editor?   317

References   338

I WRITING THE INTRODUCTION

Chapter 1
What Is the Problem?

How to write the Introduction

The introduction is certainly the most read section of any research paper, and it largely determines the reader's or reviewer's attitude toward the work. Therefore, it is probably the most delicate part of the writing of a paper. Unfortunately, many people face difficulties when writing the introduction.

The purpose of an introduction is to present the motivation behind the research, with the intention of defending it. An introduction also places your paper in a theoretical context and helps the reader to clearly understand your objectives. In addition, the introduction should grab the reader's attention completely. Below, we discuss the major components that should be included in an ideal introduction.

- A broad *theme* or *topic* of the study should be stated.
- The *academic importance* of the paper should be explained.
- The available *literature* should be summarized and previous studies that are most relevant to your research should be *cited*. In addition, if a previous study is replicated, it should be clearly stated along with an in-text citation.
- A discussion of the *knowledge gap* and *inconsistencies* found

> should follow the literature, and the *benefits* of the study's main contribution should be highlighted.
> - A clear indication of the *research question* addressed in the study, specific *objectives* that guide your research, the *context* in which the study was conducted, and the *units of analysis* used in the study should be provided in the introduction.

Simply put, an introduction should elaborate on the *Motivation, Literature Review, Knowledge Gap*, and *Research Question*.

Since the introduction should only be a brief overview of the entire paper, elaborating on the major components is not necessary. Moreover, the introduction should be composed toward the end of writing a paper, because writing the entire paper first can help in highlighting the most important points.

The different parts of the introduction are elaborated in this section. Including these steps will help you to write an effective introduction to your paper.

I. Theme or Topic

Since your paper will also be read by people outside the domain, writing the paper in a simple, yet effective way is essential for people to understand the relevance of your research. In addition, it is important that you introduce the broad theme or topic of your research in the introduction for the reader to clearly understand what the research is about. To achieve this, the following points must be followed.

- *Avoid* the use of technical jargons in the introduction.
- *Do not* begin the introduction with the research question or hypothesis.
- *Define* technical terms and constructs (concepts).

II. Academic Importance

A paper's academic importance can be determined by the lack of previous research on the topic, and by highlighting the gaps and inconsistencies in the literature. However, writing a comprehensive review of the field should be avoided.

III. Literature

A summary of the available literature should be concise and should mostly include recent studies that are directly related to the research. In addition, some studies that should be included must be from the recent past (i.e., studies from the last five years). If the research is a replication of a previous study, a brief introduction to that study along with the citation should be mentioned in this section.

IV. Knowledge Gap

Since a research aims at expanding the knowledge on a specific topic, a research should also address specific knowledge gaps, inconsistencies, and controversies in the literature. In addition, the main contribution of the study should be mentioned in this component, which will contribute to motivate the importance of the study.

V. Research Question and Objectives

This component should clearly indicate
- The research question addressed in the paper;
- The specific research objectives that guide the research;
- The context in which the study was conducted;
- The units of analysis used in the paper.

VI. Outlined Structure

This component should only include a brief outline of the flow of the entire paper.

Citing the Literature

Following is the list of most important points to be remembered when providing citations in a literature.

Citing previous studies based on these points make the citations effective to your research. However, a few mistakes commonly seen when citing literature are

> - Avoid writing a comprehensive literature review of the field.
> - Citations must be current and relevant.
> - Avoid citing studies that do not have a direct relevance to the study.
> - Studies that contradict your study or propose alternate ideas must be cited.
> - Recent studies (not older than five years) must be cited to indicate the findings. Older studies should be cited only to explain a change of thought in a particular field or the development of a particular method.

- Citing one source repeatedly;
- Citing irrelevant sources;
- Over citing definitions;
- Misattributing sources;
- Citing implications as facts;
- Too many quotations.

Literature Review

A literature review forms the theoretical basis of an article and discusses published information in a particular field. It can be just a summary of the sources, but it usually is an organizational pattern and combines the summary, critical analysis, and synthesis, i.e., a recap, evaluation, and reorganization of information. Generally, a literature review provides a new interpretation of past studies, combines new interpretations with previous interpretations, or traces the intellectual progression of the field. This helps in relating the study to previous studies in that field. A literature review can be written to provide a theoretical framework and rationale for a research.

There are four questions that first-time researchers need to examine when writing a literature review.

- Which aspects should be included in a literature review?
- How should the information in a literature review be synthesized?
- How should the literature review be structured?
- What writing style should be used when writing a literature review?

I. Which Aspects Should Be Included in a Literature Review?

An effective literature review should always include the following components:

- A brief discussion of where and how the study or research conforms to the broader view of the field.
- A definition of all the key concepts and constructs used in the paper.
- A discussion that focuses and synthesizes previous relevant research findings.
- A summary of the existing approaches explaining how previous research-measured constructs the current study measures.
- A theoretical support for the hypotheses to be tested.

Reviewers will look for these five aspects in the literature review. However, these aspects should not be used as main headings.

II. How Should the Information in a Literature Review Be Synthesized?

Since a literature review is not a chronological summary of the paper, it is necessary to synthesize existing knowledge. This should be done *without* plagiarizing or paraphrasing previous studies. This section elaborates on how to synthesize three types of information, namely definitions, lists of attributes or factors, and opposing viewpoints.

▶ Definitions

All concepts or constructs and technical terms need to be defined in the literature. It is best to define the concept or term immediately after its first mention in the paper. However, these definitions should not be borrowed from previous research; rather a reviewed definition should be provided. In addition, these definitions should not be listed consecutively in a literature review.

▶ Attributes or Factors

Generally, authors list the different attributes, factors, elements, or issues when discussing a similar topic. These factors suggest the effectiveness of a particular method or technique. However, these attributes or factors should not be merely listed in the literature review. Instead, a summary of these factors should be included in the literature review.

▶ Opposing Viewpoints

Several authors studying a similar problem will share opposing viewpoints. However, these viewpoints can be compared to as a point of discussion in a literature review. In addition, the opposing viewpoints should clearly explain the differences in these viewpoints. To further enhance the literature review, specific viewpoints that are supported should be elaborated on briefly stating reasons for accepting those viewpoints.

III. How Should the Literature Review Be Structured?

To write an effective literature review, following a logical structure is crucial. That is, the different sections and subsections of the literature review should be linked. A few points that would help in better structuring the review are listed below.

- Place the specific topic being discussed in a relevant, yet broader context and then focus the discussion on more specific issues.
- The headings should be brief and should give a detailed overview of the review. One-word titles should be avoided.
- Use relevant diagrams and discuss the comparison between several constructs crucial to the research.
- Define the technical terms and concepts clearly.
- The text provided should be relevant to the headings under which they are provided.
- Provide a brief motivation for the hypotheses of the research.

IV. What Writing Style Should Be Used when Writing a Literature Review?

Literature reviews should generally be easy to read and understand. Simply put, a literature review should be clear for a non-academic person. This should be done while avoiding technical jargons, unfamiliar terms and phrases, and undefined technical abbreviations. In addition, having a clear and concise flow in the literature can help readers understand the entire process of the research.

State the research questions in the literature review and clearly elaborate on how the attempted research responds to those questions. When doing this, briefly elaborate on the methods used and also define the ways the research develop on or provide a contrast to previous studies.

To sum up this chapter, the introduction to a research paper should provide the *Motivation, Literature Review, Knowledge Gap*, and *Research Question*. Writing the introduction based on these points help ease this otherwise complex task. Similar to the abstract, the introduction is best written toward the end of the writing process. This may help in summarizing the entire paper effectively.

> **Reviewer's Comment**
>
> *"The paper's introduction needs to first address the more general aspects of the research topic before delving into the specifics of the problem. As a reader, I find myself lost and unable to tie the problem to the larger context."*
>
> — **Reviewer, *IEEE Computing***

The reviewer in the above statement is suggesting that the author needs to first identify the more general aspects of the research, and then move toward the more specific aspects. By presenting the more general elements of the topic early in the introduction, and then focusing on more specific information that provides context, the author would have been able to help his reviewer understand the problem in a larger context.

Provide your statement of purpose and rationale. A good strategy is to write your introduction "backwards" in the beginning. This means to start with your specific purpose and then choose the context that you address in your study question. After you choose the context, you will know what general information you need to begin writing your introduction.

What Is the Problem?

Begin your introduction by clearly identifying your subject area.

In the first few sentences of the introduction, use keywords from your title to focus directly on your topic. This places immediate focus on your subject without discussing information that is too general.

Summarize other studies to provide context, key terms, and concepts so your reader can understand your research.

The key strategy is to summarize what you already know about

> the problem before presenting your experiments or studies. You can do this with a general overview of the literature, but do not include specific or lengthy explanations that you will use in the discussion. Your statement of purpose and hypothesis should focus on general information from your literature review that supports the specific topic of your study. By doing so, you will help the reader and reviewer understand your research.

Describe the Problem Investigated

I. Establishing the Importance of the General Topic
- One of the most essential current discussions in Electrical Engineering is ...
- It is becoming increasingly difficult to ignore the X, Y, and Z problem.
- X is the leading cause of color break-up in Liquid Crystal Displays.
- In the new global economy, X has become a central issue for ...
- In the history of Y, X has been thought of as a key factor in ...

II. Or, You May Begin by Emphasizing Time
- In recent years, there has been an increasing interest in ...
- Recent developments in the field of X have led to a renewed interest in ...
- Recently, researchers have shown an increased interest in ...
- The past decade has seen the rapid development of X in many ...

Summarize Other Studies to Provide *Context, Key Terms,* and *Concepts*

I. General Descriptions of Relevant Literature
- A considerable amount of literature has been published on X. These studies ...

- The first serious discussions and analyses of X emerged during the 1970s with . . .
- What we know about X is largely based on empirical studies that investigate how . . .

II. General Reference to Previous Research (usually more than one author)

- Numerous studies have attempted to explain . . . (e.g., Smith, 1996; Kelly, 1998; Johnson, 2002).
- Recent evidence *suggests* that . . . (Smith, 1996; Jones, 1999; Johnson, 2001).
- Surveys such as those conducted by Smith (1988) *show* that . . .
- Several attempts *have been made* to . . . (Smith, 1996; Jones, 1999; Johnson, 2001).

III. References to Our Current State of Knowledge

- A relationship exists between an individual's working memory and the ability to . . . (Jones et al., 1998).
- Genetically modified varieties of maize are able to cross-pollinate with non-GM varieties (Smith, 1998; Jones, 1999).
- X is one of the most intense reactions following CHD (Lane, 2003).

IV. Explaining Keywords

- While a variety of definitions of the term X have been suggested, this paper uses the definition first suggested by Thomas (1998), who saw it as . . .
- Throughout this paper, the term X refers to . . .
- This article uses the acronym/abbreviation XYZ.

V. General Keyword Meanings/Application of Meanings

- *The term X has come to refer to* . . .
- *The term X is generally understood to mean* . . .
- *The term X has been applied to situations where* students . . .
- In broad biological *terms*, X *can be defined as* any stimulus that is . . .

Simple Three-part Definitions

Biology is defined as	a branch of the natural sciences	that is concerned with the study of living organisms and their interaction with each other and their environment.
Ecology may be defined as	a scientific study	that is concerned with the distribution and abundance of life and the interactions between organisms and their natural environment.
Research may be defined as	a systematic process	that consists of three elements or components: (1) a question, problem, or hypothesis; (2) data; and (3) analysis and interpretation of data.

I. Indicating Difficulties in Defining a Term

- *Various definitions of talent* are found in the field of language teaching.
- Talent is a commonly used concept in learning, yet it is *difficult to define precisely*.
- Smith (2001) identified two abilities *that might be collected under the term* talent:
    - (1) . . .
    - (2) . . .

II. Referring to People's Definitions of Terms

- Williams (1944) was apparently the first to *use the term* . . .
- Chomsky *wrote that* a semiconductor is a "mechanical device of some sort for producing . . ." (1967, p. 11).
- *According to a definition provided by* Jones (2001), talent is the maximally . . .
- *The term "talent" was used by* Rogers (2001) to refer to . . .
- Martinez (2001) *used the term "talent" to refer to* . . .
- For James (2001), talent *means/refers to* . . .

III. General Topic Classifications

- Bone is generally classified into two types: cortical bone, also known as . . . , and cancellous bone, or . . .

- The works of Aristotle fall under three categories: (1) dialogues and . . . ; (2) collections of facts and . . . ; and (3) systematic works.
- There are two basic approaches currently adopted by research on X. One is the Y approach, and the other is . . .

IV. Specific Topic Classifications
- Smith and Johnson (2009) argued that there are two broad categories of Y, which are as follows: (a) . . . ; and (b) . . .
- According to Aristotle, motion is of four types: (1) motion that . . . ; (2) motion that . . . ; (3) motion that . . . ; and (4) motion that . . .

V. Introducing a List of Factors
- There are three reasons why language research has become so important. These are . . .
- There are generally two outcomes when a patient undergoes X. These are . . .
- The disadvantages of the new approach can be discussed *under three headings, which are* . . .

VI. Referring to Other People's Lists of Factors
- Jamison (2008) suggested three conditions for its acceptance. First, X should be . . . Second, it needs to be . . . Third, . . .
- Martinez and Rodriguez (1999) *listed* X, Y, and Z as the major causes of infant mortality.
- Patrickson and Cook (2007) argued that *there are two broad categories* of Y, *which are as follows*: (a) . . . and (b) . . .

Tenses in the Introduction

Stage 1: Current Knowledge
Use the *present tense* when stating or reporting established facts:
> Fine motor skills *require* integrating muscular, skeletal, and neurological functions.

When reporting findings from multiple previous studies, use the

present perfect tense:
> Previous studies *have indicated* the need to further examine X.

Stage 2: Literature Review
Use the *present tense* when reporting established facts:
> The salt in most oceans *is* approximately 97% sodium chloride (Ritchie, 1999).

When referring to a single, previous study, use the *past tense*:
> Kurtz (2008) *found* that instructors allocated equal time to each group.

Note that the above sentence has two verbs. The first verb, "found," describes what Kurtz did in this 2008 study. The second verb, "allocated," is in the past tense because it describes what the "instructors" in this study *did* at the time the research was conducted. If this verb (called a "verb complement") were written in the present tense, the statement would be expressing a *fact* that is true for *all* "instructors" *everywhere*. Consider the next sentence and note the tense of the second verb:
> Baggio and Klinsmann (1994) revealed that DNA polymerase *performs* a vital function in DNA replication in animal cells.

In this example, the first verb is written in the past tense, again to explain what this study *did*. However, the verb complement (the second verb in the sentence) is written in the present tense because the finding of this study was established as a fact and, therefore, *true for everyone everywhere*.

Use the *present perfect tense* when reporting findings from multiple previous studies:
> Several researchers *have studied* the relationship between classroom lighting and standardized test performance (Jens, 2006; Kirby et al., 2008; Milner, 2009).

Note how the different verb tenses used in the following three sentences slightly change the meanings: • Owen and Shearer (2002) discovered that memory load *affects* brain activity. • Owen and Shearer (2002) discovered that memory load *affected* brain activity. • Owen and Shearer (2002) suggested that memory load *may affect* brain activity.

The first sentence uses the present tense "affects" to claim this study's finding as a fact. The second sentence uses the past tense to report the finding as being limited to the circumstances of the involved study, and the third sentence uses both a tentative verb "suggested" and a modal verb "may" to describe the implications of the finding.

Stage 3: Knowledge Gap
Report facts and currently accepted methods using the *present* tense:
> Little information *is* available on the risks and benefits of X vs. Y.

Refer to multiple previous studies using the *present perfect tense*.
> However, few studies *have reported* the effects of antioxidant seeds on the endocrine system.

Stage 4: Problem Statement
Use the *present tense* when writing report-focused statements:
> The aim of this paper *is* to determine the principal mechanical parameters of thin film deposited on a circular glass substrate.

When writing research-focused statements (referring to your own study), use the *past tense*:
> The purpose of this study *was* to determine whether or not a genetic correlation exists between performance levels at high and low temperatures.

Stage 5: Rationale for Study (optional)
When expressing expected outcomes or offering future recommendations, use the *present tense* with *conditional modal verbs* (such as *could*, *may*, and *might*):
> This research *may provide* an alternative to the common field measurement of soil erosion and runoff.

Common Writing Errors and Their Corrections

A difficult and complex error has to do with using the active and passive voice. The active voice, as a rule, is favored in most contexts. Active voice sentences are generally better focused and shorter than passive voice sentences. Many international academic journals ask researchers to use the active voice whenever possible. Passive voice sentences are difficult and unclear to understand. The passive voice is recommended when we do not know who is performing the action or when what is being done is being emphasized over who is doing it. An example of this would be the methods part of the paper, which emphasizes the results more than what is creating those results.

I. What Is Active Voice?

An author may write a sentence in one of two "voices"—active or passive. The active voice emphasizes the performer (or agent) of the action:

- Wind disperses plant seeds.
- Smith et al. investigated the relationship.
- The method analyzed the results.

The active voice is direct (performer-verb-receiver), vigorous, clear, and concise. The reader knows who is responsible for the action.

II. What Is Passive Voice?

The passive voice, by contrast, emphasizes the receiver (or product) of the action:

- Plant seeds are dispersed [by wind].
- The relationship was investigated [by Smith et al.].
- The results have been analyzed [by the method].

The passive voice is indirect (receiver-verb-performer) and can be weak, awkward, and wordy. The passive voice uses a form of the *verb to be* followed by a past participle (for example, *dispersed, investigated*) and a *by* phrase. If the *by* phrase is deleted, the reader will not directly know who or what performed the action.

In addition to being awkward, sentences written in the passive voice, if not constructed carefully, may contain grammatical errors such as dangling modifiers. Changing from passive to active voice corrects the error and strengthens the sentence:

Dangling: To investigate the source of nutrients, eggshell membranes were compared. (incorrect passive)
Correction: To investigate the source of nutrients, the study compared eggshell membranes. (active)

Dangling: After analyzing the samples, the plants were measured daily. (incorrect passive)
Correction: After analyzing the samples, the researcher measured the plants daily. (active)

Despite these disadvantages, the passive voice has a function in writing. In addition to allowing an author to vary the sentence structure, the passive voice has other important functions.

III. Active and Passive Voice

More than a century ago, scientists typically wrote in an active style that included the first-person pronouns *I* and *we*. Beginning in about the 1920s, however, these pronouns became less common as scientists adopted a passive writing style.

Considered to be objective, impersonal, and well suited to science writing, the passive voice became the standard style for medical and scientific journal publications for decades.

However, there were exceptions. For instance, in 1953, one elegantly written paper began:
- We wish to suggest a structure for the salt of deoxyribose nucleic acid (D.N.A.).[1]

The opening sentence of Watson and Crick's classic article is **simple, direct, and clear**. But suppose the authors had taken the passive point of view:

- In this paper, a structure is suggested for the salt of deoxyribose nucleic acid (D.N.A.).

The emphasis is now on the receiver of the action (the structure), but at a price—the sentence has lost its clarity (who suggested?), energy (passive verb), and overall impact.

IV. Emphasize the Active Voice

Currently, most medical and scientific style manuals support the active voice.

For example, the American Medical Association's *AMA Manual of Style* recommends that "in general, authors should use the active voice, except in instances in which the author is unknown or the interest focuses on what is acted upon."[2]

The *Publication Manual of the American Psychological Association (APA)* has similar advice: "Prefer the active voice . . . The passive voice is acceptable in expository writing and when you want to focus on the object or recipient of the action rather than on the actor."[3]

These manuals and other books on science writing recommend using the active voice as much as possible. An author may decide to focus on the receiver—and thus use the passive voice—when the performer is unknown or of less importance. For many authors, this occurs most often in the methods part.

Do scientific and medical journals, in their instructions for authors, advise them to write in the active voice?

Many journals indirectly do so by referring authors to a style manual that supports the active voice, or by publishing articles in which active-voice sentences are common and acceptable.

Although some journals ask authors to limit the first-person pronouns or restrict them to certain sections, others not only encourage authors to write in an active style, but prefer them to use the first-person pronouns over passive voice. Here is a small sampling:

Behavioral Ecology: "Active voice is preferable to the impersonal passive voice."[4]

British Medical Journal: "Please write in a clear, direct, and active style . . . Write in the active [voice] and use the first person where necessary."[5]

The Journal of Neuroscience: "Overuse of the passive voice is a common problem in writing. Although the passive has its place—for example, in the methods section—in many instances it makes the manuscript dull by failing to identify the author's role in the research . . . Use direct, active-voice sentences."[6]

The Journal of Trauma and Dissociation: "Use the active voice whenever possible: We will ask authors that rely heavily on use of the passive voice to re-write manuscripts in the active voice."[7]

Nature: "Nature journals like authors to write in the active voice ('we performed the experiment . . . ') as experience has shown that readers find concepts and results to be conveyed more clearly if written directly."[8]

Ophthalmology: "Active voice is much preferred to passive voice, which should be used sparingly . . . Passive voice . . . does not relieve the author of direct responsibility for observations, opinions, or conclusions (e.g., 'The problem of blood flow was investigated . . .' vs. 'We investigated the problem of blood flow . . . ')."[9]

Science: "Use active voice when suitable, particularly when necessary for correct syntax (e.g., 'To address this possibility, we constructed an lZap library . . . ,' not 'To address this possibility, an lZap library was constructed . . . ')."[10]

IEEE: "If you wish, you may write in the first-person singular or plural and use the active voice ('I observed that . . . ' or 'We observed that . . . ' instead of 'It was observed that . . . '). Remember to check spelling. If your native language is not English, please get a native English-speaking colleague to proofread your paper."[11]

Active Voice Corrections

"Generally, I think you could improve the whole paper using more active-voice sentences. It will improve the flow and allow the reader to follow your meaning."

— 1st Reviewer, *Journal of Hydrology*

Original
Identification of poor food, bad housing, inadequate hygiene, and arge families as the major causes of poverty *was made by* Jones 2005).

Modified
Jones (2005) *identified* poor food, bad housing, inadequate ygiene, and large families as the major causes of poverty.

Original
Consideration of whether countries work well on cross-border issues such as immigration was undertaken by Raul (2007).

Modified
Raul (2007) considered whether or not countries work well on cross-border issues such as immigration.

V. Summary

For vigorous, clear writing, choose **the active voice** unless you have good reasons for choosing the passive voice.

Punctuation Point

I. When Do We Use the Passive Voice?

When should an author choose the **passive voice** over the active voice? What is the difference between them?

The passive voice emphasizes the person or object receiving the action (for example, *the ball was hit by the boy*). The **active voice**, by contrast, emphasizes the person or object performing the action (for example, *the boy hit the ball*).

Because active voice sentences are clearer, livelier, and often more concise than passive-voice sentences, most style guides advise scientific authors to **prefer the active voice** in their writing.

Notice though, that the recommendation is not to write entirely in the active voice. An all-out active writing style would be just as difficult to read as an all-out passive style: balancing the two perspectives is key.

Other than to add variety, when is **the passive voice the better choice**? Here are three good reasons to use it.

▶ The performer is unknown, irrelevant, or obvious

The passive voice is preferable if the performer **cannot easily be named** or if the performer is irrelevant to the discussion, as in the following examples:

- Up to 90% of the energy in light bulbs is wasted in the form of heat.
- The first edition of Freud's earliest writings on dreams was published in 1899.
- Drosophila melanogaster has been one of the most extensively studied species in genetics research.

In the first sentence, the author's attempts to name the performer would be awkward; in the second sentence, the author assumes the reader will not be interested in the name of the publisher; and in the third sentence, the performer (researchers) is obvious.

When naming the performer would prove difficult or unnecessary, the passive voice works well.

▶ The performer is less important than the action

When discussing an experimental procedure in the methods part, a researcher might write:

- The honeybees were kept in a humidified chamber at room temperature overnight.
- The solution was heated to 90 °C for approximately 30 minutes and then allowed to cool.

The sentences could be converted to active voice by writing the following:

- We kept the honeybees in a humidified chamber at room temperature overnight.
- We heated the solution to 90 °C for approximately 30 minutes and then allowed it to cool.

Does the active voice shorten the sentences? No (In fact, the second sentence is one word longer than it is in the original version. The active voice is not automatically more concise than the passive). Does the active voice add clarity? Perhaps the reader may be justified in assuming that the authors are also the performers.

The active voice has **changed the focus**, however, from the research to the researchers, an emphasis the author may not desire in the methods part, where the general topic is the research materials and procedures.

Conversely, when an author emphasizes the active voice over the passive in the methods (or any part), most sentences begin with *we*, which is distracting when overdone. In that case, passive sentences vary the structure and rhythm while keeping the emphasis on the work (Zeiger, 2000).

Whether in the methods or elsewhere in a manuscript, the passive voice redirects attention to the action (or the recipient).

▶ The recipient is the main topic

Choosing a passive writing style is sometimes necessary to **position crucial information** at the beginning or end of a sentence.

For instance, the subject (person, object, or idea) that the author wishes to discuss in a sentence should occur near the beginning in the **topic position** where the reader expects to find it, "first things first" (Gopen & Swan, 1990).

The following active-voice sentence begins a new part in which the topic is "green plants" (the performer):

- Green plants produce carbohydrates in the presence of light and chlorophyll.

If, by contrast, "carbohydrates" (the receiver of the action) is the opening topic, the sentence is more effectively written in the passive voice:

- Carbohydrates are produced by green plants in the presence of light and chlorophyll.

The topic of a sentence is not an isolated island; however, it has **context** in relation to the surrounding sentences and paragraphs.

The topic must not only identify the subject for the reader, but it must prepare the reader "for upcoming material by connecting it backward to the previous discussion" (Gopen & Swan, 1990).

For example, look at the first three sentences of a classic article written by Watson and Crick in 1953:

- We wish to suggest a structure for the salt of deoxyribose nucleic acid (D.N.A.). This structure has novel features which are of considerable biological interest. A structure for nucleic acid has already been proposed by Pauling and Corey. (Watson & Crick, 1953)

Notice that the authors used the active voice in the first and second sentences, but the passive in the third. If the third sentence is changed to active voice, it becomes:

- Pauling and Corey have already proposed a structure for nucleic acid.

II. Summary

Just as varying the sentence length in your scientific manuscript creates more variety and interest for your readers, so, too, does using both active and passive voice.

Choose the active voice whenever possible.

Choose the passive voice if you have a good reason to do so. Consider the passive voice when:

1. The performer is unknown, irrelevant, or obvious.
2. The performer is less important than the action.
3. The recipient is the main topic.

You can also use the passive voice to hedge (that is, to be noncommittal).

However, that is one use that cannot be recommended. (That is an example of hedging.)

Sources

1. Watson JD, Crick FHC. Molecular structure of nucleic acids. *Nature*. 1953;171:737-738.
2. Iverson C, Christiansen S, Flanagin A, et al. *AMA Manual of Style: A Guide for Authors and Editors*. 10th ed. New York, NY: Oxford University Press; 2007.
3. American Psychological Association. *Publication Manual of the American Psychological Association (5th ed.)*. Washington, DC: Author; 2001.
4. Instructions to authors. Oxford Journals Website: *Behavioral Ecology*. http://www.oxfordjournals.org/our_journals/beheco/for_authors/general.html. 2009.
5. The essentials of BMJ style. *BMJ Publishing Group Website: British Medical Journal*.
6. Westbrook G, Cooper L. Writing tips: Techniques for clear scientific writing and editing. The Society for Neuroscience Website: *The Journal of Neuroscience*. http://www.jneurosci.org.
7. Guidelines for authors. International Society for the Study of Trauma Website: *The Journal of Trauma & Dissociation*. http://www.isst-d.org/jtd/journal-trauma-dissociation-info-for-authors.html.
8. How to write a paper: writing for a Nature journal. *Nature Publishing Group Website: Nature*. http://www.nature.com/authors/author_services/how_write.html.
9. Guide for authors. Elsevier Website: *Ophthalmology: Journal of the American Academy of Ophthalmology*. http://www.elsevier.com/wps/find/journaldescription.cws_home/620418/authorinstructions.
10. Some notes on Science style. American Association for the Advancement of Science, Website: *Science*. http://www.sciencemag.org/about/authors/prep/res/style.dtl.
11. Template for Preparation of Papers for IEEE Sponsored Conferences & Symposia
12. Frank Anderson, Sam B. Niles, Jr., and Theodore C. Donald, Member, IEEE
13. Zeiger M. *Essentials of Writing Biomedical Research Papers*. 2nd ed. New York, NY: McGraw-Hill; 2000.
14. Gopen GD, Swan JA. The science of scientific writing. *American Scientist*. 1990;78:550-558.
15. Watson JD, Crick FHC. Molecular structure of nucleic acids. *Nature*. 1953;171:737-738.

The Writing Process

Writing is not easy or fun, but it can get you and your ideas noticed. The process of writing is not interesting or exciting, so do not expect it to be. To stay focused and motivated to achieve your goals, you need to think about the results of your writing instead of the process of writing. Think about all the good things that will result after you are a published writer. Imagine the increase in confidence you will have and the increase in respect others will give to you. Carry these thoughts with you to help stay focused and motivated while you are having difficulties communicating your ideas. To get your ideas out there and appreciated, you must write. The process of writing is a necessary evil to achieve your goals.

Winston Churchill, a well-known British Prime Minister and great political leader, was also a prolific writer who was known to write at least 2,000 words a day. Before, during, and after his time in politics, he wrote, painted, and practiced masonry on a daily basis. In 1927, in a letter to a friend, Mr. Churchill said, "I have had a delightful month—building a cottage and dictating a book: 200 bricks and 2,000 words per day." Showing us that focus and motivation are important factors to being published.

Why Is Technical and Academic Writing Presented in the English Language?

English is precise and Chinese is concise. This means that in Chinese you may only have one or two choices to indicate a certain kind of word usage in a specific field. In English, there could be many words that indicate the same thing, but they are specifically used within certain fields and not in other fields. English is a precise and field-specific language. In other languages, a single word has many meanings. In English, three words can have the same meaning with slightly different emphases. This makes English the ideal language to express scientific and academic thoughts. English is like an "open operating system," in that you can borrow words from other languages such as French, Italian, Arabic, Japanese, German, Tagalog, Mandarin, or Swahili. Because of this word borrowing, English becomes difficult to learn, as you are learning words from many languages. The advantage is that you have a tool for expressing precise meaning.

Tips for Journal Submission

What Journal Editors Want: Do's and Don'ts when Submitting Papers to a Journal

Below is a list of general rules for what to do when submitting to a journal and communicating with editors and reviewers.

▶ **Do examine the scope of the journal and description of its contents before submitting**

You might be amazed at the number of "inappropriate" papers editors receive and have to rapidly "desk reject" (without review, or after a quick examination by an editorial board member) simply because they don't address the interests of their audience. Some good questions to ask yourself are: Do papers like yours appear in the journal? Have you cited papers that have appeared in the journal or similar journals? If still in doubt, send only the title, author names and abstract to the journal office for a quick opinion on appropriateness.

▶ **Do format the paper appropriately**

There is the tendency amongst authors to say "I'll format the paper and reference style later, after it has been accepted." This is especially true if a paper has previously been rejected by another journal whose format is "similar." If you pay attention to the details of the appropriate format for the journal you are submitting to now, you will have one fewer thing to be criticized about by both the editorial staff and referees.

▶ **Do look into whether the journal has page charges or submission fees, or fees for color illustrations or photos, or reprint charges, and clear the expenses up front with your advisor**

You want to avoid the "good news your paper is accepted, bad news you owe us $7000" scenario. If you are "broke," many journals have an "as affordable" policy that might subsidize some of your costs if you say you are poor. Can't hurt to ask.

▶ Do prepare a cover letter that says more than that you are submitting the paper

Not only do you want to state that the paper is not being considered elsewhere, you have the permission of all the co-authors (and all that formal stuff), but you should include a sentence or two that describes the novel finding, why you are so excited about your work (the "newsworthiness factor"), and why you think it would be appropriate for the journal. Make sure you have appropriately addressed the cover letter! You would be amazed at how many letters editors receive that are addressed to the editor of another journal (obviously the last place the paper was rejected). Not a good first impression!

▶ Do suggest potential referees (up to 5 or 6) and a member of the editorial board

Of course it is the editor's choice to assign referees, but the reality is that journal staff members are overworked. If you can do a little background work to help them, it will be appreciated. Also, although journal editors and editorial board members tend to be broadly trained and interested, they do not know all fields equally well. By suggesting *appropriate* referees, you maximize the chances that your paper will get an appropriate review and not something out of your field. Of course, avoid obvious conflicts of interests. A good question to ask: "Have I cited papers by the people I am suggesting as referees?" This gives you confidence you have chosen appropriate people, and of course, the referee will be happy that you have cited him or her (assuming of course that you have appropriately and fairly represented their published findings).

Often, when a paper comes in, the editor will directly assign it to an editorial board member for a quick read (to see if it's appropriate) and to ask for referee suggestions. You don't want to make a habit of this, but you can in fact suggest people who you do not want to review your paper, because of a personal conflict, because they are an extreme competitor (not quite so much of a problem in our comparative world), or simply because you feel from prior experience that they are so opposed to your ideas as to not be able to give a fair evaluation. There is no guarantee that the editors will use any or all of your suggestions, but there times when editors look at your lists and say: "Great list, couldn't have done better myself, let's use them all."

▶ Don't assume that everything is okay once you hit the "submit" button

Good journals receive over a thousand papers a year to be reviewed. Despite their best efforts, papers get lost sometimes, electronic or hardcopy. If after a few days you don't get an acknowledgement that your paper was received, email the journal office. If you don't hear about the status of your paper in six weeks to two months, contact the journal to ask how the review is going. Most journals have electronic communication with referees, so your paper should have found suitable referees within a couple of weeks (sometimes it just takes longer to track people down though) and referees usually have a 2- to 4-week deadline.

▶ Don't interpret the editor's decision letter too literally

Unless of course the letter says something like: "All referee reports said 'accept as is', and we have sent your article to be typeset for page proofs" (this never happens), or "Your paper is most definitely rejected." Usually there are qualifiers in the decision letter like: "We can only accept your paper after major revisions" or "Your paper is not acceptable in its current form. Should you choose to revise your paper...". These are generally statements that are leaving the door open for you to revise, rebut, and resubmit.

▶ Don't take the referee comments too personally

Most seasoned referees avoid personal language, but sometimes it slips through. Remember that most editors don't take personal comments too seriously. They know who reviewed your paper, and they can often say "Oh, that's referee X, he always has strong opinions about issue Y."

▶ Don't procrastinate about revising and resubmitting your paper

Unless of course the referees have asked you to gather more data, or undertake a month's long reanalysis of your data. Get on it right away and strike while the iron is hot. Most journals have a two-month rule. If you don't resubmit within two months, it is considered a new submission and it will go out for re-review. By turning the paper around quickly, you can often avoid re-review (usually this decision rests with the referee, as they often have a box they can tick or not that says "This paper really needs to be re-reviewed" or "I'd like to see a revision please"). Also, while the paper is still fresh in the referee's mind, you might get a better reception to your revisions.

►Do make a compelling case for why your revised paper should be accepted

Assume that the referee will see your response and write it as though you are specifically responding to them. Be courteous (if there was a personal attack, or an otherwise inappropriate comment, take this up separately in your cover letter to the editor). Thank them for their input, and respond to every single point with a "We did this, see page X, line Y" or a "We respectfully disagree for the following reason(s)." Spell it all out carefully and logically so that the editors don't have to look hard for whether or not you adequately addressed the issues.

►Do bask in the glory when you get the acceptance letter

Change the paper on your *c.v.* from "submitted" to "in press" once you get the acceptance letter. Follow up to make sure you get page proofs in a timely manner and carefully check everything, including every number value and decimal point in your tables, figure axis labels and legends. Do a victory dance when your paper shows up online, and then another when the print version comes out. Do send reprints to your family.

►Do consider writing a review article

Many junior scientists think that they shouldn't be writing review articles until they are old. Fact is, after having written a dissertation, or that first grant proposal, you have reviewed and understood an enormous body of literature. You probably have some fresher perspectives than the veterans as well. But, before you do this, contact a journal editor with your idea, maybe even send a summary or abstract, and ask permission (or to ask to be invited). Journals love to have great review articles with fresh ideas and perspectives (and if not they will let you know in tactful manner). These are often the type of articles that will be highly cited and improve the journal's impact factor. You might also find yourself being asked to review for that journal, maybe eventually be invited to the editorial board. Be proactive!

Do ensure that all requested items are submitted to the journal office; you do not want to make enemies of the editorial office staff or, worse, the editor.

Do try to enlist the help of a native English-speaking colleague to assist with the preparation of your manuscripts if English is not your first language.

Do read your manuscript carefully before submission, and preferably ask several individuals to check the typescript for errors. Familiarity breeds "typo-blindness"!

Do state the hypothesis of your study prominently in the introduction section.

Do consider starting to prepare your manuscript even before all of the experiments are complete. Often, outlining the results section will alert you to gaps in the reasoning and additional experiments that can fill them.

Do provide all authors, including students, an opportunity to comment on the manuscript before it is submitted. Indeed, many journals now require a signed statement to the effect that all authors have seen and approve of the manuscript's contents.

Do try to make your study complete. Resist the temptation to submit your work as LPU-s (least publishable units).

Do try to allow your students and fellows to develop their own writing style, while maintaining quality control over the output of your laboratory.

Do participate in the peer-review process of journal manuscripts to the greatest extent possible. It is a wonderful way to learn what works (and what doesn't).

Don't rely too heavily on the spell-check feature of your word processor (but do use it!).

Don't feel that you cannot call or write to the Editor for clarification, if points raised in the review process seem unclear. However, note that some editors will only accept such inquiries if made in writing.

Don't give coauthors unlimited amounts of time to comment on the manuscript. Set them a deadline after which you will proceed with submission with or without their input.

Inappropriate Vocabulary and Improvements

As students, we should be concerned that our language is as clear as possible. We do not want to confuse the reader with words that have more than one meaning. Strong simple words are best in technical writing. A word with two or three possible meanings is not simple because the reader must "guess" which meaning the author is using. Therefore, the best words have one possible meaning.

The following are examples of "unclear words" with more appropriate substitute words listed below.

consider

A better alternative would be:

evaluate/assess

check

A better alternative would be:

verify/confirm

different

A better alternative would be:

distinct/diverse/various/varied

little/few

A better alternative would be:

seldom/slightly

problem

A better alternative would be:

limitation/restriction/obstacle/hindrance

need

A better alternative would be:

require/stipulate/necessitate

Academic Vocabulary

Headwords	Other Words in the Family
abandon	abandoned, abandoning, abandonment, abandons
abstract	abstraction, abstractions, abstractly, abstracts
academy	academia, academic, academically, academics, academies
access	accessed, accesses, accessibility, accessible, accessing, inaccessible
accommodate	accommodated, accommodates, accommodating, accommodation
accompany	accompanied, accompanies, accompaniment, accompanying, unaccompanied
accumulate	accumulated, accumulating, accumulation, accumulates
accurate	accuracy, accurately, inaccuracy, inaccuracies, inaccurate
achieve	achievable, achieved, achievement, achievements, achieves, achieving
acknowledge	acknowledged, acknowledges, acknowledging, acknowledgement, acknowledgements
acquire	acquired, acquires, acquiring, acquisition, acquisitions
adapt	adaptability, adaptable, adaptation, adaptations, adapted, adapting, adaptive, adapts
adequate	adequacy, adequately, inadequacies, inadequacy, inadequate, inadequately
adjust	adjusted, adjusting, adjustment, adjustments, adjusts, readjust, readjusted, readjusting, readjustment, readjustments, readjusts
administrate	administrates, administration, administrations, administrative, administratively, administrator, administrators
adult	adulthood, adults
advocate	advocacy, advocated, advocates, advocating
affect	affected, affecting, affective, affectively, affects, unaffected
aggregate	aggregated, aggregates, aggregating, aggregation
aid	aided, aiding, aids, unaided
allocate	allocated, allocates, allocating, allocation, allocations
alter	alterable, alteration, alterations, altered, altering, alternate, alternating, alters, unalterable, unaltered
alternative	alternatively, alternatives
ambiguous	ambiguities, ambiguity, unambiguous, unambiguously

续表

Headwords	Other Words in the Family
amend	amended, amending, amendment, amendments, amends
analogy	analogies, analogous
analyze	analyzed, analyzer, analyzers, analyses, analyzing, analysis, analyst, analysts, analytic, analytical, analytically
annual	annually
anticipate	anticipated, anticipates, anticipating, anticipation, unanticipated
apparent	apparently
append	appendix, appended, appends, appending, appendices, appendixes
appreciate	appreciable, appreciably, appreciated, appreciates, appreciating, appreciation, unappreciated
approach	approachable, approached, approaches, approaching, unapproachable

Daily Writing Schedule

Day / Time	Mon.	Tue.	Wed.	Thu.	Fri.	Sat.	Sun.
5:00 a.m.							
6:00 a.m.							
7:00 a.m.							
8:00 a.m.							
9:00 a.m.							
10:00 a.m.							
11:00 a.m.							
12:00 p.m.							
1:00 p.m.							
2:00 p.m.							
3:00 p.m.							
4:00 p.m.							
5:00 p.m.							
6:00 p.m.							
7:00 p.m.							
8:00 p.m.							
9:00 p.m.							
10:00 p.m.							
11:00 p.m.							
12:00 a.m.							
1:00 a.m.							
2:00 a.m.							
3:00 a.m.							
4:00 a.m.							
Total Minutes You Actually Worked							
What You Completed							

(Referral Belcher)

Chapter 2
Why Is the Problem Important?

Why Is the Problem Important?

I. Review Research to Provide the Reason for Why Your Study Is Important

As a researcher, one of your first and most important tasks is selling your research problem. Reviewers are not interested in reading a solution to a problem when they do not believe there really is a problem. A common reviewer comment is "The subject is of little novel interest," meaning that it is a solution to a nonexistent problem. A hero is only a hero when he can defeat a monster, or solve a big problem. You will be respected for your solution in direct relationship to the strength of the problem. Without bad guys, Superman is just a man in strange tight clothes who flies around. Make sure that your bad guy, or research problem, is big enough to earn you hero status when you solve it. Otherwise, you may have trouble getting your paper accepted by a journal. Ensure that your introduction introduces your audience to the bad guy, so they will see you as a hero when you introduce your solution.

II. Reference to Single Investigation in the Past

▶Researcher(s) as the Sentence Subject

Smith (1999)	• *found* that as levels of literacy and education of the population rise . . . • *showed* that reducing X to 190 °C decreased . . . (see Fig. 2). • *demonstrated* that when the maximum temperature is exceeded . . .

Jones et al. (2001)
- *investigated* the differential impact of formal and non-formal education on . . .
- *analyzed* data from 72 countries and concluded that . . .
- *reviewed* the literature from the period and found little evidence for this claim.
- *interviewed* 250 undergraduate students using semi-structured questionnaires.
- *studied* the effects of cytochrome P450 on unprotected nerve cells.
- *performed* a similar series of experiments in the 1960s to show that . . .
- *carried out* a number of investigations into the . . .
- *conducted* a series of trials *in which* they mixed X with different quantities of . . .
- *measured* both components of the . . .
- *labelled* these subsets as . . .
- *examined* the flow of international students . . .

When citing sources such as Smith (1996), vary your style in the following manner:

Smith (1996)		**Smith (1996)**	
	studied		considered
	investigated		described
	examined		warned
	looked at/into		contended
	evaluated		agreed
	catalogued		formulated
	listed		complained
	recorded		wrote
	tabulated		asserted
	indexed		cautioned
	tallied		stated

filed	pointed out
indicated	demonstrated
inventoried	conceived of
denoted	approached
signified	held that since
designated	proposed
specified	admitted
manifested	referred to
implied that	has shown
revealed	suggested
disclosed	thought that
exhibited	questioned
presented	accounted for
characterized	reviewed
scheduled	created
intimated	observed that
clarified	distinguished between
experimented with	made the distinction
raised the question as to	
compared the mean scores	

▶ Investigation Emphasized

- Preliminary work on X *was undertaken* by Abdul Karim (1992).
- The first systematic study of X *was reported* by Patel et al. in 1986.
- The study of the structural behavior of X *was first carried out* by Rao et al. (1986).
- Analysis of the genes involved in X *was first carried out* by Smith et al. (1983).
- A recent study by Smith and Jones (2001) *involved* . . .
- A longitudinal study of X by Smith (2002) *reported* that . . .

- A small-scale study by Smith (2002) *reached* different conclusions, finding no increase . . .
- Smith's cross-country analysis (2002) *showed* that . . .
- Smith's comparative study (2002) *found* that . . .
- Detailed examination of X by Smith and Patel (1961) *showed* that . . .
- In another major study, Zhao (1974) *found* that just over half of the . . .
- In a randomized controlled study of X, Smith (2004) *reported* that . . .
- In a large longitudinal study, Boucahy et al. (2004) *investigated* the incidence of X in Y.

▶ Research Topic as a Subject

- Classical conditioning *was first demonstrated* experimentally by Pavlov (Smith, 2002).
- The electronic spectroscopy of X *was first studied* by Smith and Douglas in 1970.
- The acid-catalyzed condensation reaction between X and Y *was first reported* by Baeyer in 1872.
- X *is* the central focus of a study by Smith (2002), in which the author found . . .
- X *was originally isolated* from Y in a soil sample from . . . (Wang et al., 1952).
- The way in which the X gene is regulated *was studied extensively* by Ho and colleagues (Ho et al., 1995, 1998).
- To determine the effects of X, Zhao et al. (2005) *compared* . . .

III. Reference to What Other Writers Have Done in Their Studies

▶ Author as a Subject

- Smith (2003) *identified* poor food, bad housing, inadequate hygiene, and large families as the major causes of . . .
- Rao (2003) *listed* three reasons why the English language has become so dominant.
- Smith (2003) *traced* the development of Japanese history and philosophy during the 19th century.
- Jones (2003) *provided* in-depth analysis of the work of Aristotle, showing its relevance to contemporary times.
- Smith (2003) *drew attention to* distinctive categories of motivational beliefs often observed in . . .

- Smith (2003) *defined* evidence-based medicine as the conscious, explicit, and judicious use of . . .
- Rao (2003) *emphasized* the need to break the link between economic growth and transport growth . . .
- Smith (2003) *discussed* the challenges and strategies for facilitating and promoting . . .
- Toh (2003) *mentioned* the special situation of Singapore as an example of . . .
- Smith (2003) *questioned* whether mainstream schools are the best environment for . . .
- Smith (2003) *considered* whether countries work well on cross-border issues such as . . .
- Smith (2003) *used* examples of these various techniques as evidence that . . .

In her major study,	
In her seminal article,	
In her classic critique of . . . ,	
In her case study of . . . ,	Smith (2004) identified five characteristics of . . .
In her review of . . . ,	
In her analysis of . . . ,	
In her introduction to . . . ,	

- Some analysts (e.g., Carnoy, 2002) *have attempted to* draw fine distinctions between . . .
- Other authors (see Harbison, 2003; Kaplan, 2004) *have questioned* the usefulness of such an approach.

IV. Reference to Other Writers' Ideas

▶ Author as a Subject

According to Smith (2003), preventive medicine is far more cost effective, and therefore better adapted to the developing world.

Smith (2003)	indicated	that	preventative medicine is far more cost effective and therefore better adapted to the developing world.
	argued		
	maintained		
	claimed		
	concluded		
	suggested		

Smith (2003)	argued for	an explanatory theory for each type of irrational belief.
	offered	
	proposed	
	suggested	

- This view is supported by Jones (2000), who wrote . . .
- Smith argued that her data supports O'Brien's (1988) view that . . .
- Smith indicated that . . .
- Elsewhere, Smith argued that . . .

Citations vs. Quotations

Citing another author means that you tell the reader in your own words what he said. Quoting is when you use another author's actual words preceded and followed by quotation marks (""). Notice that sentences using a colon do not need the word "that" before the quotation.

Some Ways to Introduce Quotations
Social Science Paper

Sachs concludes that "The idea of development stands today like a ruin in the intellectual landscape . . ." (Sachs, 1992a, p. 156).

As Smith argued: "In the past, the purpose of education was to . . . " (Smith, 2000, p. 150).

As Carnoy stated: "There are many good reasons to be skeptical." (Carnoy, 2004, p. 215)

Humanities Paper

In the final part of his thesis, Marx writes: "Philosophers have hitherto only interpreted the world in various ways; the point . . . "

Common Writing Errors and Their Corrections

Negative Transfer

Learning a foreign language is more than just memorizing new words and entering these words into our native language's grammar, it often involves learning entirely new ways of expressing ideas and unlearning what we already know from our native language. Our native language will influence how we acquire a new language, and this is referred to as *language transfer*.

For native speakers of Chinese, learning to construct simple English sentences will be relatively easy because Chinese and English have the same basic word order, which is subject-verb-object. For example, we can take the Chinese sentence 我吃苹果, translate the elements in it, and "plug" the English words into the same word order to get a grammatical English sentence: *I eat apples*. When knowledge from our native language's grammar helps us produce grammatical expressions in a foreign language, it is called *positive transfer*. By contrast, when this same knowledge causes us to produce ungrammatical expressions in a foreign language, it is called *negative transfer*.

Here are two commonly used sentence structures in Chinese that you should avoid using in English:

- 因为……所以…… (because . . . , so . . .)
- 虽然……但是…… (although . . . , but . . .)

While both are grammatical in Chinese, they are ungrammatical in English. To illustrate, you should avoid writing sentences like these:

- *Because* I am curious about the Golden Age of Mexican cinema, *so* I listen to Pedro Infante's music.
- *Although* I listen to Bollywood music, *but* I do not understand Hindi.

Using *because* . . . , *so* . . . and *although* . . . , *but* . . . in English is ungrammatical because the conjunctions in each pair make each other redundant; therefore, only one or the other must be used.

Because and *although* are *subordinating conjunctions*. Using these conjunctions makes one clause dependent upon the other:

- *Because* I am curious about the Golden Age of Mexican cinema, I listen to Pedro Infante's music.
- *Although* I listen to Bollywood music, I do not understand Hindi.

So and *but* are *coordinating conjunctions*, and they are used to join elements that are equals. They are used to connect words to words, phrases to phrases, and clauses to clauses:

- I am curious about the Golden Age of Mexican cinema, *so* I listen to Pedro Infante's music.
- I listen to Bollywood music, *but* I do not understand Hindi.

As the examples demonstrate, using these pairs of conjunctions together in one sentence as you would in Chinese is unnecessary and inappropriate in English. Using just one from each pair is enough and grammatical in English. *Because* and *so* should not be used together because they have the same function, which is to link reason and consequence. *Because is* used before the reason, and *so* is used before the consequence:

- *Because* I am curious about the Golden Age of Mexican cinema, I listen to Pedro Infante's music.
- I am curious about the Golden Age of Mexican cinema, *so* I listen to Pedro Infante's music.

As for *although* and *but*, do not use both in the same sentence because these conjunctions basically have the same meaning. Please be aware that *although* always goes before the first clause, and *but* always goes between the two clauses (do not use *but* in the beginning of a sentence):

- *Although* I listen to Bollywood music, I do not understand Hindi.
- *Although* I do not understand Hindi, I listen to Bollywood music.
- I listen to Bollywood music, *but* I do not understand Hindi.
- I do not understand Hindi, *but* I listen to Bollywood music.

Notice that the clauses are interchangeable because *although* and *but* basically have the same meaning.

Language transfer is a part of learning foreign languages, and negative transfer has probably affected anyone who has ever tried to learn a new language.

Punctuation Point

How to Use the Powerful Hyphen?

A hyphen (-) is generally used in English writing to link and separate words and parts of words. Hyphens, which should not be confused with dashes ("–" and "—"), are often used to form compound words and adjectival phrases, such as "carbon-based," "long-term," and "over-the-counter." Hyphens are also used familiarly in multiword numbers such as "twenty-three" and "eighty-nine," and in two- and three-word modifiers:

- well-researched
- high-quality
- state-of-the-art
- low-molecular-weight

However, hyphenating these phrases is necessary only when they are used as modifiers (adjectives):

- His paper presents a *well-researched* argument.
- Using the proposed method required conducting a *high-risk* assessment.
- We examined the patient in our hospital's *state-of-the-art* cardiovascular department.
- Shellac is a natural resin and *low-molecular-weight* polymer.

Note that the modifying phrases in these sentences *precede* the modified nouns. When a modifying phrase *follows* the noun it modifies, the phrase is *not* hyphenated:

- The argument in his paper is *well researched*.
- Using the proposed method required conducting an assessment that was *high risk*.
- Our hospital's cardiovascular department, where we examined the patient, is s*tate of the art*.
- Shellac is a natural resin and a polymer of *low molecular weight*.

In academic writing, hyphens are generally not used to link

prefixes to root words. This is because prefixes, by definition, are not stand-alone words. The *American Medical Association* (AMA) *Manual of Style*, for example, recommends that prefixes should not be joined by hyphens:

- nonessential
- coworker
- overproduced

Unless the usage involves a capitalized word (e.g., a proper noun), an abbreviation, or a numeral:

- Pan-Asian
- Pre-RNA molecule
- Mid-1970s

Most formal writing audiences follow this convention. However, there are exceptions:

- "Ex-" when used to mean *former*, as in "ex-husband"
- Double-vowel constructions such as in "re-edit" and "intra-aortic" (example exceptions are "cooperate" and "microorganism")
- Mitigating ambiguity (e.g., "un-ionize" and "re-formation")

Appropriate use of a hyphen enhances the clarity of writing. Conversely, inappropriate hyphen usage results in unclear wording, and the presence or absence of a hyphen can change the meaning of a statement. Consider the following example:

- The city requires a new industrial waste management system.

The wording in this sentence is ambiguous. The statement could mean that the city needs either (1) a system to manage "industrial waste" or (2) an "industrial" system to manage waste. Either of the following revised sentences would be clear and appropriate, depending on the writer's intended meaning:

- The city requires a new *industrial-waste* management system.

• The city requires a new industrial *waste-management* system.

In the first sentence, "industrial-waste" is an adjectival phrase modifying "management system," whereas in the second sentence, the adjective "industrial" modifies "waste-management," which in turn modifies "system."

Placing a hyphen after an adverb ending in "-ly" is both unnecessary and grammatically inappropriate, even in a modifying phrase:

This paper addresses the large-scale distribution of organically-grown food. (Inappropriate)

Let the "-ly" suffix do its job!

This paper addresses the large-scale distribution of organically grown food. (Appropriate)

These are but a few hyphenation conventions in academic writing; others are largely style-specific, requiring appropriate knowledge of the particular style guide on which a paper must be based. However, remaining aware of these helpful recommendations can facilitate the process of writing in any academic and technical domain.

The Writing Process
FREE WRITING

Free writing is a simple process to create ideas and get you into a writing mindset.

Free writing follows these steps:

❶ Write without stopping for a period of time (10–20 minutes).
❷ Do not make corrections as you write.
❸ Keep writing, even if you have to write something like, "I don't know what to write."
❹ Write whatever comes to your mind.
❺ Do not criticize what you are writing.

Free writing should be disorganized. In fact, if your free writing is organized, you are doing something wrong. Remember, you cannot fail in free writing. The reason for free writing is to create ideas and become creative. If you follow the above steps, your free writing will be successful.

Free writing has the following benefits:

❶ It makes you more comfortable with the act of writing.
❷ It helps you stop inner criticism which tells you, "You can't write."
❸ It releases inner stress.
❹ It helps you find things to write about.
❺ It can indirectly improve your formal writing.
❻ It can be fun.

Final Suggestions for Free Writing

1. Use the writing tool that is the most comfortable for you: a pencil, pen, computer, or whatever works best for you.
2. Do not edit anything when you are writing: write the new idea down and leave the old one.
3. Forget about punctuation. This will make your free writing faster and clearer.

Tips for Journal Submission

I. What Is a Literature Review?

A literature review discusses published information in a particular subject area, and sometimes information in a particular subject area within a certain time period.

A literature review can be just a simple summary of the sources, but it usually has an organizational pattern and combines both summary and synthesis. A summary is a recap of the important information of the source, but a synthesis is a reorganization of that information. It might give a new interpretation of old material or combine new interpretations with old interpretations. Or it might trace the intellectual progression of the field, including major debates. Depending on the situation, the literature review may evaluate the sources and advise the reader on the most pertinent or relevant source.

II. Why Do I Have to Have a Literature Review?

This is an important question. Understanding the need for the literature review allows you to know if what you're doing is worthwhile, and that you have a contribution to make. The literature review is vital to the whole thesis; it is not just a routine step taken to fulfill formal requirements. You need a good literature review because it

- Demonstrates that you know the field. This means more than reporting what you've read and understood. Instead, you need to read it critically and write in a way that shows you understand the area; you know what the most important issues are and their relevance to your work, you know the controversies, you know what's neglected, you have expectations about how it is changing. This understanding allows you to map the field and position your research within it.

- Justifies the reason for your research. This is closely connected with demonstrating that you know the field. It is the knowledge of your field that allows you to identify the gap that your research could fill.

However, it is not enough to find a gap. You must also convince your reader that what you are doing is important and needs to be done.

- Allows you to establish your theoretical framework and methodological focus. Even if you are proposing a new theory or a new method, you are doing so in relation to what has been done. The literature review becomes the foundation for the whole thesis.

III. Focusing the Literature Review

During your research and while writing a PhD thesis, you will write the literature review more than once. When trying to formulate their topic, some students first write a literature review, which is often more like a survey. This becomes more focused for your proposal. Usually, once you start to work on your own research, you will review less literature, though you should continue to read about new developments in your field.

Once you are finally writing your full thesis, the literature review needs a major revision. Now after two or three years of your own work, you will see the importance of some of the literature you read earlier. You are now ready to appreciate it and to review it critically. Also, your research findings may mean that you need to explore parts of literature that did not at first seem to be important. You may also decide to exclude whole areas of literature that are not directly related to your research.

IV. Organizing the Literature Review

The literature review should set up the reader's expectations of where your work fits; it should provide the justification of why you are doing what you are doing. If necessary, it should also establish your theoretical framework and your methodology. A chronological organization, therefore, is not usually the best way to achieve this. It is more important to focus on the issues and highlight the findings that are connected to what you are doing.

Because there is no general correct structure, you will have to try several possible arrangements. It may be frustrating and time consuming to write the whole literature review several times to see which way is best, but there are some techniques that can help you decide the best possible arrangement. Working with a diagram, concept map, or some kind of outline will capture the logic of your proposed organization and allow you to choose the clearest way before you write. Plotting out possible structures also gives you something to discuss with your supervisor or test on other readers.

V. Understanding the Literature

You need to look at your literature on two levels:

- One level is creating a system to organize the articles and develop a database for references, so you have easy access under relevant categories and do not chase the same references repeatedly.

- The other level is understanding and using the literature.

Without doing the first level, you could easily become inefficient and frustrated. You need some way of keeping track of your articles and filing them correctly.

The other task of understanding, reviewing, and using the literature can be seen in three stages.

VI. Understanding the Literature: First Stage

When you first come to an area of research, you are learning the background in a general way, getting a general understanding for the whole area (an idea of the scope), starting to appreciate the controversies (to see the key points), and become more familiar with the major authors. You need a starting point. This may come from previous work you've done. If you're new to the area, your supervisor could suggest starting points. Or you could read recent review articles to begin.

▶ Too Much Literature

At this stage there seems to be masses of literature relevant to your research, or you may worry that there seems to be hardly anything. As you read, think about and discuss articles and isolate the issues you're more interested in. In this way, you focus your topic. The more you can close in on what your research question actually is, the more you will be able to select the relevant areas of the literature. This is the only way to bring the topic down to a manageable size.

►Too Little Literature

If you can't find much literature on your research area, and you are sure that you've searched everywhere your library allows, then there are a few possibilities:

- You could be right at the cutting edge of something new and it's not surprising there is little literature.
- You could be limiting yourself to too narrow an area and not appreciating relevant material in a closely related field.
- Unfortunately, the other possibility is that there's nothing in the literature because it is not a worthwhile area of research. In this case, you need to look closely with your supervisor at what you plan to do.

►Quality of the Literature

This begins your first stage in understanding the literature. You are not closely evaluating, the literature now; you are learning through it. Sometimes at this stage, students ask how they can judge the quality of the literature if they are not experts.

You learn to judge, evaluate, and look critically at the literature by judging, evaluating and looking critically at it. You learn by practicing. There is no quick way for doing this, but here are some questions you might find useful; with practice, you will develop many others:

- Is the problem clearly spelled out?
- Are the results presented new?
- Was the research influential so that others extended and continued it?
- How large a sample was used?
- How convincing was the argument made?
- How were the results analyzed?
- What perspective are they coming from?
- Are the generalizations justified by the evidence on which they are made?
- What is the significance of this research?
- What are the assumptions behind the research?

- Is the methodology well justified as the most appropriate to study the problem?
- Is the theoretical basis clear?

In critically evaluating, you are looking for the strengths of certain studies and the significance and contributions made by researchers. You are also looking for limitations, flaws, and weaknesses of particular studies or of whole areas of research.

If you take this critical approach of looking at previous research in your field, your final literature review will not be a summary but an evaluation. It will then reflect your ability for critical analysis.

VII. Understanding the Literature: Second Stage

You will continue the process of understanding the literature by gaining more expertise that allows you to become more confident and focused on your specific research question.

You are still reading the literature. You are thinking about it as you are doing your experiments, conducting your studies, analyzing texts or other data. You are able to talk about it easily and discuss it. In other words, it is becoming part of you at a deeper level than before.

- You are now not only looking at findings but are looking at how others have arrived at their findings.
- You are looking at what assumptions are leading to the way something is investigated.
- You are looking for real differences in theories instead of differences in presentation and word choice.
- You also are gaining an understanding of why the field developed the way it did.
- You have a feeling for where it might be going.

Now what you discovered for yourself may turn out to be the key to what is important. You are getting to this understanding by taking things to pieces and putting them back together. For example, you may need to set up alongside one another four or five different definitions of the same concept, versions of the same theory, or different theories proposed to account for the same phenomenon. You may need to unpack them thoroughly, even at the very basic level of what is the implied understanding of keywords, for example "concept," "model," "principles," before you can confidently compare them, which you need to do before synthesis is possible.

Or, you may be trying to read through specific discoveries that have been variously and concurrently described by different researchers in different countries. You need to ask questions such as whether they are the same discoveries being given different names or, if they are not the same, whether they are related. You may need to do very detailed analyses of parts of the literature while maintaining the general picture.

VIII. Understanding the Literature: Final Stage

You finally understand the literature when you look back to place your own research within the field. At the final stage, you really see how your research has come out of previous work. So now you may be able to identify points or issues that lead directly to your research. You may see points you did not see at first but now you can highlight. Or you may realize that some part of your research has provided evidence to one side of a controversy. Having finished your own research, you are now much better equipped to evaluate previous research in your field. When you have finished your own research and you look back and fill in the picture, you understand the literature and you also see how it motivates your own research. When you conceptualize the literature in this way, it becomes an vital part of your research paper.

Inappropriate Vocabulary and Improvements

affect

A better alternative would be:

influence/shape

carry out

A better alternative would be:

implement/execute/promulgate/conduct

change

A better alternative would be:

modify/adjust/alter/vary

complicated

A better alternative would be:

complex/cumbersome/intricate

correct/incorrect

A better alternative would be:

precise/imprecise; accurate/inaccurate

Academic Vocabulary

Headwords	Other Words in the Family
appropriate	appropriacy, appropriately, appropriateness, inappropriacy, inappropriate, inappropriately
approximate	approximated, approximately, approximates, approximating, approximation, approximations
arbitrary	arbitrariness, arbitrarily
area	areas
aspect	aspects
assemble	assembled, assembles, assemblies, assembling, assembly
assess	assessable, assessed, assesses, assessing, assessment, assessments, reassess, reassessed, reassessing, reassessment, unassessed
assign	assigned, assigning, assignment, assignments, assigns, reassign, reassigned, reassigning, reassigns, unassigned
assist	assistance, assistant, assistants, assisted, assisting, assists, unassisted
assume	assumed, assumes, assuming, assumption, assumptions
assure	assurance, assurances, assured, assuredly, assures, assuring
attach	attached, attaches, attaching, attachment, attachments, unattached
attain	attainable, attained, attaining, attainment, attainments, attains, unattainable
attitude	attitudes
attribute	attributable, attributed, attributes, attributing, attribution
author	authored, authoring, authors, authorship
authority	authoritative, authorities
automate	automatic, automated, automates, automating, automatically, automation
available	availability, unavailable
aware	awareness, unaware
benefit	beneficial, beneficiary, beneficiaries, benefited, benefiting, benefits
bias	biased, biases, biasing, unbiased
bond	bonded, bonding, bonds
brief	brevity, briefed, briefing, briefly, briefs

续表

Headwords	Other Words in the Family
bulk	bulky
capable	capabilities, capability, incapable
capacity	capacities, incapacitate, incapacitated
category	categories, categorization, categorize, categorized, categorizes, categorizing
cease	ceased, ceaseless, ceases, ceasing
challenge	challenged, challenger, challengers, challenges, challenging
channel	channeled, channeling, channels
chapter	chapters
chart	charted, charting, charts, uncharted

Chapter 3
What Conflicts or Unanswered Questions Does Your Research Address?

This chapter helps you identify and sell your research problem. You need to find a conflict, a question, an untested population, or an untried method in the existing research of your field of study and have an experiment that addresses it. You can do this by highlighting problems or controversies or identifying a knowledge gap in your field of study. The subsections of this chapter help you develop the strategies required to define your experiment or research.

I. Highlighting a Problem or Controversy in the Field of Study

- However, these rapid changes have a serious effect . . .
- However, a major problem with this type of application is . . .
- To date, there has been little agreement on what . . .
- More recently, literature has emerged that offers contradictory findings about . . .
- There is increasing concern that some Xs are being disadvantaged . . .
- Despite its long clinical success, X has numerous problems in use.
- Despite its safety and efficacy, X suffers from several major drawbacks.
- Researchers have raised concerns about the poor . . .
- One of the most significant current discussions in legal and moral philosophy is . . .
- One observer has already drawn attention to the paradox in . . .
- In many Xs, a debate is taking place between Ys and Zs concerning . . .
- The controversy about scientific evidence for X has raged unabated for over a century.

- The issue of X has been a controversial and much disputed subject within the field of . . .
- This issue has grown in importance in light of recent . . .
- One major theoretical issue that has dominated the field for many years concerns . . .
- A major issue in early X research concerned . . .

II. Highlighting a Knowledge Gap in the Field of Study (for research)

- So far, however, there has been little discussion about . . .
- However, far too little attention has been paid to . . .
- Most studies in X have only been executed in a small number of areas.
- To date, research has tended to focus on X rather than Y.
- In addition, no research has been found that surveyed . . .
- So far, this method has only been applied to . . .
- Several studies have produced estimates of X (Smith, 2002; Jones, 2003), but there is still insufficient data for . . .
- However, there have been no controlled studies that compare differences in . . .
- Experimental data is rather controversial, and there is no general agreement about . . .

Compare and Contrast

By comparing the similarities and differences between two things, we can increase our understanding and learn more about both. This usually involves a process of analysis that compares specific parts as well as the whole. Comparison may also be a preliminary stage of evaluation. For example, comparing specific aspects of A and B can reveal which is more useful or valuable. Many paragraphs whose function is to compare or contrast begin with an introductory sentence expressed in general terms. Note the introductory sentences below:

I. Introductory Sentences: Differences

- X is different from Y in a number of respects.
- There are a number of important differences between X and Y.
- X differs from Y in a number of important ways.
- Smith (2003) found distinct differences between X and Y.
- Women and men differ not only in physical attributes, but also in the way in which they . . .

II. Introductory Sentences: Similarities

- The mode of processing used by the right brain *is similar to that* used by the left brain.
- The mode of processing used by the right brain *is comparable in* complexity to that used by the left brain.
- The effects of nitrous dioxide on human health *are similar to those of* ground level ozone.
- *Both* X and Y generally occur in a "safe environment."
- *There are a number of similarities between* X and Y.
- Numerous *studies have compared* the brain cells in man and animals, showing that these cells *are essentially identical*.

III. Comparison Within One Sentence

- *In contrast* to oral communities, it is very difficult to get away from calendar time in literate societies.
- *Compared with* people in oral cultures, people in literate cultures

organize their lives around clocks and calendars.
- Oral societies tend to be more concerned with the present, *whereas* literate societies have a very definite awareness of the past.
- Women's brains process language simultaneously on both sides of the brain, *while* men tend to process language on the left side only.
- This interpretation *contrasts with that* of Smith and Jones (2004), who argued that . . .

IV. Comparison Within One Sentence (comparative forms)

- Women are *faster/slower than* men at certain precision manual tasks, such as placing pegs in holes on a board.
- Women tend to perform *better/worse than* men on tests of perceptual speed.
- Furthermore, men are *more/less* accurate in tests of target-directed motor skills.
- The corpus callosum, a part of the brain connecting the two hemispheres, may be *more/less* extensive in women.
- Women are *more/less likely than* men to suffer aphasia when the front part of the brain is damaged.
- Adolescents are *less likely* to be put to sleep by alcohol *than* adults.
- Women tend to have *greater/less* verbal fluency *than* men.
- Men learned the route in *fewer* trials and made *fewer errors than* did women.

V. Comparison Across Two Sentences

- It is very difficult to get away from calendar time in literate societies. *By contrast*, many people in oral communities have little idea of the calendar year of their birth.
- Tests show that women generally can recall lists of words or paragraphs of text better than men. *Conversely*, men usually perform better on tests that require the ability to rotate mentally an image to solve a problem.
- Young children learning their first language need simplified, comprehensible input. *Similarly*, low-level adult L2 learners need graded input supplied, in most cases, by a teacher.
- Speech functions are *less* likely to be affected in women because the critical area is less often affected. A *similar* pattern emerges in studies of the control of hand movements.

Writing About the Past

Writing about the past in English is difficult because of a complex tense system. However, the phrases grouped below indicate the uses of the main tenses in academic writing.

I. Time Phrases Associated with the Use of the Simple Past Tense
(specific times or periods of time in the past)

• For centuries, • In the second half of the 19th century, • At the end of the nineteenth century,	church authorities *placed* restrictions on academics.

• During the Nazi period, • Between 1933 and 1945, • From 1933 to 1945, • In the 1930s and 1940s,	restrictions *were* placed on German academics.

II. Reference to Single Investigations or Publications in the Past
(simple past tense used)

- The first systematic study of X *was* reported by Patel et al. in 1986.
- Erythromycin *was* originally isolated from X in a soil sample from . . . (Wang et al., 1952).
- In 1975, Smith et al. *published* a paper in which they described . . .
- In 1990, Patel et al. *demonstrated* that replacement of H_2O with heavy water leads to . . .
- Thirty years later, Smith (1974) *reported* three cases of *Candida albicans*,

which . . .
- In the 1950s, Gunnar Myrdal *pointed* to some of the ways in which . . . (Myrdal, 1957).
- In 1981, Smith and coworkers *demonstrated* that X induces *in vitro* resistance to . . .
- In 1984, Jones et al. *made* several amino acid esters of X and *evaluated* them as water-soluble prodrugs.

III. Time Phrases Associated with the Use of the Present Perfect Tense

(for situations/actions that began in the past and continue up to the present, or for which the period of time is unspecified)

- *Over the past few decades*, the world has *seen* the stunning transformation of X, Y, and Z.
- *Since 1965*, these four economies *have doubled* their share of world production and trade.
- *Until recently*, there *has been* little interest in X.
- *Recently*, these questions *have been addressed* by researchers in many fields.
- *In recent years*, researchers *have investigated* various of approaches to X, but . . .
- *Up to now*, research *has tended to focus* on X rather than on Y.
- *To date*, little evidence *has been found* associating X with Y.
- *So far*, researchers *have identified* three factors as being potentially important: X, Y, and Z.

IV. The Present Perfect Tense May also Be Used to Describe Recent Research or Scholarly Activity with a Focus on the Area of Investigation—Usually More than One Study

- *There have been* several investigations into the causes of illiteracy (Smith, 1985; Jones, 1987).
- The relationship between a diet high in fat and poor health *has been widely investigated* (Smith, 1985; Jones, 1987; Johnson, 1992).
- The new material *has been shown* to enhance cooling properties (Smith, 1985; Jones, 1987; Johnson, 1992).
- Invasive plants *have been identified* as major contributing factors in the decline of many North American species.
- A considerable amount of literature *has been published* on X.

Common Writing Errors and Their Corrections

I. Incomplete Comparisons

Writers often think that their reader knows what two things are being compared and fail to indicate exactly what they are. When comparing two things, mention both of them in the same sentence. Always compare a verb to a verb or a noun to a noun. Do not compare a noun to a verb, because it is an incomplete comparison. Take a look at the examples below; the writer does not clearly write what is being compared.

> "Line 20 of page 2 should read, 'The finance department focuses on profits more than their department does.'"
> — 1st Reviewer, *Finance Review*

Original

The finance department focuses on profits *more than* the X department.

Modified

The finance department focuses on profits *more than* the X department *does*.

Original

Country A funds high-tech innovation *more than* Country B.

Modified

Country A funds high-tech innovation *more than* Country B *does*.

Original

The device formulated in this experiment exhibits *higher* luminance.

Modified

The device formulated in this experiment exhibits *higher* luminance *than conventional models do*.

II. Complete Comparison

Forming a comparison is crucial to satisfy two main concerns of academic writing audiences: ensuring that results are reported accurately and indicating how a study differs from previous studies. However, forming a grammatically correct, complete comparison is not easy because it involves highly specific considerations related to grammar and syntax.

All complete comparisons contain a subject, a verb, a comparative modifier, the conjunction "than" (or a prepositional phrase indicating a comparison), and a subordinate clause that mirrors the main clause.

The sentence "Men are tall" can be transformed into a comparison first by changing the adverb "tall" into its comparative form. The suffix "-er" is added to most one-syllable adjectives and adverbs (tall-er) to form a comparison, whereas most adjectives and adverbs that are greater than two syllables are preceded by "more." Comparative modifiers are frequently misused. For example, "taller"does not indicate the degree to which an object is tall (it does not mean "tall in general" or "tall but not the tallest"); "taller" is specifically used to indicate that object A is taller in comparison with object B. English is a highly specific language. Different degrees are best expressed not by modifying a word, but by determining an alternative word that precisely conveys the desired degree. Providing an accurate description often involves consulting a dictionary and taking time to choose the most appropriate word for the context.

The conjunction "than" is another word used to form a complete comparison that is often misused. Because their pronunciation is the same, "then" is frequently used in place of "than." After appropriate attention has been given to these common sources of error, a subject, verb, and subordinate clause can be added to form the following complete comparison:

- On average, men are taller than women are.

The verb at the end of this sentence is frequently omitted because it is implied. By contrast, in the incomplete comparison "Women prefer friendly doctors more than men," it is unclear whether women prefer friendly doctors more than men prefer friendly doctors, or whether women prefer friendly doctors more than they prefer men. To ensure that a comparison is complete, a writer can view a comparative sentence as an equivalent mathematical equation in which each part of speech on the left side of "than" must have a corresponding part of speech on the right side: "Women prefer friendly doctors more than men do."

In this context, the verb "do" represents the verb phrase "prefer friendly doctors." The verb in the subordinate clause of a comparison can be inserted either at the end of the sentence or after "than." The placement of the verb is mainly a matter of preference, but the placement can be altered in certain contexts to enhance clarity. Placing the verb after "than" in "Women prefer friendly doctors more than do men, who prefer serious doctors" is favorable because "men" is directly connected to a related dependent clause.

Like the verb "do," "that" and "those" are valuable in forming complete, concise comparisons, especially in comparisons involving possessives. "Girls' scores were higher than boys" incorrectly compares boys with girls' scores. "Those" must be added to complete the comparison: "Girls' scores were higher than those of boys."

"Compared to" and "compared with" can be used in place of "than," and are often used interchangeably. However, there is a distinction between these two phrases that is crucial to express an accurate comparison. "Compared to" is used to imply a similarity between two dissimilar objects, whereas "compared with" is used to indicate differences between two similar objects. Men can be compared with women, but must be compared to a machine.

In long sentences, some writers feel inclined to place a comma before "compared to" and "compared with" because a pause may be taken at this position in natural speech. However, the simple example "lymphocytes are smaller, than erythrocytes are" shows that placing a comma between the clauses in a comparison is incorrect.

Incomplete comparisons are a common source of confusion in academic writing. Without the ability to express comparisons, demonstrating how conclusions were drawn from results and how the contribution of a study differs from that of other studies is not possible. Therefore, gaining a basic understanding of these concepts is essential for success in academic writing.

Punctuation Point

The following rules cover most quotation mark usage.

1. **Use quotation marks around direct quotations, whether the quotations were originally spoken or written.**
   The police officer asked, "Who is responsible for this accident?"
   Both drivers responded, "He is!"

2. **Use a block quote for a quotation of 30 or more words (about three or four printed lines).** Begin the quote by indenting ten spaces from the left and indent the first line five spaces. This is called a "block quote." Do not use quotation marks around a block quote. Use a colon, not a comma, after the sentence introducing a block quote. Human Rights Article 18 states the following:
   Everyone has the right to freedom of thought, conscience, and religion. This right includes freedom to change his religion or belief, and freedom, either alone or in community with others and in public or private, to manifest his religion or belief in teaching, worship, and observance.

3. **Use quotation marks around the titles of newspapers and magazine articles, television and radio programs, and book chapters.** Do not use quotations marks around the titles of books or the names of newspapers. Use italics for book titles and other large publications.
   The article in the *New York Times* titled "Earning Power in 50 Industries" identifies the computer industry as the industry of choice for earning potential.

4. **Use quotation marks to emphasize words representing themselves.**
   She always mispronounces "walk" and "work."

5. **Place periods and commas inside the quotation marks.**
   I asked him, "Did you write the article, 'Time and Again,'" and he said he did.
   Note: Single quotation marks (apostrophes) are used for a

quotation inside a quotation.

6. Place colons and semicolons outside quotation marks.
She said two months ago, "Without engineering, I have no ambition"; today she studies medicine.

7. Place question marks and exclamation points inside quotation marks, unless they apply to the whole sentence and not to the quoted material.
Who wrote the article "Processes in Diluted Magnetic Semiconductors"?
I read the article, "Guess Who Murdered the English Teacher?" and I developed some ideas.

The first example has the question mark outside the quotation marks because the question mark refers not to the quoted material, but instead to the "who" question.

The second example has the question mark inside the quotation marks because the question mark is part of the title of the article.

8. Do not use quotation marks around the titles or headings of your own reports, essays, papers, or theses. Headings and titles stand alone. In addition, do not follow a title or a heading with a period. These headings and titles are not sentences; therefore, they do not end with a period.

The Writing Process
Tips for Being Productive

1. **Write regularly in a notebook.** Promise yourself a certain number of written pages for a certain number of days. Example: I will write three pages every day for the next 14 days. By recording your thoughts and ideas, you will develop a stronger relationship with your writing and your research.

2. **Make writing goals for the month/week/day.** By having your expectations in front of you, you will know when you meet them.

3. **Practice word sketching.** Sketch what you think your idea would look like if it were a picture. Sketches are quick and rough, meant as practice and to generate ideas, not perfection. Your picture may look like a graph or a flow chart and you may use it as a figure in your final paper.

4. **Take a writing workshop.** Writing is a lonely activity. Our motivation is strengthened when we learn and share with other writers. A workshop is an excellent way to learn and continue progress.

5. **Write your dreams.** Keep a notebook by your bed and write down your dreams and those wild thoughts that always show up just before you fall asleep or when you wake up. Our unconscious mind has wisdom to guide us if we stop to listen. Many successful writers claim that their dreams are valuable to their writing.

6. **Capture your good ideas.** Carry a notebook with you. Ideas come at strange times and in strange ways. Sometimes a word or phrase will come in your head while you try to arrive at a solution for something. Write down these ideas even if you do not fully understand them; you will probably not remember these ideas if you do not catch them while you can.

7. **Eliminate TV.** Take a weeklong (or longer) vacation from your

television. Watching TV is inactive. Writing is active. Choose to be active this week using your writing as a way to relax or entertain yourself.

8. **Read.** Reading is the best writing teacher. Read literature in your area and pay attention to the ways in which various writers communicate their ideas.

9. **Do not use reading as an excuse not to write.** If you spend a lot of time reading it may stop you from writing. Take a weeklong (or longer) break from reading and see how it affects your writing.

10. **Write what you want people to say about you after you die.** In 50 words or less, say not only what you did in your life but who you were. Use this as a way to show your values and then live by them. This is also a fun way to imagine how you want to improve your writing as a researcher, student, or teacher.

Tips for Journal Submission

I. Cite the Papers of Potential Reviewers in the Introduction and Compliment Them

Whether or not your paper is accepted depends on who reviews it. Important references should be mentioned on the first page. This is because the editor usually reads the first page when choosing the reviewers. The editor may choose reviewers from those mentioned in the introduction and reference section. The works of potential reviewers should be mentioned in the introduction, rather than deep in the main body. Recognize and praise the previous works of the most likely reviewers. Be kind and polite to all authors cited, but especially to those likely to be your reviewers. Explain why their research is significant to your analysis. Write one or two sentences about the contributions of each of the most likely reviewers and how their research is related to yours. This takes up less than 1% of your paper, but it can significantly increase the probability of acceptance.

II. Six Reasons to Cite the Papers of Potential Reviewers in the Introduction and Compliment Them

1. Papers are accepted on the basis of the recommendation of the reviewers.
2. Mention important reviewers on the first page, because the editor reads the paper's first page when choosing the reviewers.
3. Be nice, kind, generous, and polite when talking about potential reviewers.
4. Explain the reviewer's research as significant to your analysis.
5. Identify potential reviewers and focus one or two sentences on each of the researchers and their research.
6. This should take up about 1% of your paper, but could significantly affect the probability of acceptance.

III. Get to Know One Hundred People Active in Your Field

There are about a hundred people in your field who are likely to review your papers. Prepare a list of one hundred active people in your main research areas. Try to meet them within a five-year period. Present papers and attend at least two professional academic conferences a year. Before attending the conference, make a list of five or six possible reviewers who will be there. When presenting papers, or attending regional, national, or international academic conferences, try to meet these researchers. This is your best opportunity for building relationships. Buy them coffee and ask them about their research. Answer questions about your research and hopefully you will make a friend who will also be your future reviewer. Maintain contacts with these other researchers via telephone, fax, or e-mail. Do not send them copies of your paper unless they request it. You will also need these contacts later: they can write letters of recommendation when you seek promotion and tenure.

Inappropriate Vocabulary and Improvements

find
A better alternative would be:
determine/derive/attain/locate/identify

help
A better alternative would be:
assist/facilitate/guide/direct

important
A better alternative would be:
critical/crucial/essential/pertinent/relevant/significant/vital

improve
A better alternative would be:
enhance/upgrade/elevate

is made of
A better alternative would be:
consists of/comprises/is composed of

Academic Vocabulary

Headwords	Other Words in the Family
chemical	chemically, chemicals
circumstance	circumstances
cite	citation, citations, cited, citing, cites
clarify	clarification, clarified, clarifies, clarifying, clarity
classic	classical, classics
clause	clauses
code	coded, codes, coding
coherent	coherence, coherently, incoherent, incoherently
coincide	coincided, coincides, coinciding, coincidence, coincidences, coincident, coincidental
collapse	collapsed, collapses, collapsible, collapsing
colleague	colleagues
commence	commenced, commences, commencement, commencing, recommences, recommenced, recommencing
comment	commentaries, commentary, commentator, commentators, commented, commenting, comments
commission	commissioned, commissioner, commissioners, commissioning, commissions
commit	commitment, commitments, commits, committed, committing
commodity	commodities
communicate	communicable, communicated, communicates, communicating, communication, communications, communicative, communicatively, uncommunicative
community	communities
compatible	compatibility, incompatibility, incompatible
conduct	conducted, conducting, conducts
confer	conference, conferences, conferred, conferring, confers
confine	confined, confines, confining, unconfined
confirm	confirmation, confirmed, confirming, confirms
conflict	conflicted, conflicting, conflicts
conform	conformable, conformability, conformance, conformation, conformed, conforming, conformist, conformists, conformity, conforms, nonconformist, nonconformists, nonconformity, non-conformist, non-conformists, non-conformity

续表

Headwords	Other Words in the Family
consent	consensus, consented, consenting, consents
consequent	consequence, consequences, consequently
considerable	considerably
consist	consisted, consistency, consistent, consistently, consisting, consists, inconsistencies, inconsistency, inconsistent
constant	constancy, constantly, constants, inconstancy, inconstantly

Chapter 4
What Previous Findings Are You Challenging or Extending?

What Findings Are You Challenging or Extending?

I. Sentences for Criticizing References and Their Theories

Caution! Be aware of your reviewer's feelings. Read the tips for submission for more detail.

There is a danger in openly criticizing your references and their theories. There are some things to consider before, during, and after you decide to criticize your references. Keep these six tips in mind before you publish your criticism.

1. Never make your criticism a personal attack on the reference.
2. Your criticism should be valid, well founded, and add to the field of research.
3. Do not criticize for the sake of criticizing.
4. Realize that if your criticism is wrong, that you could damage your reputation within that field.
5. Ask other researchers in your field if they think the criticism is valid.
6. There is a hign possibility that those whom you criticize will be making decisions about your paper's acceptance.

II. Being Critical
Introducing Questions, Problems, and Limitations
(theory and author)

- One question that needs to be asked, however, is whether . . .
- A serious weakness with this argument, however, is that . . .
- One of the limitations of this explanation is that it does not explain why . . .
- One criticism of much of the literature on X is that . . .
- The key problem with this explanation is that . . .
- Existing accounts fail to resolve the contradiction between X and Y.
- However, there is inconsistency with this argument.
- Smith's argument relies heavily on the qualitative analysis of . . .
- It seems that Jones' understanding of the X framework is questionable.
- Smith's interpretation overlooks much of the historical research . . .
- One major criticism of Smith's work is that . . .
- Many writers have challenged Jones' claim on the grounds that . . .

III. Introducing Questions, Problems, and Limitations
(method/practice)

- Another problem with this approach is that it fails to take X into account.
- Perhaps the most serious disadvantage of this method is that . . .
- Difficulties arise, however, when an attempt is made to implement X.
- Nevertheless, this strategy has not escaped criticism from governments, agencies, and academics.
- One major drawback of this approach is that . . .
- The main limitation of biosynthetic incorporation, however, is . . .
- However, this method of analysis has numerous limitations.
- However, approaches of this type entail various well-known limitations.
- All of the studies reviewed thus far, however, suffer from . . .

However, all the previously mentioned methods suffer from some serious	limitations.
	weaknesses.
	disadvantages.
	drawbacks.

IV. Identifying a Study's Weaknesses

However,	the main weakness of this study is its failure to address how . . .
	this study fails to consider the different categories of . . .
	the research does not take into account pre-existing . . . such as . . .
	the author does not distinguish between X and Y.
	Smith makes no attempt to differentiate between various types of X.
	Jones fails to fully acknowledge the significance of . . .
	the paper appears to be over ambitious in its claims of . . .
	the author overlooks the fact that X contributes to Y.
	what Smith fails to do is to draw a distinction between . . .
	another weakness is the complete lack of explanation regarding . . .

V. Offering Constructive Suggestions

Smith's paper	would have been	more much more	useful convincing interesting	if he/she had	included . . . considered . . .
Her conclusions					
The study	might have been	far more	persuasive original	if the author had	adopted . . . used . . .
The findings					

- A broader study would examine a large, randomly selected sample of societies with . . .
- A more systematic study would identify how X interacts with other variables that are believed to be linked to . . .

VI. Introducing Other People's Criticisms of Your References

- However, Jones (2003) pointed out that . . .
- Many analysts have argued that the strategy of X has not been successful. Jones (2003), for example, argued that . . .
- Non-government agencies are also very critical of the new policies.
- The X theory has been vigorously challenged in recent years by a number of writers.
- Smith's analysis has been criticized by a number of writers. Jones (1993), for example, pointed out that . . .
- Smith's meta-analysis has been subjected to considerable criticism.
- The most noteworthy of these criticisms is that Smith failed to note that . . .
- Jones (2003) is probably the best known critic of the X theory. He argued that . . .
- The latter point has been devastatingly critiqued by Jones (2003).
- Critics have also argued that not only do social surveys provide an inaccurate measure of X, but they . . .
- Critics question the ability of poststructuralist theory to provide . . .
- More recent arguments against X have been summarized by Smith and Jones (1982).
- Jones (2003) criticized the conclusions that Smith drew from his findings.

Common Writing Errors and Their Corrections

I. Noun to Verb Change Corrections

Technical writers prefer verbs to nouns. Nouns are heavy and do not express action. Verbs are alive and show what happened. When students make verbs into nouns, it is necessary to add "meaningless verbs" to complete the sentence. "Meaningless verbs" are necessary because the real verbs in the sentence are inside a noun and can't do the job of showing action in the sentence. As a result, verbs like *undertaken*, *occurred*, *achieved*, *made* and *done* must be used to complete the sentence.

> *"It seems that many of your errors come from your using nouns instead of verbs. This makes your sentence longer because you need additional 'meaningless' verbs to complete your sentences."*
> — **Associate Editor, *Journal of Retailing***

Original

Enumeration of three reasons why the English language has become so important *was made by* Thompson (2006).

Modified

Thompson (2006) *enumerated* three reasons why the English language *has become* so important.

Original

Discussion of the challenges and strategies for *facilitation* and *promotion* of ERP was performed *by* Smith (2007).

Modified

Smith (2007) *discussed* the challenges and strategies for *facilitating* and *promoting* ERP.

Original

Criticism of the new policies has also been made by non-government agencies.

Modified

Non-government agencies *have also been critical* of the new policies.

II. Using "Big Words" in Scholarly Writing

Many university students and academic writers use "big words" in their writing in the belief that they make their writing "sound more academic." However, they often find that their sentences become verbose, tangled, and, at times, incomprehensible because many of those "big words" are nominalizations, which are words that are based on verbs and adjectives. While most academic jargon includes nominalizations, writers can write simple and elegant sentences that are easy to read and understand by substituting many nominalizations with the verbs and adjectives from which they originate.

Take this awkward sentence as an example:

> (a) An *obligation* is placed by the law on the citizens of the country for the correct *performance* of the *administration* of their income records.

"The obligation," "performance," and "the administration" are nominalizations of "to oblige," "to perform," and "to administer." By (reverting) these nominalizations to their original verbal forms and by eliminating the passively voiced "placed by the law" and the unnecessary "performance," we can obtain the following sentence:

> (b) The law *obliges* the citizens of the country to *administer* their income records correctly.

This sentence is even more awkward:

> (c) The *avoidance* of *the introduction* or *the removal* of toxins from rivers by industry leads to *the improvement* of the integrity of the environment and *is beneficial* to human health.

When the nominalization "the avoidance," "the introduction," "the removal," "the improvement," and "beneficial" are substituted with the verbs "remove," "improve," and "benefit" we obtain a clearer and considerably shorter sentence:

(d) Industries that *avoid introducing* or that *remove* toxins from rivers *improve* the integrity of the environment and *benefit* human health.

In addition, note that the nominalizations in sentence (d) require the use of the passive voice (e.g., "by industry") and the introduction of other terms (e.g., "leads to"). If you can write sentences in the active voice in the first place you will be less likely to use nominalizations.

However, if you have already written your paper and want to make sure that you can minimize them, you can easily spot them by looking for three things: first, look for articles in front of the nominalization. For instance, in sentence (c) "the" occurs in front of four of five nominalizations.

Second, look for the weak verb "to be," which tends to increase with the use of nominalizations. Take this sentence, for instance:

(e) The participants who **are** giving assistance with the formulation of policy ideas **are** in agreement with the researcher to offer their views.

By identifying and eliminating the unnecessary "to be" and their accompanying nominalizations, we obtain this considerably more elegant sentence:

(f) Those who assist with formulating policy ideas agree with the researcher to offer their views.

Finally, look for nouns that end in "-ization" or "-tion." This is because many (though not all) nominalizations are based on words that originate from Latin, such as "nominalization" and "ignition."

Once you have reduced the number of nominalizations, you will notice that the noun-to-verb ratio in a sentence has also decreased. For example, sentence (a) has eight nouns and one verb (8/1). Sentence (b) has six nouns and two verbs (6/2). The difference is even starker between sentence (c), which has ten nouns and two verbs (10/2), and sentence (d), which has eight nouns and four verbs (8/4).

Punctuation Point

Adjectives and Nouns Used as Such

Adjectives are words used to describe nouns and noun phrases. Expressing noun qualities, such as size, shape, color, and other characteristics, requires using adjectives, such as small, round, black, and shiny. Some adjectives are identifiable according to a suffix, a letter or group of letters attached to the end of a word to change its meaning, whereas other adjectives are simply nouns used in adjectival form. Knowing the grammatical conventions of their respective usages and determining the appropriate contextual usage are critical for producing clear and effective technical writing.

Consider traffic signs that are frequently seen along roadsides when traveling by motorcycle, car, or bus. Describing a stop sign, for instance, could involve stating that it is large and red with white script. However, other traffic signs could be described similarly. So what makes a stop sign unique? The answer is its shape. Stop signs in most parts of the world are large enough to be seen by commuters, are red to draw attention, and are printed in white script to contrast the red background. Stop signs are also generally shaped like an octagon, which is an eight-sided polygon. However, while describing a stop sign, stating that it is "large, octagon, and red" would be inappropriate. Although "large" and "red" are adjectives, the noun "octagon" is not; the appropriate adjectival usage in this context is "octagonal." Note the difference: "octagonal" (as well as "adjectival") has the suffix "-al," which generally indicates that the involved word is a descriptor or an adjective. Other common adjectival suffixes are "-ar," "-ic," "-ous," and "-y" (e.g., "polar," "economic," "momentous," and "easy"). Hence, "organizational development" and "material concepts" are more appropriate than "organization development" and "matter concepts."

Some nouns, though, do not require suffixes to be adjectives. Consider the following examples:

- A protein structure
- A silicon pore
- Student athletes

The nouns "protein," "pore," and "student" do not generally receive suffixes when used as adjectives. However, if each of these example constructions (note the adjectival use of the noun "example") is transposed, then suffixes would be necessary:

- A structural protein
- Porous silicon
- Athletic students

When using nouns as adjectives, it is imperative to remember that they must nearly always be written in singular form. The phrase "chocolate chips cookie" is inappropriate, regardless of whether the cookie has over 100 chocolate chips! In English, nouns used as adjectives must be written in singular form (e.g., "student athletes," not "students athletes"). Exceptions to this rule are the plural nouns "data" and "media," which are occasionally used as adjectives:

- Data analysis
- Data processing
- Media outlet
- Media campaign

These plural nouns do not follow the standard rule of English noun pluralization, which generally involves adding "-s" or "-es" to the end of the noun, because they are originally Latin terms adopted in English with their plural marker ("-a") preserved. "Datum analysis" and "medium campaign" would not be appropriate, simply because "data" and "media" are more commonly used than their singular counterparts and have consequently been used frequently as adjectives to describe other nouns. Another reason why the plural nouns "data" and "media" have survived as adjectives is because they do not present the phonological and morphological problems that other plural nouns used as adjectives would. The native English ear (and eye) recognizes that nouns used as adjectives must be used in their base form, or be appended with a suffix, regardless of whether the modified noun is plural. Otherwise, cumbersome pronunciations would ensue:

- Rats cages
- Injections procedures
- Substrates peptides

Using nouns as adjectives, whether by adding a suffix or using the noun in singular form, is unavoidable in technical writing, and misusing nouns to describe other nouns results in writing that is awkward, confusing, and likely to be poorly received by readers. The ability to recognize proper adjectival usage can be enhanced by practice, careful reading and listening, and more practice! Using adjectives appropriately is a reminder that, among many other aims, effective technical writing must reflect even the most basic rules of English grammar and usage.

The Writing Process
Building the Writing Habit

1. Golden Time

Try waking up at 5 a.m. and begin writing. People say the first waking hour is the "Golden Hour," where you concentrate and experience the most creativity. See if this is true for you, even if you are not a morning person. Once you form the habit of writing at a certain time, you have found your Golden Time.

2. The Same Place

Try to find a set writing place where you can focus on your topic. The purpose of this is to continually trigger your mind into a creative flow. To build an even stronger connection with writing, you might want to have a completely separate computer just for your writing. One idea is to disconnect this computer from the Internet so you will not be tempted to surf the Web, chat, check email, or play online games.

3. Idea Lists

An important part of stimulating creativity is bringing many ideas to writing. To do this, it is important to carry a notebook or a voice recorder with you throughout the day. You might be in a very unusual place when you get your great idea and you will want to capture every detail of it instead of forgetting it by trusting your memory.

4. Quiet Place

It is very important to maintain a quiet environment for writing because it takes several minutes to enter a creative state after being bothered. If it takes you 15 minutes to get into maximum productivity, and you get distracted every 20 minutes, you are not going to be productive as a writer.

5. Get Rid of Negative Thoughts

Stop all those critical thoughts that say "you have nothing to write about," "you have no fresh ideas," and "you cannot use English properly." Forget that. Put the pen to the paper, write anything that comes to mind, and see what happens.

6. Sit Alone in Silence

Create a time when you can just sit with your eyes closed for 15 minutes and think. You can concentrate on the stillness and block out all ideas. You will be surprised to find that your mind will generate the answers for you. With a clear mind, get up and write. This is especially true when you have been reading and putting a lot of information into your mind.

7. Ideas, Not Grammar, for the First Draft

Do not worry about punctuation and grammar the first time you write. Write as you normally write. Your purpose should be to make the ideas as understandable as possible and nothing more.

8. Rewrite

Revise your writing. After a one-day break, you can see your writing with fresh eyes, and you can express yourself in completely different ways. This is where you make your ideas even more understandable.

Tips for Journal Submission

I. Avoid Criticizing Your References

Papers that attack references will probably be rejected, especially when the authors or their friends are your reviewers. Journal editors use your references, especially in your introduction, to choose your reviewers.

> *"I think that the author knows his subject better than I do. I usually use his references to find a suitable reviewer."*
>
> —**Associate Editor, Journal of Retailing**

Do not emphasize the importance of your paper by belittling other papers. They are probably your reviewers and they are sensitive. Avoid using negative terms when citing other papers.

II. Examples of Offensive Citations

- The deficiency of Smith's approach is . . .
- The problems with Smith's paper are . . .
- A serious weakness with Smith's argument, however, is that . . .
- The key problem with Smith's explanation is that . . .
- It seems that Smith's understanding of the X framework is questionable.

III. A Better Citation Would Be

- Smith's model was effective for the X problem, but for Y . . .
- The X benefit of Smith's approach is not applicable to Y . . .

Using this citation style, you are not saying that Smith was an idiot, or that he did not understand his topic. You are only saying that your problem or conditions are different, necessitating a new approach.

IV. Your Research Area Is Small

It is likely that either "Smith" will be the reviewer, or one of "Smith's friends" will be. These reviewers may not like to see themselves publicly criticized for their methods and research. If you offend the reviewer with your comments, your paper and many of your future papers will have no place to go for publication. When you use a polite approach in your literature review, "Smith" will not be offended when he reads your paper, and will be more likely to recommend your paper.

V. Giving Other Reasons for Rejection

When reviewers give comments on a paper where they have been attacked, they may mention in their reviews that "Smith was taken out of context" in an effort to get the writer to modify the reference. Quite often, however, the reviewer simply rejects the paper as "outside the scope of the journal" or recommends that it be rejected because of "poor English." To be safe, be polite in your references because you never know who your reviewer will be.

Inappropriate Vocabulary and Improvements

make clear
A better alternative would be:
elucidate/clarify

make sure
A better alternative would be:
ensure/assure

meet
A better alternative would be:
satisfy/fulfill/adhere to

much / strongly
A better alternative would be:
markedly/considerably/substantially

realize
A better alternative would be:
comprehend/perceive/understand

solve
A better alternative would be:
alleviate/modify/resolve/eliminate/eradicate

Academic Vocabulary

Headwords	Other Words in the Family
constrain	constrained, constraining, constrains, constraint, constraints, unconstrained
construct	constructed, constructing, construction, constructions, constructive, constructs, reconstruct, reconstructed, reconstructing, reconstruction, reconstructs
constitute	constituted, constitutes, constituting, constitution, constitutions, constitutional, constitutionally, constitutive, unconstitutional
consult	consultancy, consultant, consultants, consultation, consultations, consultative, consulted, consults, consulting
consume	consumed, consumer, consumers, consumes, consuming, consumption
contact	contactable, contacted, contacting, contacts
contemporary	contemporaries
context	contexts, contextual, contextualize, contextualized, contextualizing, uncontextualized
couple	coupled, coupling, couples
create	created, creates, creating, creation, creations, creative, creatively, creativity, creator, creators, recreate, recreated, recreates, recreating
credit	credited, crediting, creditor, creditors, credits
criteria	criterion
crucial	crucially
culture	cultural, culturally, cultured, cultures, uncultured
currency	currencies
cycle	cycled, cycles, cyclic, cyclical, cycling
data	datum
debate	debatable, debated, debates, debating
decade	decades
decline	declined, declines, declining
deduce	deduced, deduces, deducing, deduction, deductions
define	definable, defined, defines, defining, definition, definitions, redefine, redefined, redefines, redefining, undefined
definite	definitely, definitive, indefinite, indefinitely
demonstrate	demonstrable, demonstrably, demonstrated, demonstrates, demonstrating, demonstration, demonstrations, demonstrative, demonstratively, demonstrator, demonstrators
denote	denotation, denotations, denoted, denotes, denoting

续表

Headwords	Other Words in the Family
deny	deniable, denial, denials, denied, denies, denying, undeniable
depress	depressed, depresses, depressing, depression
derive	derivation, derivations, derivative, derivatives, derived, derives, deriving
design	designed, designer, designers, designing, designs
detect	detectable, detected, detecting, detection, detective, detectives, detector, detectors, detects

Chapter 5
What Solution Do You Propose?

What Solution Do You Propose?

Briefly describe your study (hypothesis or research question), general experimental design or method, and reasons for using this method if there are alternatives.

I. Be Sure to State Clearly the Purpose or Hypothesis That You Are Investigating

The statement of purpose is usually placed near the end of the introduction, often as the topic sentence of the final paragraph. It is not necessary to use the words "hypothesis" or "null hypothesis," because these are usually obvious if you clearly state your purpose and expectations. When you are first learning to write, you can use a standard statement, such as "The purpose of this study is to . . . " or "This study investigates three possible mechanisms to explain the . . . " as a statement of purpose.

II. Provide a Reason for Your Approach to the Problem Studied

Briefly write how you approached the problem. This will usually follow your statement of purpose in the last paragraph of the introduction. Why did you choose this type of experiment or experimental design? What are the advantages of this particular model? What advantages does it have in answering the particular questions you are asking? However, do not discuss the actual techniques or protocols used in your study in the introduction. You can provide this information in the methods section, because your readers will be familiar with the usual techniques and approaches used in your field. If you use a new technique or methodology, the introduction should present the advantages of this new approach, compared with previously used methods.

III. Focus and Aim

- This paper focuses on/examines/assesses . . .
- This paper seeks to address the following questions . . .
- The purpose of this paper is to review recent research on the . . .
- This paper reviews the research conducted on . . .
- The aim of this paper is to determine/examine . . .
- The aim of this study is to evaluate and validate . . .

IV. Giving Reasons Why a Particular Method Was Adopted

- This study uses the semi-structured approach because . . .
- Smith et al. (1994) identified several advantages of . . .
- The best method to adopt for this investigation is to . . .
- A case study approach allows . . .
- The questionnaire design is based on . . .
- The X method is one of the more practical ways to . . .
- Quantitative measures usefully supplement and extend the qualitative analysis of . . .

V. Quick Points About the Introduction

- **Move from general to specific:** Connect a real-world problem to research literature, and then to your experiment.
- **Attract your reader's interest:** Answer the questions "What did you do?" and "Why should I care?"
- **Clearly present the links** between your problem and the solution, the question asked and your research design, and prior research and your experiment.
- **Use the active voice** as much as possible.

Common Writing Errors and Their Corrections

I. Creating Strong Verbs

Technical writers prefer strong verbs to weak verbs. A strong verb is a single word that shows an action. For example, *compare, consider,* and *indicate* are strong verbs. Weak verbs or helping verbs require more than one word to show an action. For example, *make a comparison, give consideration to,* and *give indication of* are all weak verbs. As students, we want to be concise and clear. Using strong verbs instead of weak verbs achieves both of these goals.

> *"Another suggestion for your paper is to find a native editor to help you with your verb use. Strong verbs move sentences. Helping verbs often confuse the reader in your technical descriptions."*
>
> – Reviewer, Journal of Technology Management

Original

Smith (2003) *asks the questions as to* whether conventional methods offer the best environment for execution.

Modified

Smith (2003) *questions* whether conventional methods offer the best environment for execution.

Original

Smith (2008) *makes use of* examples of these various techniques to prove that innovation continues.

Modified

Smith (2008) *uses* examples of these various techniques to prove that innovation continues.

II. When to Use the Verbs "Argue," "Indicate," and "Demonstrate" in Scholarly Writing

As substitutes for the word "argue," non-native writers often use the words "indicate" or "demonstrate." However, "indicate" and "demonstrate" are typically used to describe facts that are or have been proven to be indisputable; neither word expresses that a person has staked a position. "Mary Wollstonecraft indicated that women should have equal access to education," incorrectly suggests that Mary Wollstonecraft was simply, bloodlessly, pointing out an obvious fact. "Mary Wollstonecraft demonstrated that women should have equal access to education," comes closer, because she did, in fact, list reasons why society would benefit from educating women. However, this implies that Mary Wollstonecraft's reasons for educating women were more important than the fact that she staked this position, which is not the case. Her perspective arose from a belief in the equality of women, not because educating women would have concrete benefits for society. The reasons she presented for educating women supported her perspective, not the other way around. Neither of these statements is as precise as "Mary Wollstonecraft *argued* that women should have equal access to education."

It is crucial to use the word "argue" when referring to perspectives advanced in previous studies. If a study has advanced a perspective, it has "argued" that perspective. If a study has discovered an indisputable fact, it has "demonstrated" or "indicated" that fact. Effective formal English writing is unambiguous about the separation between perspectives and indisputable facts. Obscuring this difference fundamentally weakens a paper's foundation, as it is difficult for readers to properly assess an argument if they are forced to disentangle what is fact and what is argument. Certain highly technical papers, grounded completely in facts, may never require the use of the word "argue." However, perspectives and theories are argued in all fields, even in highly technical domains. Einstein argued that at certain times, light behaves as individual particles. He was not simply pointing out an obvious fact, so he did not merely "indicate" this. It would be inelegant to write that he "demonstrated" this—that would deny the theoretical nature of his activity.

Practically, the word "argue" also happens to be a convenient way for writers to avoid sounding hesitant about their findings. Results often "may indicate," "may suggest," or "may demonstrate." Certainly, there are times when hesitation is warranted. But the word "argue" effectively flags a statement as a perspective or an interpretation and invites the reader to share in that perspective, without hesitation. It is not incorrect to write, "The results may indicate that climatic change caused the extinction of the dinosaurs." However, this amounts to inviting the reader to half-believe in an unverified fact. "We argue that climatic change caused the extinction of the dinosaurs," is far stronger and clearer.

Punctuation Point

Capitalization

1. Capitalize proper nouns and proper adjectives. Use capitals for the names of specific people, places, and things.

• Names of people	⊙ Barack Obama, Abraham Lincoln
• Names of places	⊙ the United States, the Far East
• Names of public places	⊙ Yosemite Park, the Himalayas, the Midwest, Taroko Gorge
• Names of buildings	⊙ the Sears Tower, London Bridge, and Taipei 101
• Days of the weeks, months, and holidays	⊙ Tuesday, October, Thanksgiving Day, Easter, Lantern Festival, Dragon Boat Festival
• Organizations and companies	⊙ the Red Cross, General Motors, Giant
• Institutions: universities, departments	⊙ Rutgers University, the English Department
• Historical events and documents	⊙ the Gulf War, the Renaissance, the Constitution
• Religions, deities, respected people, and texts	⊙ Buddhism, Islam, Baptism, Jehovah, the Torah
• Races, tribes, nations, nationalities, and languages	⊙ Caucasian, Navajo, Spain, Spaniards, Spanish
• Registered trademark names	⊙ Nike, Xerox, Apple
• Names of ships, planes	⊙ the HMS Dreadnought, the Delta Queen, the Challenger

2. Capitalize a title before a person's name.

Example: The committee questioned *Senator Kennedy*.
Generally, a capital is not used when a title is not associated with a name. However, a capital can be used when a title substitutes for a specific person.
Example: The committee questioned *the President*.

3. Capitalize major words in titles.

For titles of published books, journals, magazines, essays, articles, and films, use a capital letter for all words except articles (*an, a, the*), coordinating conjunctions (*but, and, or, nor, so, for, yet*), "to" in an infinitive (*to* create), and prepositions (*in, on, by*) unless they begin or end a title or subtitle.
Example: *A Handbook for Writers* or *Twelve Days and Nights in Europe*.

The Writing Process
Using a dictionary and Thesaurus

Students learning to write in English are frequently advised to use a thesaurus and dictionary to appropriately vary their word choices when writing. Readers who are required to read documents that consistently use the same words can quickly become bored or frustrated and lose interest. Therefore, teachers have frequently stressed that thesauruses and dictionaries are effective tools for alleviating this problem. Teachers encourage students to use synonyms because they are words that frequently have either the same or similar meanings, depending on the context within which they are used.

Regardless, one of the goals of technical writing is to provide clear, easily understandable, and legible documents that report research results. Consequently, technical writers strongly recommend avoiding words that are colloquial, informal, over-used, vague, or dramatic. Although it is tempting to impress on readers' personal interpretations and feelings regarding research results, this is inappropriate in technical writing. Rather, studies should clearly present the reasons and aims for conducting the research, the methods used in the study, and the results and discussion in an accurate, concise, and professional manner. Formal writing necessitates restricting word choices to options that are formal, impersonal, and that reduce or eliminate any bias or personal feelings, and readers of such manuscripts appreciate that they must reach their own conclusions.

This has caused many writers to limit their word choices when writing technical documents. Nevertheless, although many words cannot be used, various applicable words remain. However, not all words are interchangeable in all situations.

For example, many authors consistently use the phrase "the results show." This phrase can be varied by using the following words: indicate, demonstrate, or depict. Such words are frequently interchangeable, but must be used with caution. They do not have identical meanings. "Demonstrate" can mean to show, but it also means to prove, present, explain, and display, depending on the context.

"Depict" is used to indicate that a representation is being used, which is frequently a picture or a diagram. "Indicate" specifically means to point information out, or to point toward a particular item or conclusion.

When employing a thesaurus, it is vital to understand that the various synonyms that are offered depend strongly on the context. A good strategy to use is to first review the definition provided for an entry. For example, the *Merriam-Webster Dictionary* defines "claim" as follows: to demand as a right, to call for or require, to take as the rightful owner, to assert as rightfully one's own. As a noun, "claim" is defined as follows: a demand for something that is due, an assertion, and a right to something.

In addition, the *Merriam-Webster Dictionary* offers additional information for people learning English as a second language. This page offers various examples and situations in which "claim" can be used including several informal and colloquial usages.

For example, when "claim" is entered on a site such as thesaurus.com, the first entry is a noun and is defined as "a property, a right reserved or demanded." All synonyms following this definition relate to this specific definition. The next entry for "claim" describes the word as a verb and is defined as "demand, maintain property or right," and all following synonyms relate to this specific definition. The entries that follow these provide synonyms for "claim" along with parts of speech and antonyms, which are words that mean the opposite of another word.

When all provided information is reviewed, it becomes clear that "claim" can be used in various contexts to indicate slightly different connotations and meanings.

For authors, reviewing all of the synonyms and antonyms for a given word is vital. When the synonyms for an entry appear to diverge from the meaning intended, the entry becomes a strong clue that the synonyms are referring to an alternate definition and cannot be used in the same context. This can be verified by reviewing the definition of a synonym in the dictionary. If the definition of the synonym does not meet the intended context, it is vital to avoid using that word.

Therefore, when using a thesaurus, it is crucial to review first the provided definition, the part of speech to ensure that the synonyms are relevant, and finally, a dictionary. By employing these strategies, authors can write effective and interesting articles that also meet the formal and restrictive requirements of technical writing.

How to Look Up Words in the Thesaurus

The Microsoft Word thesaurus provides a list of synonyms for the word you look up, and highlights the one that is closest in meaning to what you have typed, based on the context of the sentence.

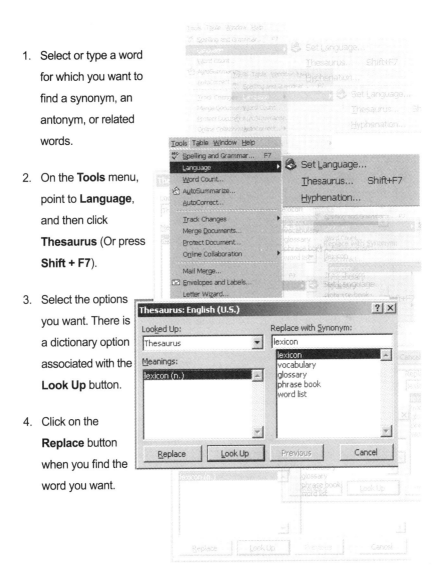

1. Select or type a word for which you want to find a synonym, an antonym, or related words.

2. On the **Tools** menu, point to **Language**, and then click **Thesaurus** (Or press **Shift + F7**).

3. Select the options you want. There is a dictionary option associated with the **Look Up** button.

4. Click on the **Replace** button when you find the word you want.

Tips for Journal Submission

I. How to Write a Title for Your Journal Paper

The title is the first part of a submitted manuscript seen by the editor, and then by the reviewers. After publication, it is the first part of the paper seen by journal readers. The title also appears in the journal issue contents page, and may also be part of an email notification or internet search result. The title therefore gives the intended audience a first impression of the author's work. If the title is unable to attract the attention of the potential reader, the rest of the article is unlikely to be read. If the title is bad, most readers do not keep reading hoping the paper will be better. They move on the next paper. Yet most journals only allow you a title of 8-15 words in length. As you craft a name for your paper, you should consider the following objectives for the title you choose. A title should:

- Describe the content of the paper;
- Distinguish the paper from others on a similar topic;
- Catch the reader's attention and interest;
- Match search queries so people will find your paper (and cite it).

We will discuss how to accomplish each of these objectives in the next section.

II. Choose a Type of Title

Titles of journal articles come in various ways and you probably have encountered most of them. For example, Hartley (2008) lists as many as 13 types, but for the sake of clarity we can summarize the most common formats in just three types (Jamali & Nikzad, 2011):

> **Declarative titles:** State the main findings or conclusions (e.g., "A three-month weight loss program increases self-esteem in adolescent girls").
>
> **Descriptive titles:** Describe the subject of the article but do

not reveal the main conclusions (e.g., "The effects of family support on patients with dementia").
Interrogative titles: Introduce the subject in the form of a question (e.g., "Does cognitive training improve performance on pattern recognition tasks?")

Each of these three types is useful and you should choose a format depending on what kind of information you want to convey to your audience. Declarative titles are generally used in research articles and they convey the largest amount of information. They are also good if you want to emphasize the technical side of the research you have carried out. Interrogative titles, on the other hand, are less common and they are more suitable for literature review articles. While the American Psychological Association (APA) states that interrogative titles are fine, other style guides such as the American Medical Association (AMA) discourage using question marks in titles. Out of the three, descriptive titles seem to be most common type in journals (Jamali & Nikzad, 2011).

III. Elements of an Informative Title

A title should answer the following questions:

- What will be researched?
- How will the topic be researched?
- With whom? Describes the research population and units of measurement.
- Where/in what context will the study by conducted?

> Main theme or research topic + Population + Geographical area
> ‖
> Informative Title

Answering the above questions should give you the three elements which are necessary for an informative article title. The *key concept*, the *device or group studied*, and *your argument*. Ideally we would also add a fourth element: *the results*. It is not always possible to add the results to the title, but it is always ideal. If you can put the results in the title, your reader can see the full impact of your work from your title alone. To put the results in the title we must find a *verb* to show the action that happened in our research and indicate the results. Below is an example of a poor title with corrections that make it complete according to our guidelines.

A poor title: *Mouse Behavior*

Why bad? We have no specific behavior and no modifying agent and no experimental organism. Basically we have no *key concept,* no *device or group studied,* and *no argument.*

A better title would be: *The Effects of Estrogen on the Nose-Twitch Courtship Behavior in Mice*
Why better? Because the key words identify a specific behavior, a modifying agent, and the experimental organism.

An even better title would give the result: *Estrogen Stimulates Intensity of Nose-Twitch Courtship Behavior in Mice*
Why better? Now we have added the results into the title by using the verb *stimulates.*

Purpose of the Title: Get Your Paper *Found* **and** *Read*
The title has served its purpose if the reader is attracted by it, has a good idea of what the article is about, and proceeds to read the abstract and the rest of the article. If the title and abstract sink an editor's interest, the rest is history. *Nature* emphasizes the importance of the title in their online section titled *How to write a paper*:

> *Titles need to be comprehensible and enticing to a potential reader quickly scanning a table of contents, while at the same time not being so general or vague as to obscure what the paper is about. We ask authors to be aware of abstracting and indexing services when devising a title for the paper: providing one or two essential keywords within a title will be beneficial for web-search results.*

IV. Titles Should Be Short

The title should accurately convey to the reader what the whole article is about with as few words as possible. Avoid lengthy titles because these may not only be difficult to decipher, but may also put off the potential reader. The subject matter should be indicated in the title. Authors should avoid the temptation of adding extraneous details, such as the objectives, methods, or results from the study.

The *Publication Manual of the American Psychological Association* (APA, 2009) recommends simplicity and the use of concise statements when formulating your title. Moreover, words that carry little or no meaning should be avoided as they increase the overall length and may mislead indexing services. The recommended length of a title is no more than 12 words (APA, 2009). Longer titles can be more difficult to remember and, as Jamali and Nikzad (2011) found, articles with longer titles are downloaded less than those with shorter titles in the biological sciences.

You can sometimes use a colon to add additional information to the title, such as the methodology that was used (e.g., "Brain activation during perception of face-like stimuli: An fMRI study"). However, using a very long subtitle can sometimes be cumbersome and counterproductive (e.g., "Self-esteem: Can it improve interpersonal relationships among community-dwelling adults in North America?"). In such cases, you can try to rewrite the title without the colon and see if any crucial information is lost (Hays, 2010).

A title should contain the fewest possible words that accurately describe the content of the paper. Omit all waste words such as:

- A study of . . .
- Investigations of . . .
- Observations on . . .

In addition, avoid starting with your article with the words "On the . . ." Starting like this implies the article is a note or short communication rather than an original research article.

For example, a title such as "A Novel Study on the Usefulness of Thermoimaging in the Diagnosis of Osteoid Osteoma of Bone: Analysis of Imaging Features and Comparison with Radiographs, Ultrasonography, Computed Tomography, and Other Conventional Imaging Techniques,

With Clinical Follow-up of Lesions in 24 Patients at the Taipei General Hospital" not only contains too many unnecessary and unhelpful words, but is boring. It can easily be replaced by "Thermoimaging in Diagnosis of Osteoid Osteoma," or simply "Thermoimaging of Osteoid Osteoma." On the other hand, a title like "Imaging of Osteoid Osteoma" or "Diagnosis of Osteoid Osteoma" will not be specific enough. You should also avoid abbreviations in the title (e.g., TI of OO).

V. Titles Should Be Active

Write in the active, not passive, voice. The active voice (where the subject acts) is usually shorter, more direct, and more precise than the passive voice (where the subject receives the action), making it better for a title of a paper. Although the passive voice has long been encouraged in scientific writing because it may be perceived as being more objective, many journals now recommend you use the active voice where possible to keep things clear and brief.

VI. Titles Should Be Understandable

The title should not be too general nor too specific. The readers you want to attract should be able to catch the central message of your paper with a quick glance at a table of contents. The target readership should be considered when constructing the title, as the title should be tailored accordingly. For a subspecialty journal, the authors can assume that the reader will be familiar with certain terms that can then be omitted from the title. In contrast, these same terms may be required to provide clarity for readers, of a general journal. However, articles that are wider in scope tend to have shorter titles, while highly specialized topics may need a longer title to fully encapsulate the subject content.

Journal editors prefer formal titles instead of cute or funny titles that may be misinterpreted. Irony, puns, and humor in the title may help you attract more readers, but they should be avoided most of the time (Hartley, 2008). The problem with them is that they may not be understood by readers who are not native speakers and they also tend to be culture-specific. Moreover, your article will probably appear less often in the search results if you decide to the replace the words carrying the main meaning with a humorous phrase.

Do not use acronyms in the title without spelling them out (Hartley, 2012). Readers who are not familiar with their meaning may simply skip your article even though it is relevant to their search.

VII. Titles Should Be Full of Keywords

Your readers will find your paper through a web search, database, or indexing service using *keywords* in the title and, to a lesser extent, the abstract. So fill your title with keywords. An improperly titled paper may never reach the audience for which it was intended, so be specific. If the study is of a particular species or chemical, name it in the title. If the study has been limited to a particular region or system, and the inferences it contains are similarly limited, then name the region or system in the title.

VIII. Titles and Search Engine Optimization

Optimizing your article for search engines will greatly increase its chance of being read and cited in other research. Citation indexes are already used in many disciplines as a measure of an article's value. The crucial area for optimization is your article's abstract and title, which are available free online. You must maximize the web-friendliness of the most public part of your article.

Each search engine, such as Google Scholar or Journal Citation Reports, has its own algorithms for ranking journal articles. Most search engines attempt to identify the topic of a journal article. To do this, some search engines still use metadata tags (invisible to the user) to assess relevant content, but most now scan a page for keyword phrases, giving extra weight to phrases in headings and to repeated phrases.

IX. SEO Key 1: Write a Clear, Descriptive Title

For search engines, the title of your article is the most interesting element. The search engine assumes that the title contains all of the important words that define the topic of the article, and thus weights words appearing there most heavily. This is why it is crucial for you to choose a clear, accurate title. Think about the search terms that readers are likely to use when looking for articles on the same topic as yours, and help them by constructing your title to include those terms. In the days of print-only journals, it didn't matter if an author published an article with an odd title in a journal because the context of the journal was clear so the reader knew the topic it was related to. On the web, people search for keywords without referencing a particular journal.

Remember that people tend to search for specifics, not just one word, e.g., *management of information systems* not just *management*. Use simple word order and common word combinations (e.g., "juvenile delinquency" is more commonly used than "delinquency amongst juveniles").

Be as descriptive as possible and use specific rather than general terms: for instance, include the specific drug name rather than just the class of drug. Avoid using abbreviations; they could have different meanings in different fields. Avoid using acronyms and initialisms (e.g., "Ca" for calcium could be mistaken for "CA," which means cancer). Write scientific names in full, e.g., *Escherichia coli* rather than *E. coli*. Refer to chemicals by their common or generic name instead of their formulas. Avoid the use of Roman numerals in the title as they can be interpreted differently: for instance, part III could be mistaken for factor III.

X. SEO Key 2: Repeat Key Phrases in the Abstract

After the title the next most important field is the text of the abstract. You should repeat the keywords or phrases from the title within the abstract itself. You know the key phrases for your subject area, whether it is temporal lobe epilepsy or website usability. Although we can never know exactly how search engines rank sites (their algorithms are closely guarded secrets and frequently updated), the number of times that your keywords and phrases appear on the page can have an important effect. Use the same key phrases, if possible in the title and abstract. Please note that numerous unnecessary repetitions will result in the page being rejected by search engines so do not do this too much. Key phrases need to make sense within the title and abstract and flow well. It is best to focus on a maximum of three or four different keyword phrases in an abstract rather than try to get across too many points. Finally, always check that the abstract reads well, remember the primary audience is still the researcher not a search engine, so write for readers not robots.

XI. When Should the Title Be Written?

Writing a paper can be a lengthy process that may take anything from a few days to several months. During this time, it is natural to decide to change some aspects of your paper or to come up with new ideas that you have not thought of before. That is why, it is a good idea to start with a draft title in the beginning and then focus on writing the rest of the paper. If you come up with a good idea in the meanwhile, just write it down and continue with your work. Once you are ready with the whole text, you can return to the title and decide on the final version. In some cases, this strategy can make a huge difference because you may get so distracted from all the editing and rewriting that you may simply forget to make changes to the title as well.

XII. Write a Few Variations of the Title

Take the time to write a few possible titles and to experiment using different types or alternative formulations (Hays, 2010). In this way, you will be able to analyze how they would function in reality and possibly generate some new ideas. Sometimes, just by looking at different variants, you can come up with a better idea that combines the best aspects of two or more tentative titles. Once you are ready with the generation of ideas, just pick the best variant and put it in the place of the draft title.

XIII. Running Title

Some journals require a "running title," which is a short version of the title. This is usually printed as a header at the top of each or alternate journal pages. The running title is limited in length by a maximum number of characters specified in the journal's author guidelines.

References

American Psychological Association. (2009). *Publication manual of the American Psychological Association* (6th ed.). Washington DC: Author.

Hartley, J. (2008). *Academic writing and publishing: A practical guidebook.* Abingdon, Oxon: Routledge.

Hartley, J. (2012). New ways of making academic articles easier to read.

International Journal of Clinical and Health Psychology, 12(1), 143-160.

Hays, J. C. (2010). Eight recommendations for writing titles of scientific manuscripts.*Public Health Nursing, 27*(2), 101-103. doi: 10.1111/j.1525-1446.2010.00832.x

Jamali, H. R., & Nikzad, M. (2011). Article title type and its relation with the number of downloads and citations. *Scientometrics, 88*(2), 653-661. doi: 10.1007/s11192-011-0412-z

Inappropriate Vocabulary and Improvements

suitable

A better alternative would be:
appropriate/adequate

tries

A better alternative would be:
attempts/aims/aspires

usually

A better alternative would be:
normally/typically/generally

very

A better alternative would be:
highly/rather/quite/extremely

way

A better alternative would be:
method/means/approach/strategy

whole

A better alternative would be:
complete/entire/comprehensive

> **figure out**
>
> A better alternative would be:
> *distinguish/differentiate/discriminate/identify*

Academic Vocabulary

Headwords	Other Words in the Family
deviate	deviated, deviates, deviating, deviation, deviations
device	devices
devote	devoted, devotedly, devotes, devoting, devotion, devotions
differentiate	differentiated, differentiates, differentiating, differentiation
dimension	dimensional, dimensions, multidimensional
diminish	diminished, diminishes, diminishing, diminution, undiminished
discrete	discretely, discreteness
discriminate	discriminated, discriminates, discriminating, discrimination
displace	displaced, displacement, displaces, displacing
display	displayed, displaying, displays
dispose	disposable, disposal, disposed, disposes, disposing
distinct	distinction, distinctions, distinctive, distinctively, distinctly, indistinct, indistinctly
distort	distorted, distorting, distortion, distortions, distorts
distribute	distributed, distributing, distribution, distributional, distributions, distributive, distributor, distributors, redistribute, redistributed, redistributes, redistributing, redistribution
diverse	diversely, diversification, diversified, diversifies, diversify, diversifying, diversity
document	documentation, documented, documenting, documents
domain	domains
domestic	domestically, domesticate, domesticated, domesticating, domestics
dominate	dominance, dominant, dominated, dominates, dominating, domination
draft	drafted, drafting, drafts, redraft, redrafted, redrafting, redrafts
drama	dramas, dramatic, dramatically, dramatize, dramatized, dramatizing, dramatizes, dramatization, dramatizations, dramatist, dramatists, dramatization, dramatizations, dramatizing

续表

Headwords	Other Words in the Family
dynamic	dynamically, dynamics
economy	economic, economical, economically, economics, economies, economist, economists, uneconomical
edit	edited, editing, edition, editions, editor, editorial, editorials, editors, edits
element	elements
eliminate	eliminated, eliminates, eliminating, elimination
emerge	emerged, emergence, emergent, emerges, emerging
emphasis	emphasize, emphasized, emphasizing, emphatic, emphatically
empirical	empirically, empiricism
enable	enabled, enables, enabling
encounter	encountered, encountering, encounters
energy	energetic, energetically, energies
enforce	enforced, enforcement, enforces, enforcing

II WRITING THE METHODS SECTION

Chapter 6
How Did You Study the Problem?

How Did You Study the Problem?

I. Materials and Methods: Introduction to the Section

This section of the paper should describe the materials used in the experiment or study, and methods employed in the study. This section should be provided under a subheading, which can be titled as *Materials and Methods, Methodology,* or *Experimental Methods*. A concise paragraph explaining a formula or step used in the procedure should be included to avoid confusing the readers.

This should be the easiest part to write; however, many students misunderstand its purpose. This section's purpose is to document the specialized materials and general procedures used in the study for other individuals to adopt either all or a few of the methods in another study or evaluate the quality of the study itself.

To further simplify this section, a list of steps on how to write an effective methods section is included below.

- Subheadings should be provided. The information can be divided under separate subsections, i.e., *methods* as one subsection and *materials* as another.
- The methods should be described in the past tense.
- Novel methods must be described so that the research or experiment can be replicated by another researcher.
- The methods already established in the field should be referenced.
- Finally, the statistical methods should be described.

Below listed are steps to write an effective materials section.

- The materials should be described in a separate section only if this section needs to be distinguished from the methods in the study.
- The description of the materials should include specialized equipment or supplies not commonly found.
- Do not include commonly found supplies such as test tubes, beakers, or standard lab equipment such as centrifuges.
- If the use of a specific piece of equipment is critical to the success of the experiment, then it should be provided in this section along with the source or manufacturer information.

II. Style Used in the Materials and Methods Section

The use of active voice should be avoided, as it draws the reader's attention to the researcher instead of the work. Therefore, passive voice should be used in this section.

III. Sampling, Data Collection, and Measures

Three important components of the materials and methods, namely sampling, data collection, and measures, are elaborated below.

▶Sampling

This subsection should be included in experimental procedures. In this subsection, the following points should be included.
- A clear description of the target population and/or participants, the research description, and the units of analysis used in the study should be provided.
- The sampling method should be mentioned. This section should also include:

- Description and motivation of the sampling method used;
- Disadvantages related to the use of the sampling method used in the paper;
- Description of how the sampling method was used;
- Finally, include the target sample size, how the sample size was determined, the realized sample size, the response rate, and the number of usable responses.
- Provide a demographic and/or behavioral profile of the participants in the study.

▶ Data Collection

This subsection should discuss the following points:
- A brief description of the data collection method(s) and the pretesting method should be included.
- A description of how the data was collected should be provided and should include:
    - Description and motivation of the data collection method(s);
    - A reference to the instrument used for data collection;
    - Description of the data collection process;
    - Indication of the time period of the data collection.

▶ Measures

This subsection should describe the scales of measurement and define the questionnaires used in the study. This component could also be included under a separate subheading titled *Measurements*.

The points listed below should be included when writing this subsection.

- Only the scales used to measure the main concepts should be described.
- The description should include the
    - Basic scale design, e.g., Likert;
    - Number of scale items or points;
    - Labeling of the scale points and items in the study;
    - Number of subdimensions;
    - Defining the score(s) of the scale used;
    - Cross-reference to the scales or questionnaires;
    - Reference for the scales adapted;
    - Method(s) used to calculate the scores;
    - Indication of the consistency reliability of multiple rating scales;
    - Comparison of the values obtained in the study.

Using Verb Tenses to Describe Materials and Data

Previously, we discussed the appropriate use of verb tenses when explaining your research. For instance, we recommended using the **present tense** when stating or referring to an **established fact**.

- Subcutaneous injections *are highly* effective in administering vaccines and medications.

We also suggested using the **past tense** when describing the **methods** of your study. For example:

- A questionnaire **was administered** to evaluate the current impact of nursing innovation in neonatal intensive care units.

When describing **materials** in your study, the verb tense you use depends on whether you changed the materials in any way. For instance, when explaining the essential details of **conventional** (unmodified) materials used in your study, write in the **present tense**.

- The scanning electron microscope (SEM) generally *contains* a tungsten hairpin filament, which *serves* as an electron source.
- Silicon *is* the core component of most semiconductor devices, and *demonstrates* electrochemical properties in aqueous solutions.

When describing materials in your study that you **modified, altered,** or **changed** in any way, use the **past tense**.

- A scanning electron microscope (SEM) *was modified* by adding large-field vector deflection to examine remote radioactive specimens.*

- The silicon *used* in this study *was* an n-type silicon *obtained* from 100-mm diameter ingots *grown* using the Czochralski method.*

* Note the appropriate use of passive voice to describe methods.

Using verb tenses when reporting data also depends on whether the information is an established fact, or is a finding that you derived from your research. For example, use the **present tense** when reporting facts about a **general** population:

- The population density of Shanghai *is* approximately 2,657 people per square kilometer.

- Nearly 80% of Singaporeans *are* literate in English as either their first or second language.

- Graduate students from other countries *total* 1,073, or 27.6% of enrolled MS candidates.

When reporting **sample** data obtained through the research **you conducted** or from **your literature review**, use the **past tense**.

- According to a 2009 survey conducted by the Institute of Higher Education, Keio *was* the top-ranked private university in Tokyo; the next highest *were* Juntendo, Waseda, and Nihon.

- One-third of Internet users in Europe *were* infected by malware in 2010.

- The students surveyed in this study *were* not a randomly selected population and may not, therefore, be representative of all students at the University.

Knowing which verb tense to use when describing materials or reporting particular data is a critical step toward ensuring that your reviewers clearly understand your research.

How Did You Study the Problem?

Briefly explain the general type of procedure you used.

I. Describing the Different Methods Available

- To date, various methods have been developed and introduced to

measure X . . .
- Most recent studies measure X in four ways.
- Radiographic techniques are the main non-invasive methods used to determine . . .
- Different authors have measured X in various ways.
- Previous studies have based their selection criteria on . . .
- Several methods are used to assess X. Each has its advantages and disadvantages.

II. Giving Reasons Why a Particular Method Was Adopted

- The semi-structured approach was chosen because . . .
- Smith et al. (1994) identified several advantages of the case study . . .
- The best method to adopt for this investigation is to . . .
- A case study approach was chosen to allow a . . .
- The questionnaire design is based on . . .
- The X method is one of the more practical ways to . . .
- Quantitative measures supplement and extend qualitative analysis.

III. Indicating a Specific Method

- X was prepared according to the procedure used by Patel et al. (1957).
- The synthesis of X was conducted according to the procedure of Smith (1973).
- X was synthesized using the same method that was detailed for Y, using . . .
- This compound was prepared by adapting the procedure used by Zhao et al. (1990).
- This study used X to explore the subsurface of . . .

What Did You Use?

(This section may be a subheading, e.g., Materials)
Describe what materials, subjects, and equipment you used.

I. Indicating Sample Size and Characteristics

- The initial sample *consisted of* 200 students, but 13 did not complete all

of the interviews.
- All studies that described using some sort of X procedure *were included* in the analysis.
- All of the participants *were aged* between 18 and 19 at the beginning of the study . . .
- Two groups of subjects *were interviewed*, namely X and Y. The first group was interviewed . . .
- A random sample of patients with . . . *was recruited* from . . .
- Forty-seven students studying X *were recruited* for this study.
- The students *were divided* into two groups based on their performance on . . .
- The project *used* a convenience sample of 32 first-year modern language students.
- Just over half the sample (53%) *were* female, of which 69% were . . .

II. Indicating Reasons for Sample Characteristics

- A small sample was chosen *because of* the expected difficulty in obtaining . . .
- The subjects were selected *on the basis of* their homogeneity in . . .
- Criteria *for* selecting the subjects *were as follows*: . . .

Common Writing Errors and Their Corrections

I. Avoid Starting Sentences with the Words "It" and "There"

One key difference between writing at an undergraduate level and graduate level is the number of words students use in written projects. Undergraduate students try to fill the paper with as many words as possible because their professors tell them to have at least 500 words for a written project. This emphasis on quantity over quality hurts technical writing. Technical writers emphasize their ideas, instead of their words, by making their sentences as clear and short as possible. Technical writers do not want to fill their papers; instead, they want their papers to be filled with simply structured sentences, so the research stands out.

> *"Your sentences are too long, especially your methods part! Try cutting them into individual units of complete thoughts instead of stringing together thoughts without stopping for breath."*
>
> — Reviewer, Journal of Water Resource Management

> *"Look up the rules on using 'it.' This word should not appear at the beginning of every sentence."*
>
> — 2nd Reviewer, Journal of Usability Studies

Original

It is possible that participants between the ages of 18 and 19 responded differently than those between the ages of 20 and 21.

Modified

Participants between the ages of 18 and 19 *may* have responded differently than participants between the ages of 20 and 21.

Original

There is a need for implementation of the policy on a larger scale by the president of the association.

Modified

The association president *must* implement the policy on a larger scale.

Original

It could happen that a decision to modify the model is made by the researcher.

Modified

The researcher *may* decide to modify the model.

Original

There is a necessity for a semi-structured approach to be chosen.

Modified

A semi-structured approach *must* be chosen.

Original

It was vital that quantitative measures would usefully supplement and extend the qualitative analysis.

Modified

Quantitative measures *must* usefully supplement and extend qualitative analysis.

Original

It is necessary that the best method to adopt for this investigation is determined by the committee.

Modified

The committee *must* decide the best method to adopt for this investigation.

II. Overuse of "It" Structures

In conversation and informal writing, the pronoun "it" can be the sentence subject. The "impersonal it" can refer to time, the weather, or temperature. For example, "It is 9:25," or "It is hot today."

In formal writing, another kind of "it," the "anticipatory it," should not be used. This is also called a "fake subject" because the "it" appears to be the subject of the sentence, but the subject is actually in the sentence. Here are some examples:
- It was important for the government to intervene.
- It is essential that the model be revised.
- It will be necessary to rebuild the economy.

The anticipatory "it" in each of these sentences is acting only as a fake subject. Because the anticipatory "it" is really meaningless, good writers will rewrite these sentences. Students often overuse this structure in their writing, but removing "it" is simple. Just move the subject of the sentence and drop the needless "it." Consider the revised sentences below:
- The government must intervene.
- The model must be revised.
- Rebuilding the economy is necessary.

These sentences allow the true subject to be placed in a clear position, while creating more direct action. Avoid using these wordy phrases beginning with "it."
- It is known that . . .
- It is considered that . . .
- It demonstrates that . . .
- It could be said that . . .
- It follows that . . .

Punctuation Point

I. Active Verbs for Describing Analysis and Phenomenon in the Research Paper

When writing, we often automatically make lazy choices, especially when choosing verbs. We feel enticed by generic all-purpose verbs such as "deal with" or "show," which on the surface can sound snappy and technical. However, the more these verbs are used in a particular paper, the more meaningless they become. Even in journal articles, these verbs put in a shocking number of appearances and return for many unsolicited encores. Yet these words convey no analytical meaning at all and are barely informational. Much to the reader's frustration, "deal with" and "show" are often merely thinly disguised excuses for much more active analytical verbs such as theorize, suggest, imply, and propose. For the reader, "Chen dealt with" or "Figure 1 shows" are far less meaningful than "Chen hypothesized" or "Figure 1 represents." As always, you should choose exact words in favor of nonspecific ones, especially when you can use an active verb.

In technical writing, learning to deploy active verbs on the page is one of the most obvious and easiest ways to improve your style. Active verbs—whether in present or past tense—are especially meaningful as you describe work that another author or you have completed or are in the process of completing. As a rule, you should try to choose active verbs in the following circumstances:

1. As you prepare a literature review, where your job is to describe the work of others in concise, analytical terms.

> Phillip Chang (2008) proposes a mechanism explaining increased silica solubility in the presence of two small organic acids.

2. As you interpret your own experimental work, where your job is to explain observed trends.

> The results of this study challenge findings from similar studies about analytic concentration varying with sample location.

3. As you present a thesis or objective statement, where your job is to forecast information that will follow in the paper.

> This study characterizes wetlands by their water chemistry and postulates that water chemistry varies with water source and wetland type.

4. As you refer to figures, tables, or equations, where your job is to define the purpose of the figure, table, or equation.

> Figure 4 depicts grain growth that occurred after the ceramic was sintered for three hours.

What follows is a substantial list of active verbs. I assembled this list by scanning journal articles to see how the best authors described their work or the work of others. Each of these words is packed with individual, analytical meaning. When using this list, be sure to choose the best verb for the situation—verbs such as "construct," "challenge," and "extrapolate" are obviously completely different from each other, so you must use them with meaningful care.

Active Verbs that Describe Work and Analytical Thinking

yield	illustrate	illuminate	reveal	employ
mean	suggest	clarify	indicate	represent
prove	insist	propose	imply	assert
postulate	consider	infer	state	extrapolate
estimate	define	classify	invoke	analyze
compare	hypothesize	synthesize	summarize	disagree
generalize	narrate	evaluate	simplify	measure
note	predict	introduce	report	challenge
delineate	depict	construe	interpret	provide
acknowledge	distinguish	inform	specify	restrict

determine	detail	sum up	designate	point out
set forth	deduce	derive	characterize	guide
maintain	believe	speculate	present	organize
investigate	assess	determine	calculate	support
devise	construct	evaluate	attribute	obtain
assume	argue	reiterate	discover	decide

II. Describing Phenomena with Active Verbs

Which do you prefer—the phrase "to cut or split something into two theoretically and essentially equal parts," or the simple verb "bisect"? Which is easier to write and to read—the phrase "unite into what is essentially one body," or the simple verb "coalesce"? As you explain scientific phenomena, your readers will be highly pleased with you if you offer them lively, exact, direct, robust, vibrant, single-word verbs. Furthermore, your writing will be less wordy and more clear. However, many writers are tempted in the other direction. Trying to sound impressive, some would write "The device is prone to the submission of one pulse every 12 seconds" instead of the much simpler and more accurate "The device transmits one pulse every 12 seconds." Always beware of overcomplicating your verbs, and remember that their function is to describe actively and efficiently.

Many verbs are used continually in one field but rarely in another, so it is essential that you become familiar with those verbs that are standard vocabulary in your field. The verb "induce," which means "to produce an electric current or magnetic effect by induction," should be standard vocabulary for someone in physics or electrical engineering, while the verb "sinter," which means "to weld without melting," should be familiar and useful to those in metallurgy (it also doubles as a noun in geology).

Plenty of meaningful single-word verbs are out there just waiting for you to use them. One easy way to choose the best verb is to consult the brief (and certainly not exhaustive) list that follows to search for the kinds of active verbs that the best writers choose. The verbs are organized randomly to stress that they are not interchangeable nor to be used arbitrarily. Even though the exact verb that you need to describe a phenomenon may not be on this list, the verbs on the list do suggest the kind of verbs that you should choose. Many students tell me they turn to this list as they write a paper just to keep their minds tuned-in to using single-word active verbs. For efficiency, accuracy, and your own credibility as a technical writer, always aim for the best and simplest verb. If you are unsure of a verb's exact meaning, be sure to look it up.

A Short List of Active Verbs that Describe Phenomena

discharge	overlie	emanate	radiate	scatter
exchange	separate	surround	combine	eliminate
emit	transmit	carry	bombard	exert
exude	interact	behave	exchange	absorb
converge	extend	constrain	force	elongate
contract	trend	plunge	occur	fracture
continue	mix	slow	quicken	produce
bond	interlock	fuse	deteriorate	migrate
encompass	access	traverse	join	dominate
deposit	underlie	overlap	originate	isolate
invade	permeate	evolve	divide	sinter
reclaim	restore	abandon	contain	accrue
precede	influence	saturate	circulate	forecast
orient	distribute	allow	lag	terminate
activate	cease	record	form	transect
condense	enrich	invert	convert	alter
link	superimpose	rotate	rupture	streamline
appear	require	ascend	descend	collapse
superpose	crystallize	bisect	cede	coalesce
disperse	disseminate	disintegrate	propel	repel
accelerate	transfer	penetrate	halt	curb

The Writing Process
Writing Support Groups

I. What Is the Purpose of Writing Support Groups?

Being a productive, motivated writer can be difficult when working alone. Writers need the supportive and competitive energy of other writers. Writing support groups can help you develop your academic writing and editing skills for class papers, proposals, dissertations, and publications. Working with a group of other writers encourages you to set goals and deadlines for your writing, revising, and project completion. You are responsible to the group to complete and share your writing. You are not just responsible to yourself; you are responsible to others. Writing support groups also help you d evelop skills by offering feedback on your ideas and writing. Writing groups let you know you are not alone.

II. What Are the Mechanics of Writing Support Groups?

Your group can meet every two weeks, once a month, or on any schedule the members choose. The more time between meetings, the bigger your goals should be. Each member agrees to email their writings to the members several days before the next meeting. The papers are then read by the members who offer feedback, questions, comments, and editing suggestions. The group can choose one or two writing samples for everyone to read at each meeting or can assign a sample to each member beforehand. This way, everyone's work is read and everyone receives feedback. The group should continue to meet as long as its members benefit. New and replacement members can be added as time passes.

Tips for Journal Submission

I. Understanding New Words when Reading an Academic Paper

When reading an academic paper, it is best not to interrupt your reading process to look up every difficult word right away in the dictionary. Mark unfamiliar words with a penciled mark, not with anything permanent, but try these techniques for making an "educated guess" at the meaning as you go. You will acquire some real understanding of how words are used rather than just long vocabulary lists and an overused dictionary. Eventually you will confirm your guesses with a dictionary.

1. First, sound the word out. Use simple phonics to attempt saying the word—try a couple of ways. You might recognize the word when you say it out loud.
2. Next, examine the structure of the word. Look for familiar word parts, and see if you can tell how the prefixes and suffixes shape the root meaning.
3. Then look at the context of the word. Guess at the word's meaning from the way it is used in the sentence. You may find that an informal definition is included with the word. Or maybe you will see the meaning in the next idea, or just be able to tell the meaning by the way the sentence continues.
4. Only then, check the dictionary. If you cannot understand what you are reading after using the above steps, pause and turn to the dictionary or the textbook's glossary list. When you find your word, skim through the whole entry and find the most relevant meaning. Check the pronunciation too.
5. Then reinforce your understanding by writing a usable brief definition or synonym in the margin of the paper you are reading—in pencil, because you won't always need it there.

You should also use the dictionary as a final step even if you have been able to guess well enough to keep going in your reading. When you stop after a section of reading to make notes, check your understanding of any words that are not yet clear. Read the dictionary entry carefully—look for analysis of the word's derivation and structure and for examples of its usage. Then make a marginal note.

II. A Method for Reinforcing New Vocabulary Words

When you have learned a new word, make it part of your active store of words. A list helps you review; note cards are even better to let you deepen your command of important words. The following method keeps the words in context. It also calls on both sight and hearing so that you learn in various ways at once. Keep returning to your cards and repeat this method until you feel comfortable using the word. You won't do this for all your new words. Choose a few to work on intensively.

1. Say the word out loud according to the dictionary pronunciation guide. Look up the key to pronunciation symbols at the front or back of the dictionary if necessary.
2. Write down the word and mark it up to show its inner structure (root word + prefixes or suffixes). Keep saying it over aloud (or at least in your head).
3. On the other side of the card, write down a brief definition. Then copy out the sentence where you saw the word used—and say it aloud as you write. You will probably find sentences from other readings to add later.
4. Read over the card periodically. Eventually try writing a sentence of your own using the word. When you can do this without even looking at the card, you've arrived!

III. Further Tips for Building Vocabulary Skills

The best way to increase and deepen your general vocabulary is to spend time reading about a topic you already enjoy or need in English: a newspaper or popular magazine will be fine, as long as you read with an active interest in the words that you find there. Do not just buy an English grammar book and try to read it. You may succeed the first time you read it but because the topic is not interesting to you, studying a grammar book will not be sustainable. Better to read English comic books or play English computer games, if this is what you already enjoy. Because you enjoy these topics reading them will be more interesting for you. As your vocabulary from reading increases, you will begin to be comfortable actually using these new words in speech or writing. In fact, you may not need to use them deliberately; you will simply find them in your command when you need them. If they're established through a true understanding, they belong to you.

Inappropriate Vocabulary and Improvements

As students, we must use clear vocabulary and avoid unnecessary phrases or strings of words that can easily be replaced with a single word. The following phrases are examples of complicated word strings that should be replaced with shorter, one-word substitutes.

is found to be

A better alternative would be:
is

is capable of

A better alternative would be:
can

in view of the fact that

A better alternative would be:
because

in this case

A better alternative would be:
here

in some cases

A better alternative would be:
occasionally

in no case

A better alternative would be:
never

Academic Vocabulary

Headwords	Other Words in the Family
enhance	enhanced, enhancement, enhances, enhancing
enormous	enormity, enormously
ensure	ensured, ensures, ensuring
entity	entities
environment	environmental, environmentalist, environmentalists, environmentally, environments
equate	equated, equates, equating, equation, equations
equip	equipment, equipped, equipping, equips
equivalent	equivalence
erode	eroded, erodes, eroding, erosion
error	erroneous, erroneously, errors
establish	disestablish, disestablished, disestablishes, disestablishing, disestablishment, established, establishes, establishing, establishment, establishments
estate	estates
estimate	estimated, estimates, estimating, estimation, estimations, over-estimate, overestimate, overestimated, overestimates, overestimating, underestimate, underestimated, underestimates, underestimating
ethic	ethical, ethically, ethics, unethical
ethnic	ethnicity
evaluate	evaluated, evaluates, evaluating, evaluation, evaluations, evaluative, re-evaluate, re-evaluated, re-evaluates, re-evaluating, re-evaluation
eventual	eventuality, eventually
evident	evidenced, evidence, evidential, evidently
evolve	evolution, evolved, evolving, evolves, evolutionary, evolutionist, evolutionists
exceed	exceeded, exceeding, exceeds
exclude	excluded, excludes, excluding, exclusion, exclusionary, exclusionist, exclusions, exclusive, exclusively
exhibit	exhibited, exhibiting, exhibition, exhibitions, exhibits
expand	expanded, expanding, expands, expansion, expansionism, expansive
expert	expertise, expertly, experts
explicit	explicitly

续表

Headwords	Other Words in the Family
exploit	exploitation, exploited, exploiting, exploits
export	exported, exporter, exporters, exporting, exports
expose	exposed, exposes, exposing, exposure, exposures
external	externalization, externalize, externalized, externalizes, externalizing, externality
extract	extracted, extracting, extraction, extracts
facilitate	facilitated, facilitates, facilities, facilitating, facilitation, facilitator, facilitators, facility
factor	factored, factoring, factors
feature	featured, features, featuring
federal	federation, federations

Chapter 7
How Did You Proceed?

How Did You Proceed?

Key Questions to Answer

Document and explain the steps of your experiment. Use a subheading such as "Methods" or "Procedures" to signify this part. Use the infinitive of purpose to describe your processes in the experiment.

Methods

1. Report the methodology that you used in your research and intend to write about in your paper.

2. Describe the methodology completely and specifically. Include all relevant information that will help your reviewers and other researchers to understand your methods.

3. Use headings focused on specific procedures or groups of procedures that present your methods clearly and concisely.

4. Report how your procedures were conducted in general terms. Do not describe day-to-day events. Always think about what would be important to other researchers working in your field of study.

5. If you used a well-known procedure, then report it by name with a reference to it. Keep it simple, short, and concise.

What to Avoid

6 Avoid writing this section as a list of instructions.

7 Remove all explanatory information and background—save that for the discussion.

8 Remove information that is not important to other researchers, such as the color of the instruments you used, or who recorded the data.

Explain the Steps You Took in Your Experiment

I. Describing the Process: Infinitive of Purpose

- *To identify* the T10 and T11 spinous processes, the subjects were asked to . . .
- *To understand* how X regulates Y, a series of transfections were performed . . .
- *To enable* the subjects to see the computer screen clearly . . .
- *To see* if the two methods performed the same measurement . . .
- *To control* for bias, measurements were performed by another person.
- *To measure* X, a question asking . . . was used.
- *To determine* whether or not . . . , KG-1 cells were incubated for . . .
- *To establish* whether or not . . .
- *To increase* the reliability of measures, each X was tested twice with a 4-min break between the trials.
- The vials were capped with . . . to *prevent* volatilization.
- In an attempt to *make* each interviewee feel as comfortable as possible . . .

II. Describing the Process: Other Phrases Expressing Purpose

- *For the purpose of* measuring height, subjects were asked to stand . . .
- *For the purpose of* analysis, two segments were extracted from each . . .
- *For estimating* protein concentration, 100 µL of protein sample was mixed with . . .

III. Describing the Process: Typical Verbs

(use of the passive voice)
- Data management and analysis *were performed* using SPSS 8.0.
- The experiments *were performed* over the course of the growing period from . . .
- Injection solutions *were coded* by a colleague to reduce experimenter bias.
- Drugs *were administered* by ICV injection under brief CO_2 narcosis.
- The mean score for the two trials *was subjected* to multivariate analysis of variance to determine . . .
- The subjects *were asked* to pay close attention to the characters whenever . . .
- Prompts *were used* as an aid to Question 2 so that . . .
- The pilot interviews *were conducted* informally by the trained interviewer . . .
- Blood samples *were obtained* from 314 Caucasian male patients . . .
- Independent tests *were carried out* on the X and Y scores for the 4 years from . . .
- This experiment *was* then *repeated* under different conditions to improve the poor signal-to-noise ratio.
- Significance levels *were* set at the 1% level using the Student's t-test.
- A total of 256 samples *were taken* from 52 boreholes (Fig. 11).

IV. Describing the Process: Sequence Words and Phrases

- *Prior to* commencing the study, ethical clearance was obtained from . . .
- *In the end*, the EGO was selected as the measurement tool for the current study.
- *After* "training," the subjects were told that the characters stood for X and that their task was to . . .
- *After* collection, the samples were shipped back to X in . . .
- *After* conformational analysis of X, it was necessary to . . .
- *Once* the Xs were located and marked, a thin clear plastic ruler . . .
- *Once* the positions had been decided on, the Xs were removed from each Y and replaced by . . .
- *Once* the exposures were completed, the X was removed from the Y and placed in . . .
- *On completion* of X, the process of model specification and parameter estimation was carried out.

- *Following this*, the samples were recovered and stored overnight at . . .
- Ratings were *then* made for the ten stimuli applied to the subject.
- The analysis was evaluated when initially performed and *then* evaluated again at the end of . . .
- The subjects were *then* shown a film and asked to . . .
- The soil was *then* weighed again, and this weight was recorded as . . .
- The results were corrected for the background readings and *then* averaged *before* being converted to . . .
- *Finally*, questions were asked as to the role of . . .

V. Describing the Process: Adverbs of Manner

- The soil was then placed in a furnace and *gradually* heated to . . .
- The vials were shaken *manually* to allow the soil to mix well with the water.
- The medium was then *aseptically* transferred to a conical flask.
- The resulting solution was *gently* mixed at room temperature for 10 minutes.
- A sample of the concentrate was then *carefully* injected into . . .
- The tubes were *accurately* reweighed to six decimal places using . . .

VI. Describing the Process: Passive Verb + Using . . . for Instruments

- Fifteen subjects *were recruited using* email advertisements requesting healthy students from . . .
- All of the computer work *was carried out using* Quattro Pro for Windows and . . .
- Data *were collected using* two high spectral resolution spectroradiometers.
- Data *were recorded* on a digital audio recorder and transcribed *using* . . .
- Semi-automated genotyping *was performed using* X software and . . .
- Statistical significance *was analyzed using* analysis of variance and t-tests, as appropriate.

VII. Describing the Process: Giving Detailed Information

- Compounds 3 and 5 were dissolved in X at pH 2.5 to yield concentrations of 4 mM . . .
- . . . and the solutions were degraded at 55 °C or 37 °C for 42 hours.
- At intervals of 0.5 min, 50 μL of the X was aliquoted into 0.5 mL of cooled boric acid buffer (pH 7.5) to . . .

Quick Points About the Methods Section

1. **Provide enough detail** for another researcher to repeat your experiment. For example, a journal article on zoology should include the genus, species, strain of organisms, their source, living conditions, and care; a chemistry paper should include the sources (manufacturer locations) of chemicals and apparatuses.
2. **Order** procedures by time and by the type of procedure. Use a subheading to distinguish times within the types of procedure.
3. **Use past tense** to describe *what you did*.
4. **Quantify**: concentrations, measurements, amounts (all metric); times (24-hour clock); temperatures (centigrade).

What to Avoid

1. **Do not** include details of common statistical procedures.
2. **Do not** mix results with procedures.

Common Writing Errors and Their Corrections

Avoid using unclear terms to identify controls, treatments, or other study parameters that require more specific terms to be understood. These terms must be explained so that readers can understand exactly what is happening without trying to remember what the terms mean.

Original

"A Spec 20 was used to measure A600 of Tubes 1, 2, and 3 immediately after chloroplasts were added (Time 0) and every 2 min. thereafter until the DCIP was completely reduced. Tube 4's A600 was measured only at Time 0 and at the end of the experiment."

Modified

"A Spec 20 was used to measure A600 of the reaction mixtures exposed to light intensities of 1500, 750, and 350 uE/m^2/s immediately after chloroplasts were added (Time 0) and every 2 min until the DCIP was completely reduced. The A600 of the no-light control was measured only at Time 0 and at the end of the experiment."

Punctuation Point

Misplaced and Dangling Modifiers

It is early Monday morning. You are waiting for the MRT when a headline in the *Taipei Times* grabs your attention: "Lions maul Elephants with three in the ninth, win 6-5." Referring to the previous night's baseball game between Tainan City and Taipei, the article recounts how the Uni Lions won the game in the last inning.

> *After falling behind in the count, 0-2, designated hitter Liu Fu-Hao hit a single off second baseman Fong Shen-Shien's leg, which then rolled into right field. Before the right fielder could retrieve it, pinch-runner Hsu Fong-Bing crossed home plate with the winning run.*

You drop the newspaper, suddenly overcome with sadness. Not over the Elephants' loss (you are a Lions fan, after all), but rather over the loss suffered by the second baseman. "What a way to lose a leg," you bewail.

Yes, a leg was indeed lost. However, it was caused not by Liu Fu-Hao's base hit, but by the sportswriter committing one of the most common English writing errors. It is called a "misplaced modifier."

A misplaced modifier is a word or phrase that modifies an *unintended* word in the sentence. This happens because of the misplacement of either the *modifier* or the *noun* that it is inadvertently modifying.

> Liu Fu-Hao hit a single off second baseman Fong Shen-Shien's leg, <u>which then rolled into right field</u>.

The underlined phrase must, by the sacred laws of English syntax, refer to the subject that immediately precedes it; i.e., "Fong Shen-Shien's leg." Of course, this is not the sportswriter's intended meaning. Nevertheless, by this simple, unconscious slip in the arrangement of sentence parts, he has caused the poor second baseman to lose a valuable appendage (and a whole host of readers to cry in despair).

To fix this error, of course, is easy: "Liu Fu-Hao hit a single off the second baseman's leg and the ball rolled into right field."

Here is an example that causes complete ambiguity.

> I was told that I will be awarded the scholarship by my professor.

Did the professor do the *telling* or will he do the *awarding*? Either assumption is reasonable.

These kinds of mistakes occur so often in English writing, they seemingly generate on their own, like microwave magnetic envelope solitons in magnetic films (physicists, you understand me). Yet another example reveals how easily the error can go unnoticed, even by editors prior to publication. This one is from an actual newspaper report about king crabs, written in 2011:

> A team led by Dr. Craig Smith from the University of Hawaii at Manoa found the crabs using a remotely operated submersible.[1]

Where do you suppose those crabs obtained their engineering degrees? It is great comedy, but such a mistake should never be published unless it is for satirical newspapers such as *The Onion* or *Not the Nation*.

If not always easy to spot, these mistakes are certainly easy to fix. The previous atrocity can be rewritten correctly as:

> A team led by Dr. Craig Smith from the University of Hawaii at Manoa used a remotely operated submersible to find the crabs.

Or perhaps it could be reconstructed this way:

> Using a remotely operated submersible, crabs were found by a

team led by Dr. Craig Smith from the University of Hawaii at Manoa.

It is the same mistake slightly altered. Technically, this is what is known as a "dangling modifier" or "dangling participle," which usually appears with the use of *–ing* or *–ed* verbs (participles) and at the beginnings of sentences, as in: "Plunging hundreds of feet into the gorge, we saw Yosemite Falls." (Nice way to die.) It is called a dangling modifier because the clause hangs alone with uncertainty (it "dangles"), having no clear connection to an appropriate noun. The comma separator further signifies its "aloneness."

In some fields, when the meaning is obvious, misplaced and even dangling modifiers may actually be acceptable. In English Literature, for instance, grammar and syntax will sometimes be violated in seeming defiance of rules (e.g., "sleeping in mine orchard, a serpent stung me" is a line from, of all people, William Shakespeare). However, in academic writing, misplaced modifiers are a sign of carelessness.

In science papers, for example, writers will often produce misplaced or dangling modifiers when discussing experiments or the results of their studies. Take this simple line from a chemistry paper:

> After combining the reactants, the reaction mixture was stirred at room temperature for 3 h.

This kind of error may occur because experiments or results are typically referred to in the passive voice (e.g., experiments "are conducted," they do not "conduct"). As soon as an active clause is written ("after combining the reactants"), an author may suddenly and accidentally replace a *subject* that would normally perform such an action (e.g., "we" or "researchers") with the *object* that is the focus of the section ("the reaction mixture"). A dangling modifier is the unintended result.

As with all dangling modifiers, two main solutions are possible for the previous sentence:

1. Replace the subject that is being inappropriately modified ("the reaction mixture") with the appropriate subject ("we"), thus

producing: "After combining the reactants, we stirred . . ."
2. Because the current subject of the second clause is passive (i.e. is being acted upon), change the verb in the first clause to the passive voice, thereby yielding: "After the reactants *were combined*, the reaction mixture was stirred . . ."

Misplaced and dangling modifiers can be quite amusing. Unfortunately, professional journal editors accept only articles that possess perfect or near-perfect English and consider misplaced and dangling modifiers publishing no-nos.

Sources

1. http://www.independent.co.uk/environment/climate-change/climate-change-sees-giant-crabs-invade-the-antarctic-2350959.html

The Writing Process
10 tips for Forming Good Writing Habits

I. Have a Schedule

If you try and tag writing on at the end of the day when all tasks are done, there'll never be any writing time. It just won't happen. So make sure it's part of your schedule every day. Try and carve out a block of writing time every single day. Plan for it ahead of time by blocking it out in your diary/calendar. Even setting aside 15 minutes of uninterrupted writing time can make a huge difference if you focus for that time. And to be honest, starting small is often best. Add small chunks of writing time to your schedule and build up once you get in the habit.

II. Make a Habit of It

OK, so you've learned to plan the time and sit down and work. Now you just keep doing that over the next few weeks. These don't have to be long torturous sessions; it's best to keep them brief and productive. But keep them going. You'll peak and trough during that time of course. There will be some days when the time flies by and you finish with extreme satisfaction at having written well. Other times even though you've only got 15 minutes to write something, it'll seem like forever. You'll have trouble formulating ideas and words won't flow. Well guess what?
  (a) That was still productive time because even if the words aren't there, the thinking has been done and
  (b) You stuck to a routine. And that's the really important part!

If you carried on regardless of the difficulties, it means it'll be all the easier to sit down tomorrow and get more work done. Try to keep this daily writing routine no matter what else is going on. So, even if you're traveling, consider setting aside just a small amount of time to do some writing, even if you're just pecking letters into the notes app on your smartphone.

III. Plan

Never sit down to write without knowing ahead of time what you're sitting down to write! Many people believe that writer's block and or procrastination come from an empty or muddled mind. Even if you've set aside some writing time, shut down all distractions, and approached your desk rested and after drinking coffee, you might still stare at a blank screen for the next five hours if you don't know what it is you're supposed to be writing. Firstly, you can help this by making sure you're well prepared. It can help to schedule reading time in advance of writing time. Some people find that they write best in the morning and read well in the afternoon. If this is the case, when you have your afternoon reading session, end it by making a brief plan of what you'll write up the next day. But whatever happens, make sure you keep an up-to-date plan of what needs writing next. If you're working on a literature review, list the books and amount of writing time you'll allocate to each and tick them off. If you're working on another section, divide it up and again allocate portions of time for each.

IV. Have a Backup Plan

Sometimes with the best will in the world you can't quite wrap your head round your work. Even the worst writing session can pay off if it means you've somehow thought something through, even if you didn't realize it. You might not have many words on a page to show for it but they'll fall out of your fingers next time you write. However, if you really think you're being unproductive or you think it'll break your writing spirit to sit another minute without having achieved something tangible, go to your backup list of tasks. This is a list you'll make of things that always need doing. This might mean doing some research, editing a section, checking footnotes . . . Have this backup list so you never lose momentum. You should only use it when you really need to feel productive; otherwise this will become another way to procrastinate from writing.

V. Limit Desk Time

The less time you have at your desk the more productive you'll be when you are there. Don't do all your socializing and online shopping at your desk and then try to work from it too; all you'll feel is that you've been at your desk for hours. Try to use another tool or location for your online life (a tablet, a smartphone) and keep your desk as "pure" as possible. If you have to use the one machine/location for all, absolutely don't do it in the same sitting. Make sitting down to work a "fresh" thing to do.

VI. Limit Hours

Even if you can write all day, you can't be productive all day, so think about how much of that time has been wasted on words you won't use. Limit the amount of time you work to manageable chunks. You only have about two productive working hours of writing in you per day. So sit down to write, and write more or less for 2 hours. That said, it's also a good idea to keep to brief time slots and refresh yourself in between.

One of the best methods for this is the *Pomodoro Technique*. The Pomodoro Technique is a productivity method that applies to almost any task. You take a timer (the technique is named after the iconic tomato-shaped kitchen timers), set it for 20 minutes and go full throttle. Stop for five to visit the toilet and get refreshments. This 25-minute slot is called a "pomodoro." If you try to divide your working hours into these tomato-timed units, you'll stay refreshed and productive throughout. And now here's the thing. When you're done for the day, you're done. Walk away. Even if–actually, especially if–you've reached a thorny subject. Leave it! Even if–actually, especially if–you've hit your stride. Make notes for the next day and leave it! Don't over do it or burn out because it'll take its toll in another writing session and erode the habit you're building.

VII. Limit Words

Maybe writing in time slots doesn't work for you. Perhaps the timer goes off just as you get going. Try instead to set word-count-based targets for yourself. But be kind! Some people can dash off a thousand words in an hour and will go back and edit it later. Other people plan each word on the page and might take an hour to hit 50 words. First, notice which way you write. Then test yourself over a week or so. Record how many words you've written at the end of each day, average it and there's your word count for each day of the next week. Record your results and decide if you need to drop your target word-count to make it easier to achieve, or if you can put it up a bit to stretch yourself. Just don't push too far. Try to stay within the realms of the realistic word-count-base target or you'll break your writing spirit.

VIII. Just Do It!

If you schedule writing time and sit down ready to write (even if you've been doing urgent work email for the last hour, get up, get a quick break, and signal your good intentions by sitting down refreshed for this important new task), you must now write. This sounds so easy in theory and it's so much harder in reality, but block out those nagging thoughts of failure and don't you dare touch that browser address bar. Remind yourself you've only got to get 25 minutes of work done and just do it. Get up, get a coffee. Sit down and do it again. If you force yourself to stick to this simple act of just starting (and remember, starting anywhere is fine) you'll soon find you can get work done and–crazy as it may sound– repeatedly get work done without much stress.

IX. Write Anything

Writing regularly is the key. It almost doesn't matter what you're writing because regular writing will improve your communication skills in all areas of your work and ward off that dreaded writer's block. And let's face it; there's always writing to be done in academia, whether it's your thesis, a paper, a lesson plan, or a conference abstract. If tackling your thesis is too much to begin with, use your allotted writing time/space to work on anything that needs to be written. Every bit of writing we do helps hone our craft. But as soon as you start to nail your writing habit, phase in some project writing. Perhaps alternate to start with going backwards and forwards between two pieces of work.

X. Remember that Routine?

The single most important killer of procrastination is having a routine and sticking to it. OK, so we've all sat down to work, let our minds wander and ended up 2 hours/40 videos later feeling like we're worthless academic failures. Maybe that's going to happen now again. But if you set aside productive time, and keep it that way, the video might never come to call. Keeping to set times and not focusing on one task for too long helps you to make sure you are productive (and then who cares what you do with the rest of your time. Although, ever noticed how a successful writing session kills any desire to search for videos?) In fact, have you ever noticed how being productive in one area propels you forwards into being productive in another area. You might find that a great writing session ends with a bunch of errands run in record time and an evening or a weekend doing something truly fulfilling.

Tips for Journal Submission

I. Work with other authors

Collaborate with experienced authors with publication experience and share the credit. Work with your advisors, at least for the first few years after receiving your PhD. Writing alone is a risky strategy, especially right after graduate school. With experienced authors, the probability of acceptance will double. By collaborating with other authors, you may be introduced to an experienced group of researchers. You also may learn how to write better papers. However, remember that you have to become independent at some point.

II. Weight of Coauthored Articles

The following weights may be used as a guide to estimate the overall impact of coauthored articles:
1 = an article (one author).
0.75 = first author in a coauthored paper.
0.7 = second author in a coauthored paper.
0.5 = an author in a paper with three authors.
$1/n$ = four or more authors.

Avoid being the fourth author, except in certain areas. You will be included in "et al.," which is used for all authors after the first three authors.

III. Agree on Coauthor Contributions in Advance

When collaborating on a paper, it is best to divide the work with coauthors in advance. This reduces the chance of some authors getting a free ride after the paper is written or already accepted. Be considerate when determining the order of authors. To assure a long-term relationship, take turns being the first author of a paper, especially when the contributions are equal.

IV. Maintain Collaboration

If a personality conflict develops, collaboration may not work. It takes time and effort to cultivate a relationship with another author. If you have found a good working relationship, do not change it to obtain small benefits.

V. Be Patient with Inactive Coauthors

Be kind to your coauthors. Removing an inactive coauthor from the paper may not be best, especially if it is done insensitively. If a coauthor does not contribute anything, be careful in handling the situation. Often the hatred created is not worth the benefit. If a collaborative paper is being ended because of unexpected changes, clearly define who owns the paper. This avoids problems later.

Inappropriate Vocabulary and Improvements

the question as to

A better alternative would be:
whether

subsequent to

A better alternative would be:
after/following

serves the function of

A better alternative would be:
is

reach a conclusion

A better alternative would be:
conclude

put an end to

A better alternative would be:
end

provided that

A better alternative would be:
if

> **prior to**
> A better alternative would be:
> *before*

Academic Vocabulary

Headwords	Other Words in the Family
fee	fees
file	filed, files, filing
final	finalize, finalized, finalizes, finalizing, finality, finally, finals
finance	financed, finances, financial, financially, financier, financiers, financing
finite	infinite, infinitely
flexible	flexibility, inflexible, inflexibility
fluctuate	fluctuated, fluctuates, fluctuating, fluctuation, fluctuations
focus	focused, focuses, focusing, refocus, refocused, refocuses, refocusing
format	formatted, formatting, formats
formula	formulae, formulas, formulate, formulated, formulating, formulation, formulations, reformulate, reformulated, reformulating, reformulation, reformulations
found	founded, founder, founders, founding, unfounded
foundation	foundations
framework	frameworks
function	functional, functionally, functioned, functioning, functions
fund	funded, funder, funders, funding, funds
fundamental	fundamentally
gender	genders
generate	generated, generates, generating
generation	generations

续表

Headwords	Other Words in the Family
globe	global, globally, globalization
goal	goals
grade	graded, grades, grading
grant	granted, granting, grants
guarantee	guaranteed, guaranteeing, guarantees
guideline	guidelines
hierarchy	hierarchical, hierarchies
highlight	highlighted, highlighting, highlights
hypothesis	hypotheses, hypothesize, hypothesized, hypothesizes, hypothesizing, hypothetical, hypothetically
identical	identically
identify	identifiable, identification, identified, identifies, identifying, identities, identity, unidentifiable
ideology	ideological, ideologically, ideologies

III WRITING THE RESULTS SECTION

Chapter 8
What Did You Observe?

What Did You Observe?

Observations are important for the results section of your paper. You should carefully and briefly explain your experiment and avoid including any details you mentioned in your methods section. Report your results as supported by your data, and avoid restating the methods section.

In the following section, we discuss the general guidelines that must be followed when reporting the results.

- Present the results as concisely as possible, and provide sufficient details to justify your conclusions.
- Briefly explain the multivariate statistical methods used in non-technical terms for the reader's clarity, for example, two-way ANOVA, multiple regression analysis, and factor analysis.
- In the text, you should summarize and discuss the information presented in the figures and tables.
- Clear cross-references for the figures and tables should be provided for clarity. In addition, the reference should precede the specific figure or table.
- When presenting a figure or table in the text, you should clearly guide

the readers indicating the content of the specific figure or table, for example, "The first column of Figure 1 presents . . . "
- Table captions and figure legends should stand alone and help the readers understand the contents of the table without having to refer to the text.
- Finally, you should specify how the results of the study answered your research question(s) stated in the beginning of the paper.

I. Style

- Arrange all the results in a **logical order**, except when referring to the figures and tables.
- Use the term *figure* when it is used at the beginning of the sentence, for example, "*Figure 1 indicates* . . . " You can use the shortened form in the rest of the text, e.g., Fig. 1.
- Number the figures and tables well and place them in their numerical order at the end of the sentence. Figures and tables can be placed in the text if preferred.

The points mentioned above clearly specify the structure of the results section. However, certain domains require the results section to address specific points. We have elaborated on these points further for better clarity. Most domains follow a set pattern or style, and style guides for these domains generally employ this pattern. However, sometimes, it becomes difficult to refer to multiple sources when writing this section. To simplify your task further, we have provided a concise and easy-to-write recipe for this section.

▶ Sciences and Engineering

There are seven points that should be carefully followed when writing this section of the paper. A brief elaboration on each of these points will help you write a substantial *results* section.

- Start the section by *revisiting the research's aim* to remind the readers of the purpose.
- Provide a *general overview* of the results.
- *Present the results obtained* by the methods employed or the experiments conducted. This would also include referencing *figures, tables, equations, and graphs*.
- Briefly elaborate on the *specific or key results* of the paper.
- Provide a *comparison of the results* with previous studies.
- State the *problems, deficits, and/or invalidations* of the results.

- List the implications and future applications of the results.

▶ Social Sciences

This section, for papers relevant to the domain of social sciences, summarizes and reports the results of the hypotheses tested in the paper, and answers the research questions posed in the paper through the results. Below, we have listed a few points that will help in structuring the results section in this domain.

- Begin this section by restating the hypotheses proposed in your paper.
- Provide a paragraph that states the primary issue tested by your specific hypothesis, and state your acceptance or rejection of the formulated hypotheses.
- State the hypothesis test employed in your study, for example, independent sample t-test, and provide the level at which the hypotheses were tested.
- Use relevant descriptive representations, such as figures and graphs, wherever necessary, and provide an interpretation of these representations clearly indicating whether they are in line with the hypotheses proposed.
- Indicate the parametric and nonparametric significance tests considered in the study and how they supported your hypothesis.
- After providing the results of each of the tests employed, clearly indicate which test is most appropriate to your study and why.
- Finally, briefly provide the implications of your findings.

Next, we will examine the steps to construct effective tables, figures, and graphs.

▶ Figures/Tables/Graphs

Figures, tables, and graphs are graphical representations of the data provided in your paper, and become crucial in helping readers understand the results and comparisons of your study. Hence, it is important that these representations are made with utmost care. To help you clearly understand how to prepare your figures, tables, and graphs, we have listed a few important points that should be considered when preparing these representations.

▶ Figures

- Visual representations, including diagrams, photographs, drawings, and maps, are all part of figures.
- Use figures only when you are providing primary data that are in the form of an image, diagram, or any other visual representation.
- Depending on the data they provide, include a concise legend explaining the contents of the figure.

- Always construct a legend that is standalone, and place it below the figure.
- Offer the readers a clear, well-defined image of the values used in the paper, and how they set your paper apart from the rest.
- If you are providing photographs or diagrams, make sure that they are enlarged and clear enough for the readers to be able to understand what the images include.
- When referencing the figure in the text, you can either use the complete term, e.g., Figure 1, or the shortened version of the term, Fig. 1.

▶ Tables

- Large amounts of repetitive data that cannot be avoided should be compressed and represented in a table.
- Do not include a table when the information can be provided in a sentence or two.
- Include brief labels for the tables, for example, table and column headings and table entries.
- The tables should only be as large as the content it includes.
- Do not include data that are unnecessary to the paper and digress from the main point mentioned in the paper

▶ Graphs

- Use graphs when data included show trends that are best represented in the form of graphs.
- Do not use a graph to present data that are dull, when the data satisfies the expectations of the paper, and when the data compared in the paper is similar.
- When preparing a graph, select the type of graph that is most appropriate for the data being presented.
- Eliminate all unnecessary lines in the graph and keep the content large enough for the readers to clearly understand the content of the graph.
- For table headings and graph and figure legends, use complete grammatical sentences that end with periods.
- The headings and legends should indicate the information the readers are looking for in the figure or table.
- Do not include unnecessary information in the figures, tables, and graphs, as it may make it difficult for the readers to interpret this information.
- Enlarge or highlight data that is most crucial to a representation and to add emphasis.
- For mathematics and statistics, always start the numerical axis at zero.
- Delete all unnecessary details included in these representations.
- Use keywords and highlight them in the table or figure for emphasis.

▶ To Help Indicate Statistical Data Better
- Indicate the parameters described in the paper, for example, mean ± S.D.
- Indicate the statistical tests used in the paper to analyze the data.
- Report exact p values, for example, $p = .42$ instead of $p < .50$.
- Use the term significant only when describing statistically significant differences.

II. Describing Results: Verb Tenses

When presenting the findings, use the past tense:
- Subjects in this study *spent* more time engaged in activities that matched their interests and skill levels.
- Participants in each reward trial *selected* the high-probability stimulus significantly more often than the low-probability stimulus ($P < 0.05$).

Use the present tense when comparing results with those of other studies:
- As opposed to previous research using noncontact specular microscopy, our Orbscan II measurements *are* significantly smaller.
- Conversely, our results *demonstrate* improved performance over previously proposed methods.

When presenting different types of results, use the past tense:
- The highest incidence of cardiac events *was* discovered among women with high severity of induced ischemia.
- Costs *showed* a tendency to decrease over the 18-month period.

Use the present tense to refer to tables and figures:
- Table II *lists* the results of the independent t-test.
- Figure 3(c) *displays* the chemical reaction scheme used to synthesize the copolymer.

Use present tense tentative verbs or modal verbs when commenting on results:
- Managerial accountants *seem* to be generally averse to outsourcing.
- Managerial accountants *might* be generally averse to outsourcing.

When discussing the implications of your results, use the present tense with tentative or conditional modal verbs:
- Urea nitrogen concentrations of less than 7 mg/dL *indicate* a deficiency in dietary protein.
- Reactive impurities of 1 ppm *could contribute* to the measured decay rates of the hydroxide concentration.

Briefly Describe Your Experiment(s) Without the Detail of the Methods Section (a sentence or two is enough)

Reference to Aim/Method

- The Y questionnaire was used to assess X.
- To distinguish between these two possibilities . . .
- Repeated measures of ANOVA were used to assess Z.
- Regression analysis was used to predict the . . .
- Changes in X and Y were compared using . . .
- The average scores of X and Y were compared to . . .
- Nine items on the questionnaire measured the extent to which . . .
- The correlation between X and Y was tested by . . .
- The first set of analyses examined the impact of . . .
- Simple statistical analysis was used to . . .
- A scatter diagram and Pearson's product-moment correlation were used to determine the relationship between . . .
- T-tests were used to analyze the relationship between . . .

Report Main Result(s), Supported by Selected Data

I. Location and Summary Statements

Table 1	shows	the experimental data on X.
	compares	the results obtained from a preliminary analysis of X.
Figure 1	presents	
	provides	the intercorrelations among the nine measurements of X.

	are shown	in Table 1.
The results obtained from the preliminary analysis of X	can be seen	
	are compared	in Fig. 1.
	are presented	

As shown in Figure 1,	
As can be seen from Table 1,	the X group reported
It can be seen from the data in Table 1 that	significantly more Y than the other two groups.
From Figure 1, we can see that	

| Table 1 illustrates | some of the main characteristics of the ... |
| Figure 1 shows | the breakdown of ... |

II. Statement of Results (positive)

- Strong evidence of X was found when ...
- This result is significant at the p = 0.05 level.
- There was a significant positive correlation between ...
- There was a significant difference between the two conditions ...
- On average, Xs were shown to have ...
- The mean score for X was ...
- Interestingly, for those subjects with X ...
- A positive correlation was found between X and Y.
- Further analysis showed that ...
- Further statistical tests revealed ...

III. Statement of Results (negative)

- No increase of X was associated with ...
- No significant differences were observed between ...
- No substantial differences were found between ...
- No increase in X was detected.
- No difference greater than X was observed.
- The chi-square test did not show any significant differences between ...
- None of these differences were statistically significant.
- Overall, X did not affect males and females differently in these measures ...

IV. Transition Statements

- Turning now to the experimental evidence on . . .
- Comparing the two results, it can be seen that . . .
- Evaluating the two results reveals . . .

V. Highlighting Significant, Interesting, or Surprising Results

- The most striking result to emerge from the data is that . . .
- This correlation is related to . . .
- The correlation between X and Y is remarkable because . . .
- The single most striking observation to emerge after comparing the data was . . .

VI. Reporting Results from Questionnaires and Interviews

- The response rate was 60% at six months and 56% at 12 months.
- Of the study population, 90 subjects completed and returned the questionnaire.
- Of the initial cohort of 123 students, 66 were female and 57 male.
- The majority of respondents felt that . . .
- Over half of those surveyed reported that . . .
- Seventy percent of those who were interviewed indicated that . . .
- Almost two-thirds of the participants (64%) said that . . .
- Approximately half of those surveyed did not comment on . . .
- A small number of those interviewed suggested that . . .
- Only a small number of respondents indicated that . . .
- Of the 148 patients who completed the questionnaire, just over half indicated that . . .
- A minority of participants (17%) indicated . . .
- In response to Question 1, most of those surveyed indicated that . . .
- When the subjects were asked . . . the majority commented that . . .
- Other responses to this question included . . .
- The overall response to this question was poor.

Common Writing Errors and Their Corrections

Use Pronouns Clearly
(for example, *they, which, them, this, it, he, and she*)

Reviewers frequently complain about unclear pronouns. What "it" represents may be perfectly clear to you, but the reviewer, editor, and reader often have no idea. Pronouns are best avoided whenever possible. Pronouns force the reader to guess which noun the writer is talking about. Because the main goal of technical writing is to be clear, you do not want the reader to guess your meaning. Instead, you want him or her to know the meaning without any doubt. Therefore, rewrite sentences as necessary to avoid using confusing pronouns.

> *"Line 12 on page 3 of your paper is an example of your ongoing problem using pronouns clearly. There are at least 3 different nouns 'it' could refer to. You must make your pronoun references clear!"*
>
> — 3rd Reviewer, **IEEE Transactions on Advanced Packaging**

Original

A case study approach was chosen; *this* allowed a closer observation of a single specimen.

Modified

A case study approach was chosen *to* allow a closer observation of a single specimen.

➡ **Original**

In most recent studies, *they* have measured X in four different ways.

Modified

Most recent studies have measured X in four different ways.

➡ **Original**

X substantially alters Y. *This* suggests that Y can be modified using the proposed model.

Modified

X substantially alters Y. *This occurrence (finding, observation, phenomenon, event)* suggests that Y can be modified using the proposed model.

➡ **Original**

The response rate was 60% at six months and 56% at 12 months, *which* indicates that the overall response to this question was poor.

Modified

The response rate was 60% at six months and 56% at 12 months, *indicating* that the overall response to this question was poor.

Punctuation Point

Gender Bias in Pronouns

A person should not show gender bias in technical writing. Pronouns of gender include he, she, his, her, and him. Try to avoid using these pronouns. Consider this biased example followed by methods for revising the sentence.

Example:
When a politician campaigns for office, *he* must spend considerable money to compete with *his* opponents.

revising sentences about people and roles using one of the following methods:

❶ **Use plural instead of a singular noun: they and their.**
When politicians campaign for office, *they* must spend considerable funds to compete with *their* opponents.

❷ **Rewrite the sentence removing pronoun usage.**
A politician *who* campaigns for office must spend considerable funds to compete with opponents.

❸ **Use both singular pronouns: he and she.**
When a politician campaigns for office, he or she must spend considerable funds to compete with his or *her* opponents.

This last example can sound bad, especially if there are several sentences using the same pattern. Only use this option when the sentence is short. Do not use slash marks (/), such as s/he or he/she in academic writing. Slash marks confuse readers and indicate lazy writing.

The Writing Process

Writer's block is an excuse we all use sometimes. It is also a lie. Writing and other forms of artistic talent are not magical gifts showing themselves only when they want to take over our minds.

What Is Writer's Block?

Writer's block is the inability to continue work on a specific project. There is no complete loss of creativity or talent, but the writer loses the ability to produce a sentence. There are reasons for writer's block. Once you find the cause of your writer's block, you can solve it. The three reasons are:

❶ Weak Motivation
Weak motivation has several forms, from waiting for "inspiration" to finding other more interesting tasks.

❷ Poor Planning
Poor planning causes writer's block when the writer has no idea what to do next in his or her writing. In this case, the writer may not have done the valuable prewriting exercises or collected enough raw material for the paper.

❸ Perfectionism
Perfectionism causes terrible writer's block. Remember that a paper can be revised. Finish a draft before worrying about minor details.

Use the Following Cures to Help Fight Writer's Block

Many writers and artists have natural talents or gifts to create, but an unused gift is worthless. Writing is a skill and a talent, the same as the ability to analyze complex mathematics. We never hear about "scientist's block." Both scientific skills and writing skills are learned and improved through practice. Do not allow yourself to use "a lack of inspiration" as an excuse for not writing. Do you think that famous painters started painting only when inspiration came? They worked to earn money. Most of these artists were not working for free. Even though Picasso realized that his talents were special, he had to earn money. Every project, even if it is not ideal for you, is an opportunity to practice these skills. Professional researchers and academics write. They go to work on a schedule and meet deadlines. If you are an academic writer, you must have this self-discipline.

Tips for Journal Submission

I. Questions to Ask When Reviewing a Journal
- Is the journal peer reviewed?
- Is the journal in the recommended publishing outlet category?
- Does the journal have a solid reputation?
- Does the journal have a reputable publisher?
- How old is the journal?
- Is the journal carefully produced?
- Does the journal come out on time?
- Are the authors who are published in its pages diverse?
- Does the journal publish more than five or six articles a year?
- Is the journal online or indexed electronically and where?
- Does it take a long time to get published once you submit your manuscript?
- Is the journal going through a transition?
- Who reads the journal?

II. Matching Your Article to the Journal
- Does the journal have an upcoming theme or special issue on your topic?
- Does the journal have word or page length limits that you can meet?
- Does the style of your article match the journal style?
- Do you know any of the journal editors?
- How does your journal require articles to be submitted?

III. Questions to Ask the Managing Director
- How many submissions a year does your journal receive?
- What is your journal's turnaround time?
- What is your journal's backlog?

Journal Review Form

Journal title	_____			
Editor's name/email	_____			
Managing editor's name/email	_____			
Editorial office address	_____			
Journal web address	_____			
Peer reviewed	❏ Yes	❏ No	❏ Not sure (find out)	
SCI or SSCI	❏ Yes	❏ No		
Type of journal	❏ Disciplinary	❏ Interdisciplinary	❏ Trade/practitioner	
	❏ Field-based	❏ Edited vol.	❏ Conf. Proceeding	
Electronic and print	❏ Yes	❏ No		
US-based ed. office	❏ Yes	❏ No, based in _____		
Reputation	❏ Solid	❏ Medium	❏ High	❏ Low
Publisher type	❏ Large (e.g., univ., commercial, assoc.)		❏ Small	
Publisher name	_____			
Longevity	❏ <2 years	❏ <8 years	❏ <15 years	
Production	❏ Carefully produced		❏ Sloppy	
Timeliness	❏ Issue on time	❏ >1-year delay	❏ >2-year delay	
Contributors	❏ Open (often outsiders)		❏ Closed (mostly insiders)	
	❏ Mixed	❏ High (profs.)	❏ Low (mostly graduate students)	

No. of articles a year	❏ <8 articles	❏ >12 articles	❏ >20 articles	
Indexed electronically	❏ No	❏ Yes, on _____		
Backlog (guess)	❏ Articles' latest cites dated this year or last			
	❏ Older citations _____			
Themed/special issues	❏ No	❏ Yes, on _____		
Word limits	❏ <5,000	❏ <9,000	❏ No limit	❏ Not stated
Page limits	_____ pages of shortest article		_____ pages of longest article	
Board members I know or my professor knows				
Rejection rate	❏ <40%	❏ <60%	❏ <80%	❏ Over 80%
Turnaround time	❏ <1 month	❏ 3 months	❏ <9 months	❏ Over 9 months
Backlog	❏ <6 months	❏ <1 year	❏ <2 years	❏ Over 2 years
Submission guidelines	_____			
Style manual	❏ Chicago	❏ MLA	❏ APA	❏ Other _____
Documentation style	❏ Cite in text	❏ Cite in notes	❏ Other _____	
Hard copies to submit	❏ 0	❏ 1	❏ 3	❏ Other _____
Electronic copies	❏ Yes	❏ No	❏ Send by e-mail?	
Include self-addressed envelope	❏ Yes	❏ No		

Inappropriate Vocabulary and Improvements

come to a conclusion

A better alternative would be:
conclude

by means of

A better alternative would be:
by

in a position to

A better alternative would be:
can

be deficient in

A better alternative would be:
lack

at this point in time

A better alternative would be:
now

at the present time

A better alternative would be:
now

Academic Vocabulary

Headwords	Other Words in the Family
ignorant	ignorance, ignore, ignored, ignores, ignoring
illustrate	illustrated, illustrates, illustrating, illustration, illustrations, illustrative
image	imagery, images
immigrate	immigrant, immigrants, immigrated, immigrates, immigrating, immigration
impact	impacted, impacting, impacts
implement	implementation, implemented, implementing, implements
implicate	implicated, implicates, implicating, implication, implications
implicit	implicitly
imply	implied, implies, implying
impose	imposed, imposes, imposing, imposition
incentive	incentives
incidence	incident, incidentally, incidents
incline	inclination, inclinations, inclined, inclines, inclining
income	incomes
incorporate	incorporated, incorporates, incorporating, incorporation
index	indexed, indexes, indexing
indicate	indicated, indicates, indicating, indication, indications, indicative, indicator, indicators
individual	individualized, individuality, individualism, individualist, individualists, individualistic, individually, individuals
induce	induced, induces, inducing, induction
inevitable	inevitability, inevitably
infer	inference, inferences, inferred, inferring, infers
infrastructure	infrastructures
inherent	inherently
inhibit	inhibited, inhibiting, inhibition, inhibitions, inhibits
initial	initially
initiate	initiated, initiates, initiating, initiation, initiations, initiative, initiatives, initiator, initiators
injure	injured, injures, injuries, injuring, injury, uninjured

续表

Headwords	Other Words in the Family
innovate	innovation, innovated, innovates, innovating, innovations, innovative, innovator, innovators
input	inputs
insert	inserted, inserting, insertion, inserts
insight	insightful, insights
inspect	inspected, inspecting, inspection, inspections, inspector, inspectors, inspects
instance	instances
institute	instituted, institutes, instituting, institution, institutional, institutionalize, institutionalized, institutionalizes, institutionalizing, institutionally, institutions
instruct	instruction, instructed, instructing, instructions, instructive, instructor, instructors, instructs

Chapter 9
How Can You Describe Quantities?

How Can You Describe Quantities?

I. Highlighting Data in a Table or Chart

- It is apparent from Table 2 that very few . . .
- Table 1 is quite revealing in several ways. First, unlike other . . .
- Data from this table can be compared with the data in Table 4, showing that . . .
- The data in Fig. 9 shows that the length of time remaining between . . .
- From Table 1, we can see that Experiment 2 resulted in the lowest value of . . .
- The histogram in Fig. 1 indicates that . . .
- What is noteworthy in Figure 2 is that . . .
- In Fig. 10, there is a clear trend of decreasing . . .
- As Table 3 shows, a significant difference (t = -2.15, p = 0.03) exists between the two groups.

II. Describing High and Low Points in Figures

- Floodwaters *reached a peak* of 5.2 meters.
- The *peak* temperature is markedly affected by changes in technique.
- Oil production *dipped* in 2006.
- Natural gas production reached a (new) *low* in 2000.

Sentences for Describing Quantities

I. Describing Ratios and Proportions

- The proportion of live births outside marriage reached *one in ten* in 1945.
- The birth rate dropped from 44.4 to 38.6 per 1,000 per annum.

II. Describing Fractions

- Of the 148 patients who completed the questionnaire, slightly over half indicated that . . .
- The response rate was 60% at six months but only *one-fourth of* that (15%) at 12 months.
- Over half of those surveyed indicated that . . .
- Four out of five interviewees indicated that . . .
- Approximately half of those surveyed did not comment on . . .
- Nearly half of the respondents (48%) agreed that . . .
- Less than a third of those who responded (32%) indicated that . . .
- The number of first marriages in the United Kingdom fell by *nearly two-fifths*.

III. Describing Percentages

- Precisely 13.1% of men and 23.1% of women who had married said that they . . .
- Returned surveys from 51 radiologists yielded a 34% response rate.
- The response rate was 60% at six months and 56% at 12 months.
- East Anglia had *the lowest proportion* of single parents, at only 14 percent.
- An 18% *increase* in stolen kidneys contributed to the survival rate.
- The mean income of *the bottom* 20% of US families families declined from $10,716 in 1970 to . . .
- A study in Java found that of 2,558 abortions, 58% were for young women aged 15-24 years, of whom 62% were . . .
- Less than 10% of the articles cited in either study reported that . . .
- In 1998, *just over* 5% of all female deaths in Hong Kong were tobacco

related.

IV. Describing Averages

- Figure 2 can be viewed as the *average* life expectancy at various ages.
- The proposed model suggests a steep decline in *mean* life expectancy ...
- Roman slaves probably had a lower than *average* life expectancy.
- The *average* of 12 observations from X, Y, and Z is 19.2 mgs/m ...
- The *mean score* for both trials was subjected to multivariate analysis of variance to determine ...
- The corresponding *mean distance* between negative charges on the semiconductor ... nanoparticle surface was estimated using ...

V. Describing Ranges

- The evidence shows that life expectancy from birth *lies in the range of 20-30 years*.
- *Between a depth of 575 and 590 meters*, the sea floor is extremely flat, with an average slope of only 1:400.
- The mean income of homeowners in the UK, declined *from $18,080 in 1995 to $15,830 in 2005*.
- The respondents had practiced for an average of 15 years (*ranging from 6 to 35 years*).
- The participants *were from 19 to 25 years old*, and were from both rural and urban areas.
- They calculated the *ranges of* journal use to be from 10.7%–36.4% for the humanities, and 25%–57% for the ...
- Rates of decline ranged from 2.71 to 0.08 cm day-1 (Table 11) with a mean of 0.97 cm day-1.

Common Writing Errors and Their Corrections

I. Linguistic Redundancy

The objective of both academic and technical writing is the clear and concise communication of information for brief and to-the-point text that captures the attention of readers, presents accurate data, and demonstrates credibility and authority. These objectives can be achieved by eliminating redundancy.

Redundancy is defined as the construction of a phrase, clause, or sentence using more words than required. Although redundancies in speech are often employed unintentionally, in rhetoric, they are considered improper and are best avoided. The main culprits of redundancy in writing are repetition, unnecessary words, meaningless jargon, contradictory wording, and the use of pretentious sentences.

For writers desperate to reach a specific word count, the lengthy phrase "at this point in time" may seem more attractive compared to "now." However, cluttering text with repetitive or overlapping terms reduces the quality of the information. Conveying the same information by using fewer words saves readers' time. Furthermore, the saved space can be used to elaborate points, provide additional evidence, and include opposing views.

Redundancy in writing typically results from the following four sources:

- **Wordy set phrases** (a multiword phrase that can be reduced to a single word without loss of meaning)
  For example, "in view of the fact that" can be replaced with "because."

- **Obvious qualifiers** (where a word is implicit in the word it modifies)
  For example, "advance planning," "completely finish," or "young

boy" are qualifiers in which the meaning is already implied.

- **Scattershot phrasing** (where two or more synonyms are compounded)
  For example, "thoughts and ideas" or "actions and behavior" (What is the difference between the two terms, and does the writer mean to use it?)

- **Hidden verbs** (where a verb is used as the head of a noun phrase)
  For example, "take into consideration" is a nominalization of the word "consider."

  Several classic wordy set phrases and their suggested substitutes are presented below.

in view of the fact that	since, because
at this point in time	then
in accordance with your request	as requested
in the near future	soon
at this current time	now, currently
to the fullest extent possible	fully
predicated upon the fact that	based on
take cognizance of the fact that	realize
with regard to	regarding
until such time as	until
has the ability to	can
that being the case	therefore

Verbs are the only part of speech that can serve as a sentence; for example, Stop! Wait! Run! The verb conveys the action. Too often, however, the action is hidden in other parts of speech, resulting in weak and bloated phrasing. Common examples of hidden verbs that should be avoided are as follows:

- be in agreement   agree

- draw a conclusion   conclude
- make a decision   decide
- is dependent upon   depends on
- cause the destruction of   destroy
- is an indication of   indicates
- place an order   order
- give a sign   signal

By employing fewer well-chosen words that emphasize the substance, writers can communicate with their readers more effectively. Another source of redundancy is the use of verbose, clichéd, or outdated phrases in an attempt to impress. This is detrimental in the fields of academic and technical writing, where the subject may already be complex. The following are examples of such phrases:

- At this point in time . . .
- For the most part . . .
- For the purpose of . . .
- In a manner of speaking . . .
- In the final analysis . . .
- As far as I am concerned . . .
- Be that as it may . . .
- In order to . . .

A common example is the phrase "the authors would like to thank" included in the Acknowledgments. This construction informs the reader that the authors wish to thank the contributors, but why not just thank them instead? The following are suggestions of options that are more appropriate:

- The authors thank . . .
- The authors are thankful to . . .
- The authors are grateful to . . .
- We thank . . .
- We appreciate . . .
- We are grateful to . . .
- Thanks are due . . .
- . . . is gratefully acknowledged.

Concise writing conveys information to readers while avoiding verbiage. Always check for repetitive and redundant words, phrases, or expressions that can be removed. Less is more. To avoid repetition, apply the rule that if one word conveys the meaning of the other words, then use that word alone.

Writers should also avoid constructions that are likely to be misunderstood, even if they are arguably "correct" according to a dictionary or style manual. Strive for brevity. Every extra word or letter costs time to write, review, and print. Thus, cut words and simplify sentences whenever possible. Simple direct sentences (subject + verb + object) convey thoughts efficiently and reduce the likelihood of grammatical errors. More attentiveness to the elements of good writing increases the precision and clarity for your readers, thereby encouraging them to consider your writing seriously.

II. Deleting Redundancy and Extra Words

"The whole paper should be shorter. I am confident that you could say everything you need to say in 30% less space."

— Reviewer, IEEE Journal of Engineering Management

Original

After *the end of* World War II, the Japanese government *began the process of rebuilding* the nation.

Modified

After World War II, the Japanese government *rebuilt* the nation.

Original

There are as many sets of force data as force structure data.

Modified

The sets of force data *equal* the force structure data.

Original
Just by a lucky chance, the sailors had enough pure drinking water unpolluted by any impurities.
Modified
Fortunately, the sailors had enough pure water.

Original
It is evident that information systems alter organizations in various ways.
Modified
Information systems alter organizations variously.

Original
It may be said that there are *more than one* explanation *which could produce* this result.
Modified
Several explanations for this result are possible.

Original
The current study was unable, *insofar as we could determine*, to analyze these variables.
Modified
The current study was unable to analyze these variables.

Original
It is the systems analyst *who makes a determination of the question as to* whether the program *should be executed*.
Modified
The systems analyst *determines* whether to *execute* the program.

The following list of common phrases are redundant, but can be reduced to a shorter form:

- adding together .... adding
- cancel out .... cancel
- combine into one .... combine
- cubic meters in volume .... cubic meters
- different varieties .... varieties
- final outcome .... outcome, conclusion
- first and foremost .... first
- goals and objectives .... goals
- initial introduction .... introduction
- joined together .... joined
- mixed together .... mixed
- past history .... past
- personal opinion .... opinion
- physical size .... size
- point in time .... time, period
- reason why .... reason
- refer back to .... refer to
- repeat again .... repeat
- small in size .... small
- this particular instance .... this case, this instance
- triangular in shape .... triangular
- true fact .... a fact, true, the truth

Punctuation Point

How to Use Essential and Nonessential Clauses in Academic Writing

Essential and nonessential clauses are a common source of confusion and error in English writing. However, if expressed appropriately, they enable writers to present both essential and nonessential information in a clear and organized manner. The appropriate expression of essential and nonessential clauses involves choosing the correct pronoun to begin a clause and correctly placing commas.

An essential clause is a clause that cannot be omitted without affecting the meaning of the sentence. By contrast, a nonessential clause, although it may contain valuable information, can be omitted without changing the meaning of the sentence.

The pronouns "which" and "that" are indicators of whether clauses are essential or nonessential. In general, "which" begins a nonessential clause, and "that" begins an essential clause:

- Honey, *which* is sweet, is a natural food source.

In this sentence, "which is sweet" does not limit the meaning of honey. The clause is designated supplementary information by using commas, and the focus of the sentence is the use of honey in foods.

- Honey is typically produced by bees *that* belong to the genus Apis.

In this example, the clause beginning with "that" clearly limits the meaning of "bees"; therefore, it is essential to the sentence.

In addition to pronouns, commas are critical indicators of whether a clause is essential or nonessential. As shown in the examples, a nonessential clause is designated using commas, whereas an essential clause is not. Although identifying essential and nonessential clauses based on these rules of pronoun use and punctuation rules is easy, applying commas appropriately during the writing process is often challenging.

The pronoun "who" can begin both essential and nonessential clauses; therefore, clauses beginning with "who" are excellent examples demonstrating appropriate comma use:

- Beekeepers, *who* are also called apiarists, sometimes keep bees to satisfy scientific curiosity.

Commas are used in this sentence because "who are also called apiarists" is a nonessential clause. It can be removed without changing the meaning of the sentence. The commas separate the supplementary information from the necessary information, enabling the emphasis to be placed on the beekeepers' motivation for keeping bees.

- Researchers *who study bees* must have a thorough understanding of honey production.

Commas must be omitted in this sentence because "who study bees" is an essential clause; removing it would change the meaning of the sentence. If commas were used in this sentence, it would imply that all researchers must understand honey production, which is false. Therefore, expressing essential and nonessential clauses appropriately by using correct punctuation is crucial in academic writing to ensure that information is reported accurately.

Understanding and applying these rules enables writers to communicate effectively; however, there are exceptions. Determining whether or not to use commas to enclose a clause beginning with "such as" or "including" is particularly difficult because these clauses are often punctuated inconsistently. In the following example, the essential and nonessential clauses are punctuated in a manner that contradicts the rules:

- Honey from flowers, *such as* heather or manuka, exhibits unusual viscous properties including thixotropy.

This is an acceptable and conventional approach to punctuating this sentence, mainly because of the relationship between spoken and written English. By representing the natural pauses taken when speaking or reading, commas facilitate clarity and flow in writing. This is especially true in long sentences, which must be broken into readable segments. Therefore, although "such as heather or manuka" is an essential clause, commas are used to indicate a pause. Commas do not enclose the nonessential clause, "including thixotropy," because it ends the sentence and no pause is taken.

Although there are exceptions, two rules apply in all cases: "that" is used in essential clauses; "which" and commas are used in nonessential clauses. Applying these two rules consistently prevents the confusion and error that result from the incorrect use of essential and nonessential clauses.

Understanding Relative Clauses

The three most common relative pronouns are *who*, *which*, and *that*. The choice of pronoun depends on the noun the clause refers to and the type of relative clause.

I. Who

- Refers to a person or people
- Can be used for clauses that make a noun specific (restrictive relative clauses)
- Can be used for clauses that provide additional information (nonrestrictive clauses)

Examples

People *who* live in New York lead very busy lives.
My sister, *who* works for the YMCA, leads a very active life.

II. Which

- Refers to a thing or concept
- Typically used for restrictive relative clauses

- Occasionally used for nonrestrictive clauses in formal writing

Example
<u>The Empire State Building</u>, *which* used to be the tallest building in the world, remains a popular tourist attraction.

III. That

- Only appropriate for restrictive relative clauses
- Refers to a thing or concept

Example
<u>The book</u> *that* you gave me was stolen.

IV. Where and When

- Used for clauses that refer to a place or time
- Can be used for restrictive relative clauses
- Can be used for nonrestrictive relative clauses

Examples
<u>The hospital</u> *where* the research was conducted is a privately funded institute.
<u>After the participants had retired</u> was the time *when* they experienced the strongest feelings of loneliness.

In conclusion, relative clauses are extremely useful because they allow writers to be more specific with the information conveyed and increase the sophistication of their writing. However, adequate consideration should be allocated to identifying the type of relative clause and selecting an appropriate relative pronoun.

The Writing Process

Choosing the Right Search Terms When Looking for Journal Articles in Academic Databases

Whether you are searching research databases or conducting general online searches, the search terms and phrases you use will determine what information you find. Following some basic search term guidelines can make the process go smoothly. When searching for articles within a database, start by using keywords that relate to your topic.

Example: alternative energy

To expand your search, use synonyms or components of the initial search terms.

Synonym Example: renewable energy
Component Example: algae energy, wind energy, biofuel

Another technique you can use is to refine the presentation of your search terms by using suggestions in the following table.

| Use multiple words. | Use multiple words to more narrowly define your search. | renewable energy instead of energy |
| Use quotation marks. | Place quotation marks around two or more words that you want to search for only in combination, never individually. | "renewable energy" |

Use "AND" to connect words.	Use "AND" between words when you want to retrieve only articles that include **both** words.	algae AND energy
Use "OR" to choose one or the other.	Use "OR" to find information relating to one of two options but not both. This option works well when you have two terms that mean the same thing and you want to find articles regardless of which term has been chosen for use.	ethanol OR ethyl alcohol
Use "NOT" to eliminate likely options.	Use "NOT" to eliminate one category of ideas you know a search term will likely generate.	algae NOT food
Use "*" or "?" to include alternate word endings.	Use "*" or "?" to include a variety of word endings. This process is often called using a "wildcard."	alternate* energy
		alternate? energy
Use parentheses to combine multiple searches.	Use parentheses to combine multiple related terms into one single search using the different options presented in this table.	(renewable OR algae OR biofuel OR solar) AND energy

When you find a helpful article or Internet site, look for additional search terms and sources that you can follow up on. If you don't have time to follow up on them all when you find them, include them in your research log for later follow-up. When possible, copy and paste terms and links into your log. When you have to retype, take great care with spelling, spacing, and most of all, attributing direct quotations to their original source.

The aforementioned tips are general ideas for keyword searching.

When you are searching within a database or a certain search engine, pay attention to any search tips or help screens that present methods that work well with the specific database or search engine. For example, you may have the option to narrow your search to "full text" entries only or to refine it to texts published within a certain time frame.

Key Points to Remember

A quick and easy way to increase your search results is to try synonyms of your initial search term, such as "ethanol" for "ethyl alcohol." A similar step is to try components of an idea such as "wood," "ethanol," and "algae" when you are searching for biofuel.

You can use special techniques to more accurately target your search. Using multiple words will typically narrow your search more specifically to the information you want. For example, "ethyl alcohol" will bring up a wide range of uses of ethyl alcohol, such as fuel, drinking alcohol, chemistry, and lotions. A search for "ethyl alcohol as fuel" will limit the results to only the use of ethyl alcohol as fuel. Similarly, the use of quotation marks will limit search results to a complete term rather than to individual parts of a term. For example, within quotations, "algae energy" returns only results that include both words. Following a word with an asterisk or a question mark produces results including alternate endings of the word and using parentheses allows you to combine multiple searches.

Using "AND" allows you to make sure a search includes identified words. Inserting "OR" between two words lets you conduct two individual searches at once. Placing "NOT" between two words excludes all results including the second word.

Tips for Journal Submission

Dealing with a Negative Review

We are often taught in PhD programs how to succeed, but not how to handle rejection. So how do you get over the feeling of rejection, especially as an early career researcher? Here are some tips in getting over the barrier of rejection in journal publishing.

• Give yourself a week before you do anything after reading a rejection. It takes some time to disassociate your emotions (rejection, anger, disappointment) from the piece you have written. It is necessary to disassociate them when you need to make decisions about your next step. After you have given yourself a week, reread your rejection letter/email for any feedback, and then reread your submitted to piece. This allows you to analyze what your next step will be.

• You have three choices: Rewrite and resubmit the piece; submit the piece as is to another journal; or scrap the piece for a better time.

• If you decide to resubmit, you will need to do some additional work. You may want to email the editor to see if you can get specific direction in how to make the manuscript more acceptable. If your manuscript has made it to the peer review process, review each comment. I find having a table that addresses each point helps in your revision, but also in the follow-up letter you will submit with your new manuscript. If the manuscript was rejected outright (without indication of revisions), you will need to justify how the revised manuscript is substantially different than the original. In your follow-up letter you will need to address each comment made by editors/peer reviewers.

You do not have to revise everything a reviewer comments on, but you do have to address it. For example, one of the reviewers of an article

I co-wrote used a different theoretical framework in his analysis of our research. We maintained our methodology and justified it in our comments (and why we DID NOT use the methodology he would prefer).

- You may decide to submit the same article to another journal or publisher (Note of warning: you should not have the same manuscripts at two different places at the same time). One possibility is to email the journal from which you were just rejected for recommendations for other places in which your piece might be more appropriate. This does two things: (1) it ensures that the other journal knows you are withdrawing your article and will be submitting it elsewhere so they will not be allowed to print it in the future; (2) you may receive some additional feedback so you can make adjustments in your next submission.

If you decide to go to a different publisher, you need to do a little more homework. Based on your rejections, try to identify a publisher by which your ideas will be accepted. In reviewing the list of reviews and the authors' names, you may discover that there were very few outside of Ivy League/top 20 international universities represented in the articles and none represented as a reviewer. Your assumption should be that because you are not from one of these institutions, nor a leading researcher in the field, editors may filter your article out. Often they will have 100-200 submissions a month, so this helps decrease the workload for reviewers. Now when you look for new journals to submit to, you should look at readership, topics (usually they have a description on their website), reviewers, and any professional organizations they are affiliated with.

There are two areas you MUST change when you resubmit to another journal. The first is the style (most websites have a style guide). The other is your introduction. You need to always include in your introduction how your article will be of interest for the journal's readership.

- If you decide not to resubmit your manuscript, you should consider how you can still communicate your research. You might want to consider submitting a paper to a conference (even having it published as a conference proceeding), upload it to a public depository (such as Academia.edu or your university's working papers depository), or blog about it. Make sure you save the article.

As an early career researcher, an article that was not accepted is a good starting point for collaboration or new research. So do not think of the unpublished manuscript as a failure, but rather a future starting point. It is important to continue to work even if you have had numerous articles rejected. If you feel that you are not getting anywhere with publishing, work with a mentor in your field who can give you direction on places to publish, ways to make your manuscripts more marketable, and motivation to continue to submit for publication.

Inappropriate Vocabulary and Improvements

notwithstanding the fact that

A better alternative would be:
although

manner in which

A better alternative would be:
how

make inquiry regarding

A better alternative would be:
ask about/inquire about

it is possible that

A better alternative would be:
may/might/could/can

is in a position to

A better alternative would be:
can

Academic Vocabulary

Headwords	Other Words in the Family
integrate	integrated, integrates, integrating, integration
intelligent	intelligence, intelligently, unintelligent
intense	intensely, intenseness, intensification, intensified, intensifies, intensify, intensifying, intension, intensity, intensive, intensively
interact	interacted, interacting, interaction, interactions, interactive, interactively, interacts
internal	internalize, internalized, internalizes, internalizing, internally
interpret	interpretation, interpretations, interpretative, interpreted, interpreting, interpretive, interprets, misinterpret, misinterpretation, misinterpretations, misinterpreted, misinterpreting, misinterprets, reinterpret, reinterpreted, reinterprets, reinterpreting, reinterpretation, reinterpretations
interval	intervals
intervene	intervened, intervenes, intervening, intervention, interventions
intrinsic	intrinsically
invest	invested, investing, investment, investments, investor, investors, invests, reinvest, reinvested, reinvesting, reinvestment, reinvests
investigate	investigated, investigates, investigating, investigation, investigations, investigative, investigator, investigators
invoke	invoked, invokes, invoking
involve	involved, involvement, involves, involving, uninvolved
isolate	isolated, isolates, isolating, isolation, isolationism
issue	issued, issues, issuing
item	itemization, itemize, itemized, itemizes, itemizing, items
job	jobs
journal	journals
justify	justifiable, justifiably, justification, justifications, justified, justifies, justifying, unjustified
label	labeled, labeling, labels
labor	labored, laboring, labors
layer	layered, layering, layers

续表

Headwords	Other Words in the Family
lecture	lectured, lecturer, lecturers, lectures, lecturing
legal	illegal, illegality, illegally, legality, legally
legislate	legislated, legislates, legislating, legislation, legislative, legislator, legislators, legislature
levy	levied, levies, levying
liberal	liberalize, liberalism, liberalization, liberalized, liberalizes, liberalizing, liberalization, liberate, liberated, liberates, liberation, liberations, liberating, liberator, liberators, liberally, liberals

IV WRITING THE DISCUSSION SECTION

Chapter 10
What Do Your Observations Mean?

What Do Your Observations Mean?

Writing the Discussion Section

The discussion section of a research paper interprets and describes the significance of your findings and compares it with what was already known about the research problem being investigated. In addition, it should explain any new understanding or insights about the problem after having taken the findings into consideration. The discussion also connects to the rest of the paper, as it discusses the research questions or hypotheses posed and the literature reviewed. However, the discussion should not only simply repeat the information in the paper but also explain how your study has advanced the reader's understanding of the research problem.

The discussion section is important to your paper, as it effectively demonstrates your ability to critically think about an issue, develop solutions to the problems based on the findings, and formulate a deeper understanding of the research problem reported in your study. Moreover, the discussion section is where you explore the implications of your results in other areas of study, and evaluate any improvements that can be made to further develop your research.

To further help you write this section effectively, we have listed a few key points that should be considered.

- Begin the section by briefly restating the study's main results.
- Restate the importance of your study and its findings by comparing it with results from previous research.
- Briefly summarize the results of each problem or hypothesis tested in your paper and assert their general application.
- State and provide an association of the results with the literature and the results reported by previous research.
- Provide a brief explanation for the failures or drawbacks of your research's findings.
- Highlight the main limitations that could influence the validity of your study.
- Finally, discuss the opportunities that will be helpful for future research on the issue discussed.

However, the discussion should not just restate the results or report additional findings that have not been mentioned in the paper before. Instead, the discussion section should focus on highlighting the implications of the results and relate them with findings from previous research.

The Do's and Don'ts of the Discussion Section

Many authors, especially those writing a research paper for the first time, are often puzzled by the technicalities of writing any section of the paper. This confusion is specifically seen in the discussion section, as stating the importance of their entire research in less than 1000 words becomes more of a challenge. To prevent this dilemma, we have listed certain do's and don'ts that can be followed when writing this section.

- *Do* not include entire sentences restating your results. Should you

- need to remind the reader of the finding to be discussed, use "bridge sentences" that relate the result to the interpretation.
- Recommendations for further research can be included in either the discussion or conclusion of your paper. However, *do not* repeat your recommendations in both sections.
- *Do* not introduce new results in the discussion.
- Use of the first person is acceptable; however, too much use of the first person may actually distract the reader from the main points. Hence, try *avoiding* the use of the first person.
- Interpret your data in appropriate depth. This means that when you explain a phenomenon, you *must* describe reasons for your observations, especially when your results differ from your expectations. If your results agree with your expectations, then describe the theory your study supports. It is never good to only mention "the data agreed with expectations."
- Decide if each hypothesis is supported, rejected, or if you cannot make a decision with confidence. *Do not* merely say that a study or part of a study was "inconclusive."
- Research papers are not accepted if the work is incomplete. Conclude what you can based on the results that you have and complete the paper.
- *Do* suggest future directions, such as how the experiment might be modified to achieve another objective.
- *Do* explain your observations thoroughly, focusing on mechanisms.
- *Do* decide if the experimental design answered the hypothesis, and whether it was properly controlled.
- *Do* try to offer alternative explanations if they exist.
- No single experiment completely answers a broad question; hence, it would be best to elaborate your next steps. In addition, it is very crucial *to state* the questions that remain to be answered.

Finally, to recap this section, writing the discussion section mainly involves:

- Reiterating the research problem and stating the major findings
- Explaining the meaning of the findings and stating why they are important
- Relating your findings to the results of similar studies conducted in the past
- Considering and providing alternative explanations of the findings
- Acknowledging and explaining the study's limitations
- Providing suggestions for further research in the field

Verb Tenses in the Discussion Section

When explaining findings, use the present tense with modal verbs or use the past tense:
- These results indicate that company size *influences* corporate reporting patterns.

As addressed in the recommendations for using verb tenses in the introduction, the above example describes the function of "company size" in the present tense (*influences*) because the sentence is written to establish a *fact*. Note the verb tense usage in the sentence below:
- These results indicate that company size *influenced* corporate reporting patterns.

In this example, the verb describing "company size" is written in the past tense (*influenced*) because the finding is limited to this study alone and may not be true (or has yet to be proven) elsewhere.

When referring to the purpose, hypothesis, or when restating the findings, use the past tense:
- This research *attempted* to assess and compare three models of audio-visual fusion.
- We *discovered* distant metastases in 12% of head and neck carcinomas.

When explaining the limitations of findings, use the past tense or present tense with modal verbs:
- The sample *involved* only children aged three to five years.
- Surveying other departments *may produce* different results.

Use present tense verbs when comparing findings:
- This outcome *corresponds* with that of Rundle et al. (2008).
- Our findings *agree* with those of both Cherundolo (2002) and Dempsey (2010).

When stating the implications, use the present tense with tentative or conditional modal verbs:
- Spirochetes *appear* to grow preferentially on the external surface of subgingival plaque.
- This antigen *could behave* as an adhesion molecule in NK-target cell interaction.

Use the present tense and modal or tentative verbs when offering recommendations or describing applications:
- The approach outlined in this study *should be replicated* in more diverse academic environments.
- We *suggest* that the approach outlined in this study be replicated in more diverse academic environments.

Examples of Tentative Language for the Discussion Section

- **Adjectives**
  apparent, certain, consistent with, few, many, most, possible, presumed, probable, several, some, supposed

- **Adverbs**
  about, apparently, arguably, fairly, in general, largely, likely, more or less, mostly, often, perhaps, possibly, presumably, probably, quite, rather, somewhat, unlikely, usually

- **Nouns**
  appearance, indication, inference, likelihood, possibility, probability, suggestion, tendency, to our knowledge

- **Verbs**
  aim, appear, assume, can, could, estimate, indicate, infer, intend, may, might, presume, propose, seem, seen as, should, speculate, suggest, suppose, tend

Quick Tips About the Discussion Section

1. **Move from specific to general.** Move from your findings to other literature, to general theories, and then to practice.
2. **Do not ignore or bury the major issue.** Did the study achieve the goal (resolve the problem, answer the question, support the hypothesis) presented in the introduction?

3. Provide complete explanations.
   * Give evidence for each conclusion.
   * Discuss possible reasons for expected and unexpected findings.

What to Avoid
1. Avoid overgeneralizing.
2. Do not ignore deviations in your data.
3. Avoid guessing about what cannot be tested in the near future.

What Do Your Observations Mean?

Background information (reference to literature or to research aim/question)
- A strong relationship between X and Y has been reported in the literature.
- Prior studies highlight the importance of . . .
- A review of the literature reveals no data on the association between X and Y.
- As mentioned in the literature review . . .
- Little was found in the literature on the question of . . .
- This study began with the aim of assessing the importance of X in . . .
- The third question in this research was . . .
- A previous study hypothesized that participants with a history of . . .
- The present study was designed to determine the effect of . . .

Discussion Section: Statement of Results

(usually with reference to the results section)

- The results of this study indicate that . . .
- This experiment did not detect any evidence of . . .
- On the question of X, this study shows that . . .
- The experiments in the current study revealed that . . .
- The most compelling finding is that . . .
- Another crucial finding is that . . .
- The results of this study do not show a significant increase in . . .
- In the current study, comparing X with Y shows that the mean degree of . . .
- In this study, Xs were found to cause . . .

- X comprises the largest set of significant clusters of . . .
- Note that in all seven cases of this study . . .

What Conclusions Can You Draw?

For each major result:
Describe the patterns, principles, and relationships your results show. Explain how your results relate to expectations and to literature cited in your introduction. Do they agree or contradict? Or, are they exceptions to the rule? Explain plausibly any agreements, contradictions, or exceptions.

Explanations for Results

- Several explanations for this result are possible.
- These differences can be explained in part by the proximity of X and Y.
- A possible explanation for this might be that . . .
- Another possible explanation for this is that . . .
- This result may be explained by the fact that . . . /by a number of different factors.
- This result is difficult to explain, but it might be related to . . .
- Quite possibly, these results are due to . . .
- The reason for this is not clear, but it may have something to do with . . .
- These students may have benefited from . . .
- This discrepancy may be due to . . .
- This rather contradictory result may be caused by . . .
- These factors may explain the relatively strong correlation between X and Y.
- However, this study derived other possible explanations.
- The possible interference of X cannot be ruled out.
- The observed increase in X can be attributed to . . .
- The observed correlation between X and Y might be explained by . . .

Unexpected Outcomes

- Surprisingly, X was revealed to . . .
- An unanticipated finding was that . . .
- It is somewhat surprising that no X was noted in this condition . . .

- What is surprising is that . . .
- Contrary to expectations, this study did not find a significant difference between . . .
- However, the observed difference between X and Y in this study was not significant.
- However, one-way ANOVA results show that this outcome is not statistically significant.
- This finding was unexpected, suggesting that . . .

Reference to Previous Research

I. Supporting

- This study produced results that corroborate the findings of several previous studies in this field.
- The findings of the current study are consistent with those of Smith and Jones (2001), who discovered that . . .
- This finding, which also links X and Y, supports previous research on this area of the brain.
- This study confirms that X is associated with . . .
- It is encouraging to compare this figure with the findings of Jones (1993), who showed that . . .
- Noteworthy similarities exist between the attitudes expressed by X in this study and those described by both Smith (1987; 1995) and Jones (1986).
- These findings further support the idea of . . .
- Increased activation in the PCC in this study corroborates earlier findings.
- These results are consistent with those of related studies, and suggest that . . .
- The present findings seem to be consistent with the findings of previous research, showing that . . .
- This also agrees with our earlier observations, which demonstrated that . . .

II. Contradictory

- However, the findings of the current study do not support previous research.
- This study was unable to demonstrate that . . .
- However, this result has not previously been reported.
- In contrast to earlier findings, no evidence of X was detected.

- Although these results differ from some published studies (Smith, 1992; Jones, 1996), they are consistent with those of . . .

Advising Cautious Interpretation

- These findings must be interpreted with caution because . . .
- These results must therefore be interpreted with caution.
- However, with a small sample size, caution must be applied, as the findings might not be transferable to . . .

Suggestions for Future Work

- Describe how additional research might resolve these contradictions or explain exceptions.
- However, more research on this topic needs to be undertaken before the association between X and Y can be clearly understood.
- Further research should be conducted to investigate the . . .
- Research questions that could be asked include . . .
- Future studies on the current topic are, therefore, recommended.
- Further study with a greater focus on X is suggested.
- Additional analyses that account for these variables will need to be performed.
- Further work is required to establish this X.
- In future investigations, it might be possible to use a different X in which . . .
- This is a critical issue for future research.

Common Writing Errors and Their Corrections

How to use "As," "Because," and "Since" in Scholarly Writing

In technical writing, clarity is one of the most crucial aspects. Although many words have similar meanings, some that have the same meaning in one context may have another in a different context. Significant debate has raged over the proper use of the following words: "because, "since," and "as."

The *Merriam-Webster* Dictionary definitions are listed as follows:

I. Because

The *Merriam-Webster Dictionary* defines **because** as a **conjunction** (a word that is used to join two sentences, clauses, phrases, or words) as follows:
1. For the reason that: SINCE
2. The fact that: THAT

II. Since

The *Merriam-Webster Dictionary* provides several definitions and functions for this word. **Since** is defined first as an **adverb** (a word that modifies or describes a verb):
1. From a definite past time until now
2. Before the present time
3. After a time in the past: SUBSEQUENTLY

Since is also defined as a **conjunction**:
1. At a time in the past after or later than **or** from the time in the past when (something happened or some period occurred)
2. In view of the fact that: BECAUSE (As you can see, both since and because can be used to define each other in this context.)

Finally, **since** may also be used as a **preposition** (a function word that is typically combined with a noun phrase to form a phrase that is usually used to express a modification or prediction):

1. In the period after a specified time in the past **or** from a specified time in the past

Thus, although **since** and **because** are often used interchangeably, **since** can be applied in several other situations.

III. As

The *Merriam-Webster Dictionary* describes no less than *five* functions for this word. We shall examine the first three. The first usage is as an **adverb**.

1. To the same degree or amount
2. For instance
3. When considered in a specified form or relation—usually used before a preposition or a participle (a word that functions as an adjective but has verbal characteristics, such as tense, voice, and the ability to take an object).

The second usage of **as** is a **conjunction**:

1. AS IF
2. In or to the same degree in which
3. In the way or manner that
4. In accordance with what or the way in which
5. WHILE, WHEN
6. Regardless of the degree to which
7. For the reason that
8. That the result is

The third usage of **as** is as a **preposition**:

1. LIKE
2. In the capacity, character, condition, or role of

Because we can use **as** and **since** in various ways, for technical writing, many style guides recommend using each word to have only one meaning. Thus, we seldom use **since** or **as** to mean **because**. We use **since** only for situations that refer to time.

The sixth edition of *The Publication Manual of the American Psychological Association* states the following: "**Since** is more precise when it is used to refer only to time (to mean 'after that'); otherwise, replace with **because**" (p.84). For example:

She had not been able to answer her phone since she was in class.

Does this mean she did not answer her phone **since** the time she had been in class, or **because** she was in class?

A better way to rephrase this sentence is to write: She had not been able to answer her phone **because** she was in class.

Similarly, the tenth edition of the *American Medical Association Manual of Styles* states the following: "*As, because,* and *since* can all be used when 'for the reason that' is meant. However, in this construction, *as* should be avoided when it could be construed to mean *while*" (p. 386). For example:

He could not accurately examine the patient as he was looking at another patient's chart.

Does this sentence mean he could not examine the patient **while** he was looking at another patient's chart, or **because** he was looking at another patient's chart? The meaning is unclear.

A better way to rephrase this sentence is to write as follows: He could not examine the patient **because** he was looking at another patient's chart.

Clarity is crucial in technical writing to avoid confusion and misinterpretation. We can achieve this by applying such consideration when we write.

Punctuation Point

General Rules About Using Numbers in Academic Writing

I. Never Start a Sentence with a Numeral

Spell out the number or modify the word order so that a numeral does not begin the sentence. A sentence can begin with a date, but it is generally better to rewrite the sentence.
- Nine days passed after he received the news.

II. Use Commas to Separate Thousands, Millions, and Billions

English readers are used to this visual aid in reading numbers. Do not use periods in place of commas. The period mark is actually called a "point" and is used for decimals.
- 25,000 units, not 25.000

III. Write Numbers in the Millions As Numerals or As Numerals Plus the Word "Million"

The word million is not plural when used after a number. When writing about money, use a numeral followed by the word "million" or "billion." When referring to money, remember to use the dollar sign ($) (or other currency symbol) before the number, not after it.
- 2.5 million people or 2,500,000 people
- $2.5 million/billion

IV. Spell Out Numbers from One to Ten. Then Use Numerals for All Numbers 11 and Above

However, when expressing a range that involves numbers of both types, write all numbers numerically.

- The final incubation periods varied from 8 to 12 days.

V. Write the Percent Symbol (%) After Numerals

Some writers prefer the percent symbol and others prefer to spell out the word percent. When in doubt, consult your specific journal submission guidelines.
- 52% or 52 percent

Optional usage
Spell out money or percentage expressions when they contain fewer than four words. For example: seventy-five percent, twenty-four dollars.

VI. Pluralizing Numerals

Avoid using an apostrophe for numerals written in plural form.
- In the 1980s . . . (not the 1980's)

VII. Place a Hyphen between a Numeral and a Unit of Measurement When They both Modify a Noun

- 25,000-volt charge, 15-inch steel rod, one-ton tank, 60-foot boat

VIII. When Numbers Are Used Together in the Same Phrase, Write One As a Word and the Other As a Numeral

- Each experiment required twenty 5-centiliter tubes.

IX. Centrally Align and Numerically Designate Equations on a Separate Line in the Document, unless They Are Short and Simple

- The general first-order linear equation is $dy/dx = p(x)y + q(x)(1)$, and the general second-order linear equation is $d^2y/dx^2 + p(x)dy/dx + q(x)y + r(x)(2)$

The Writing Process

Imitate Skillful Writers

Observe how successful writers introduce their topic, cite literature, and present their writing. Imitate their words and phrases, and modify them to fit your paper and research. It is easier to imitate what someone else has written than to create a completely new sentence.

However, Do Not Plagiarize

Plagiarism is stealing words and ideas from someone else. In Webster's Third International Dictionary, to plagiarize means to "steal and pass off as one's own the ideas and words of another." Many students plagiarize because they feel overwhelmed, having waited until the last minute, or did not otherwise use effective time management strategies during the research phase of their project. They may intentionally plagiarize to finish a project by a deadline or they may feel their own words are not good enough. They may unintentionally plagiarize words or ideas because they were confused about or did not use consistent citation styles; they paraphrased original texts in their notes, and then copied them in their paper; they were unable to locate a primary source for their paper, but still used the information; or they were just confused about what was expected of them. There is also a cultural consideration as well. It is a Western idea that individuals can own ideas and words. Other cultures in the world, especially, those with a more a collectivist identity, may see that these words and ideas are communally used or are community property.

Therefore, if you are quoting statements made by another writer, use quotation marks. Some people suggest that you should not copy more than three consecutive words without identifying quotation marks. This is extreme advice that few people can follow. Do not copy, but summarize contributions of other writers in your own words as they relate to the subject of your paper. Mention the cited author with the year of publication in the text, and provide the citation details in the reference section.

Tips for Journal Submission

How do journals compare to each other? This question is frequently asked by researchers and graduate students who wonder where to submit their papers. The quality of your research is often judged by the quality of the journal in which it is published. Therefore, do not ignore the journal rankings. What is a good journal choice? Should it be based on the reputation of a journal, its selectivity, or its most recent impact?

Citation Statistics

Journal Citation Reports (JCR), published annually by the Institute for Scientific Information in Philadelphia, Pennsylvania, provides statistical information about sufficiently large or established journals. Among the citation statistics, three are especially important: Total Citations, Cited Half-Life, and Impact Factor.

Total Citations (TC) is the number of all citations of papers published in the journal during a year. A large TC may indicate a journal's importance in the field, and also contains common multidisciplinary journals (such as *Nature*) and journals focusing on a wide field. A small TC may indicate a journal's weakness or less frequent publication. However, a small TC is also typical for narrow-specialty journals.

Cited Half-Life (CHL) is the number of journal publication years going back from the current year, accounting for 50% of the total citations received by the cited journal in the current year. CHL indicates the age of its average cited articles. A large CHL may imply longevity of the published information. However, a relatively small CHL may reflect a journal's emphasis on cutting edge research and its timeliness.

Impact Factor (IF) is the ratio between the number of all current citations of papers published in a journal during the previous two years to the total number of articles that the journal published during that time. It can also be viewed as the frequency with which the "average article" in the journal has been cited in a particular year. The IF reflects the influence on its field of an average article published in the journal. It is also believed to be a fair quality measure that "tends to discount the advantage that large, frequently issued, older journals have over smaller, less frequently issued, newer journals" (McDonnell, 1997). Of the three statistics, IF is generally considered the most strongly connected to a journal's quality.

Although citation statistics are often interpreted as measures of journal quality, the Institute for Scientific Information (1995) warns that "The quantitative data it reports are intended to complement, not replace, traditional quantitative and subjective inputs, such as peer surveys and specialist opinions." Dagan (1989) further cautions ". . . citation habits differ among fields, and comparison of journals belonging to different areas is not warranted." This may also be true even for journals covering the same field, yet catering to different audiences.

Of course, the citation statistics cannot be used to judge the quality of a single article. They only reflect the nature of an average article. Hence, you can expect to see some poor-quality contributions published in top journals as well as great articles published in low-ranked journals.

Inappropriate Vocabulary and Improvements

in most cases

A better alternative would be:
usually

in many cases

A better alternative would be:
often

in large measure

A better alternative would be:
largely

is in excess of

A better alternative would be:
exceeds/surpasses

in proximity to

A better alternative would be:
near

> **in case**
>
> A better alternative would be:
> *if*

Academic Vocabulary

Headwords	Other Words in the Family
license	licenses, license, licensed, licensing, licenses, unlicensed
link	linkage, linkages, linked, linking, links
locate	located, locating, location, locations, relocate, relocated, relocates, relocating, relocation
logic	illogical, illogically, logical, logically, logician, logicians
maintain	maintained, maintaining, maintains, maintenance
major	majorities, majority
manipulate	manipulated, manipulates, manipulating, manipulation, manipulations, manipulative
manual	manually, manuals
margin	marginal, marginally, margins
mature	immature, immaturity, maturation, maturational, matured, matures, maturing, maturity
maximize	max, maximized, maximizes, maximizing, maximization, maximum
mechanism	mechanisms
mediate	mediated, mediates, mediating, mediation
medical	medically
mental	mentality, mentally
method	methodical, methodological, methodologies, methodology, methods
migrate	migrant, migrants, migrated, migrates, migrating, migration, migrations, migratory

续表

Headwords	Other Words in the Family
minimal	minimalization, minimalize, minimalizes, minimalized, minimalizing, minimalist, minimalists, minimalistic, minimally
minimize	minimized, minimizes, minimizing
ministry	ministered, ministering, ministerial, ministries
minor	minorities, minority, minors
mode	modes
modify	modification, modifications, modified, modifies, modifying, unmodified
monitor	monitored, monitoring, monitors, unmonitored
motive	motivate, motivated, motivates, motivating, motivation, motivations, motives, unmotivated
mutual	mutually
negate	negative, negated, negates, negating, negatively, negatives
network	networked, networking, networks
neutral	neutralization, neutralize, neutralized, neutralizes, neutralizing, neutrality

Chapter 11
How Do Your Results Fit into the Broader Context?

How Do Your Results Fit into the Broader Context?

1. **Describe** the theoretical implications of your results.
2. **Suggest** practical applications of your results.
3. **Extend** your findings to other situations or other subjects.
4. **Give** the big picture: Do your findings help us understand a broader topic?
5. **Present** trends and projections.
6. **Suggest** the theoretical implications of your results.

Noting Implications

- This finding has important implications for developing . . .
- An implication of X is the possibility that . . .
- One of the issues that emerges from these findings is . . .
- Some of the issues emerging from this finding relate specifically to . . .

Commenting on Findings

- However, these results are not encouraging.
- These findings are rather disappointing.
- The test was successful as it was able to identify students who . . .
- The present results are remarkable in at least two major respects.

Extend your findings to other situations or other subjects. Give the big picture: Do your findings help us understand a broader topic?

Suggesting General Hypotheses

- The value of X suggests that a weak link may exist between . . .
- It is, therefore, likely that such connections exist between . . .
- It can be suggested, therefore, that . . .
- It is possible to hypothesize that these conditions are less likely to occur in . . .
- Therefore, it is probable that . . .
- Hence, it could conceivably be hypothesized that . . .
- These findings suggest that . . .
- It may be the case that these variations . . .
- In general, it seems that . . .
- It is possible, therefore, that . . .
- Therefore, X could be a major factor, if not the only one, in . . .
- It can, therefore, be assumed that the . . .

Describing Trends and Projections

A trend is a description of change over time. A projection is a prediction of future change. Trends and projections are usually illustrated using line graphs in which the horizontal axis represents time. The following section provides some of the language commonly used for writing about trends and projections.

I. Describing Trends

This graph shows that there has been a [slight / gradual / steady / marked / steep / sharp] [increase / rise / decrease / fall / decline / drop] in the number of divorces in England and Wales since 1981.

II. Describing High and Low Points in Figures

- The graph in Figure 2 indicates a *marked increase* in withdrawals since 2001.
- The numbers and bars in Fig. 3 represent *steady* median values.
- This chart shows a *gradual decline* of extinction probabilities for marine life.
- The upper graph illustrates three *sharp decreases* in false diagnosis.

III. Projecting Trends

The number of Xs	is projected to	decline steadily	after 2020.
The amount of Y	is expected to	drop sharply	
	is likely to		
The rate of Z	will probably	stabilize	

IV. Writing Conclusions

The conclusion section is a relatively short part of an academic paper that usually serves two functions. First, the conclusion summarizes and arranges the main areas covered in the text, in a manner similar to "looking back." Second, the conclusion provides a final comment or judgment on the overall study. Final comments may also include suggestions for improvement and speculation regarding future research.

In dissertations and lengthy research papers, conclusions are more complex and may also include sections on the significance of the findings and recommendations for future work. Conclusions may be optional in research articles where the discussion section summarizes the study and its implications. However, a conclusion is expected in dissertations and essays.

V. Summarizing the Content

- This paper provides a description of, and the reasons for, the widespread use of X . . .
- This essay has argued that X is the best instrument to . . .

VI. Restatement of Aims

- This study sought to determine . . .
- The present study was designed to determine the effect of . . .
- The aim of this investigation was to assess . . .
- The purpose of the current study was to determine . . .
- This project was undertaken to design . . . and evaluate . . .
- Returning to the hypothesis posed at the beginning of this study, it is now appropriate to state that . . .

VII. Summarizing the Findings

- This study shows that . . .
- These findings suggest that in general . . .
- One of the more significant findings to emerge from this study is that . . .
- It was also shown that . . .
- This study determined that generally . . .
- The following conclusions can be drawn from the present study . . .
- The relevance of X is clearly supported by the current findings.
- The second major finding was that . . .
- The results of this investigation show that . . .
- The most obvious finding to emerge from this study is that . . .
- X, Y, and Z emerged as reliable predictors of . . .
- Multiple regression analysis revealed that the . . .

VIII. Suggesting Implications

- The evidence from this study suggests that . . .

- The results of this study indicate that . . .
- The results of this research support the idea that . . .
- In general, it seems that . . .
- Taken together, these results suggest that . . .
- An implication of X is the possibility that . . .
- The findings of this study suggest that . . .

IX. Significance of the Findings

- The X that we thus identified increases our understanding of the role of . . .
- These findings enhance our understanding of . . .
- This research serves as a basis for future studies and . . .
- The current findings add substantially to our understanding of . . .
- The current findings add to a growing body of literature on . . .
- The methods used for this X can also be applied to other Xs in . . .
- Overall, these findings suggest that X plays a role in promoting Y.

X. Limitations of the Current Study

- Finally, numerous consequential limitations must be considered. First . . .
- Several caveats must be noted regarding the present study.
- The most critical limitation lies in the fact that . . .
- This current study was limited by . . .
- This study was unable to analyze these variables.
- However, this study was not designed to evaluate factors related to . . .
- The current study only examined . . .
- The project was limited in several ways. First, the project used a convenience sample that . . .
- However, with a small sample size, caution must be applied in . . .

XI. Recommendations for Future Work

- This research raises many questions that require further investigation.
- Further study must be conducted to determine whether or not . . .
- Further research should be undertaken in the following areas.
- Further experimental investigations are required to estimate . . .
- What is now needed is a cross-national study involving . . .
- On a broader scale, research must also determine more precisely . . .
- The association of these factors should be investigated in future studies.
- Further research might explore how . . .

- Further research in this field regarding the role of X would be of great help in . . .
- Further investigation into and experimentation of X is strongly recommended.
- Future studies performing the same experiment could . . .
- Assessing the effects of both X and Y would be enlightening if . . .
- More information on X would help establish a greater degree of accuracy in . . .
- For the debate to advance, a clearer understanding of X must be developed.
- Before X is promoted, a study similar to this should thoroughly assess . . .
- These findings provide the following insights for future research.
- Considerably more work is required to determine . . .

XII. Implications and Recommendations for Practice or Policy

- These findings suggest several courses of action for . . .
- An implication of these findings is that both X and Y should be accounted for when . . .
- The findings of this study have several crucial implications for future practice.
- Therefore, a definite need remains for . . .
- However, numerous critical changes must be made.
- Another noteworthy practical implication is that . . .
- Furthermore, additional Xs should be made available to . . .
- Other types of X could include (a) . . .
- Unless governments adopt X, Y will not be attained.
- This information can be used to develop targeted interventions aimed at . . .
- A reasonable approach to tackle this issue could be to . . .

Common Writing Errors and Their Corrections

How to Use Initialisms and Acronyms in Scholarly Writing

Abbreviations are an integral part of technical writing. When writing academic papers, the wide variety of concepts and terms in diverse fields of research necessitates using abbreviations such as initialisms and acronyms, which must be appropriately introduced in a paper by providing the accompanying "expansion": for instance, "The effects of using 'diphenyl phosphate (DP)' in an aqueous solution were investigated."

"Initialisms," which are abbreviations formed from initial letters (such as "FAQ" for "frequently asked question" and "IEEE" for "Institute of Electrical and Electronics Engineers"), are often mistaken for acronyms, even in academia, to indicate any arrangement of initials that represent a particular multi-word term. Although some initialisms are certainly acronyms, not all of them are. When considering the terms "atomic force microscopy," "English as a second language," and "full width at half maximum," the abbreviations "AFM," "ESL," and "FWHM" are technically not acronyms because they are not pronounced as newly formed, stand-alone words; they are pronounced by enunciating each letter separately: "ay-ef-em," "ee-es-el," and "ef-double-you-aitch-em." By contrast, an acronym specifically involves initials that represent the first letters of words (or initials that spell key syllables) in a particular phrase to form a new, *phonetically pronounced* word:

- laser = **l**ight **a**mplification by **s**timulated **e**mission of **r**adiation
- radar = **ra**dio **d**etection **a**nd **r**anging
- scuba = **s**elf-**c**ontained **u**nderwater **b**reathing **a**pparatus

Note that the terms in these three examples are so well known that that they have transcended scientific spheres to become commonly used words, which is why they are generally no longer expressed as "LASER," "RADAR," and "SCUBA." Examples of acronyms that are generally written in all capital letters are "MET" for "mobile equipment technology" and "PIN" for "personal identification number." Distinguishing an acronym from an initialism is crucial because of how they are pronounced in speech, thus affecting how they are used in writing. When writing either acronyms (e.g., "AIDS") or initialisms (e.g., "HIV"), the abbreviated terms are still grammatical elements that must be represented appropriately.

For instance, although "HIV" begins with the consonant letter "H," it requires the general article "an" because it is read with a beginning vowel sound ("aitch-eye-vee"). Consider the following example:

♦ Our institute has implemented *an* HIV testing and counseling program.

When writing out the full term the initialism represents, use the general article "a":

♦ Our institute has implemented *a* human immunodeficiency virus testing and counseling program.

Treating abbreviations with grammatical appropriateness is essential to ensure readers and reviewers that the author thoroughly understands the terms he or she uses. However, exceptions to this recommendation exist. Some initialisms represent pluralized terms and are written without plural markers because the pluralized term is generally treated as a singular noun. Examples of this usage are "IS" for "information systems" and "GM" for the corporation "General Motors." Writing "ISs" or "GMs" would be inappropriate and misleading in nearly any context.

A mistake to avoid when using initialisms and acronyms is the error of redundancy. When using "RIE" to represent "reactive-ion etching" a technical writer should avoid the construction "RIE etching," which literally means "reactive-ion etching etching!" Other redundantly used abbreviations are "PIN number," "ATM machine," and "RAM memory." This phenomenon is so common in speech and writing that it has earned its own abbreviated term, the redundant initialism "RAS syndrome" (RAS = redundant acronym syndrome)! Although remarking on such redundancies can be enjoyable and enlightening, creating them in technical writing should be conscientiously avoided.

Another frequent error in academic writing is to employ acronyms that do not exist. One such error entails referring to the corporation "Sony" as "SONY," because their logo shows all four letters capitalized. However, such representation is inappropriate, because "Sony" is not an acronym—it is simply the name of the company; therefore, only the first letter requires capitalization.

Finally, the most common misrepresentation involving initialisms and acronyms in technical writing is the belief that all capital letters must represent capitalized words; but this is not true. For example, the business management philosophy "total quality management" is abbreviated as "TQM." However, its expansion is often written inappropriately as "Total Quality Management," because some authors forget that the term is not a proper noun, or worse—the authors are never completely knowledgeable about the term to begin with! Remember, knowing the meaning and origin of terms is vital before abbreviating them in text, because how an author treats initialisms and acronyms in an academic paper often reveals how much he or she knows about the terms they represent.

Technical writers must often use abbreviations or acronyms. Sometimes, students use so many abbreviations and acronyms that their writing can become unclear, even for knowledgeable readers.

Look at the following example, which was taken from a thesis:

> The Resource Sponsors present their *SPPs* to the *IR3B* for review. Because the *SPPs* are consistent with planning guidance, they are compiled by *N80* into a *POM* proposal. The *ESC* reviews the proposal for policy issues. The *CNO* then approves the Tentative *POM (T-POM)*. The *T-POM* is presented by *N80* and the Marine Corps *DCS* for programs and resources to the *DPSB*. After finishing the review by the *DPSB* and signing by the *SECDEF*, the *DoN POM* is submitted to the *OSD* for review.

In this example, some of the abbreviations and acronyms should be spelled out because they look more like code than English. Another option here is a process chart that would provide this information in graphical form.

Punctuation Point

How to Use Dashes in Academic Writing

Today's topic is dashes: when to use them and when not to use them. I am going to start with the distinction between hyphens and dashes. A hyphen joins two words into a unit (e.g., "on-site coordinator" or "high-tech company") or indicates a word break at the end of a line of text. A short dash (often called an en-dash because it is the width of the letter "n") separates items such as dates or page numbers (e.g., 1611–1676 or pp. 136–8). A long dash (often called an em-dash because it is the width of a letter "m") is what we will be talking about below. A hyphen is produced by a simple keystroke on your keyboard; dashes are symbols that can be inserted into a document from the symbols menu in your word processor.

I am now going to talk about using dashes in your writing. First, we will look at single dashes, which I do not believe are formal enough for academic writing, although some would disagree. Here is an example:

- One task is more important than any other to the junior scholar and will determine whether he receives funding, promotion, and tenure—academic publishing.

This dash could be replaced by either a comma or a colon. I would suggest a colon because a colon signals clearly that what follows will complement or complete what precedes it. A comma would work, but because commas play so many roles in our writing, I generally choose a colon instead of a comma when I have a choice. Here is another example:

- The range of activities an academic must participate in compete for his time to write—such activities are important but should not be allowed to take the place of scholarly writing.

In this case, you could replace the dash with either a semicolon or a period. Generally, a semicolon will work best since it will provide the closeness that the author was trying to show with the dash.

I am only arguing against the single dash in academic writing—it is absolutely fine in a more casual context—like a newsletter. My reason for this advice is that the dash can play the role of a comma, colon, or period without doing anything unique. Nothing special is added and something may be lost. You may lose clarity, and you will certainly lose formality. Personally, I don't think the single dash has any place in academic writing, of course, others may disagree. One possible defense of the single dash in academic writing is the drama of the single dash; because it breaks up a sentence in an unconventional manner, it does draw real attention to what follows it. Now let's turn to the use of double dashes.

Double dashes are used instead of commas (or parentheses) to interrupt a sentence. The phrase separated by dashes must be grammatically inessential, by which I simply mean that the sentence will still work without that phrase. Here is an example:

- The issues that prevent doctoral students from writing—most importantly, their lack of familiarity with academic vocabularies—are a serious concern for advising professors.

It is often said that we use dashes to signal that something crucial is being added to a sentence and use parentheses to signal that the interruption is relatively unimportant (e.g., to give dates or citations or examples). In this schema, commas fall somewhere in the middle. There is some truth to this division, but I find the next three principles more helpful in deciding whether to use double dashes:

1. Most importantly, double dashes can be used to add an element to a sentence that already has enough commas.
2. Double dashes are very common in some fields (most humanities fields, for instance) and rare in others (in many scientific fields, for instance). If they are rare in your field, it is unlikely that you would want to use them.
3. Regardless of field, double dashes are a stylistic variant and should be used sparingly; they draw attention to themselves, and the audience will grow tired of them if they are overused.

Overall, I suggest using double dashes—if they are appropriate to your field of study—in moderation and replacing single dashes with colons, commas, or even periods, if only in your formal writing.

The Writing Process

I. Do Not Use the Word "I" in Technical Writing

Using "I" makes the writer appear proud. Reviewers generally do not like proud people. "The paper achieves . . . " sounds softer and more humble than "I did this." In particular, avoid starting a paragraph with "I."

II. Avoid Citing Your Own Works Extensively

Reviewers may think you are self-centered if you focus on your own studies too much. Other researchers have contributed to the literature, as well. If the first page mentions only your work, and not that of others, it means you are either researching an area in which no one else is interested (which is bad), or you are proud and do not care about the contributions of others, which is even worse.

III. Do Not Apologize

You should acknowledge the limitations of the approach only once in the conclusion. Do not apologize for what the paper cannot do. The more you talk about this to reviewers, the less contribution your paper seems to make.

Tips for Journal Submission

I. Cite Current Papers

If your most recent references in a paper are more than ten years old, publishing your page will be difficult. You are probably exploring a dead issue. Do not start such a paper! If the most recent references closely related to your paper are five years old, it may be a dying issue. Editors hesitate to accept such papers, (even if the reviewers recommend publication), because they are interested in new research. It is also difficult for an editor to find suitable reviewers for old topics. Having no new references implies that you have either not read the literature or that other researchers are not interested in your topic. Either way, a paper citing old references is unlikely to get published.

II. Do Not Write Papers on Breakthrough Ideas at First

In the early stages of your career, avoid writing about your breakthrough ideas unless your mentor is the editor of a major journal. Papers with breakthrough ideas are often not published. Wait until you gain tenure to tackle breakthrough ideas.

Chapter 11 How Do Your Results Fit into the Broader Context?

> *"I told my own young colleagues that they should preferably start off with the received wisdom with some changes until they get their tenure."*
>
> — Douglas North, 1993 Nobel Laureate in Economic Science(Nyaw and Yu, 1995).

After you have gained tenure or built a solid reputation in your field, you can tackle breakthrough ideas. Until then, you need to focus on minor but important ideas as you gain experience. In the beginning, it is better to extend existing literature. The majority of papers published today are modifications of existing papers or tests of existing theories. Of course, there must be something in your paper and your research that is original and unique. Copying is not extending knowledge.

Inappropriate Vocabulary and Improvements

in all cases

A better alternative would be:
always

a number of

A better alternative would be:
several/many/numerous

if conditions are such that

A better alternative would be:
if

happens to be

A better alternative would be:
am/is/are

give indication of

A better alternative would be:
indicate/suggest

give consideration to

A better alternative would be:
consider

Academic Vocabulary

Headwords	Other Words in the Family
norm	norms
normal	abnormal, abnormally, normalization, normalize, normalized, normalizes, normalizing, normality, normally
notion	notions
objective	objectively, objectivity
obtain	obtainable, obtained, obtaining, obtains, unobtainable
obvious	obviously
occupy	occupancy, occupant, occupants, occupation, occupational, occupations, occupied, occupier, occupiers, occupies, occupying
occur	occurred, occurrence, occurrences, occurring, occurs, reoccur, reoccurred, reoccurring, reoccurs
odd	odds
offset	offsets, offsetting
option	optional, options
orient	orientate, orientated, orientates, orientation, orientating, oriented, orienting, orients, reorient, reorientation
outcome	outcomes
output	outputs
overlap	overlapped, overlapping, overlaps
panel	paneled, paneling, panels
paradigm	paradigms
paragraph	paragraphing, paragraphs
parallel	paralleled, parallels, unparalleled
parameter	parameters
participate	participant, participants, participated, participates, participating, participation, participatory
partner	partners, partnership, partnerships
passive	passively, passivity

续表

Headwords	Other Words in the Family
perceive	perceived, perceives, perceiving, perception, perceptions
percent	percentage, percentages
period	periodic, periodical, periodically, periodicals, periods
persist	persisted, persistence, persistent, persistently, persisting, persists
perspective	perspectives
phase	phased, phases, phasing

Chapter 12
How Can You Describe Causes and Effects?

How Can You Describe Causes and Effects?

Academic writing often involves understanding and suggesting solutions to problems. Particularly in applied fields such as engineering, students find specific problems to study. However, solutions cannot be suggested unless the problem is fully analyzed, and this involves understanding the causes of the problem. Useful sentences for explaining causes and effects are listed below:

I. Verbs Expressing Causality

Lack of protein	*may cause* *can lead to* *can result in*	mental retardation.
Low levels of chlorine in the body	*stem from*	high blood pressure.
Much of the instability	*stems from*	the economic effects of the war.

Kwashiorkor is a disease	*caused by*	insufficient protein.
Beriberi is a disease	*resulting from*	vitamin deficiency.
Scurvy is a disease	*stemming from*	a lack of vitamin C.

II. Nouns Expressing Causality

The most *likely causes* of X are poor diet and lack of exercise.

A *consequence* of vitamin A deficiency is blindness.

Physical activity is an important *factor* in maintaining fitness.

Many other medications have an *influence* on cholesterol levels.

Another reason *why* Xs are considered crucial is that . . .

III. Prepositional Phrases Expressing Causality

| Over 200,000 people per year become deaf | *because of* | a lack of iodine. |
| | *as a result of* | |

IV. Sentence Connectors Expressing Causality

If undernourished and retarded children survive to become adults, they have decreased learning ability.	Therefore,	when they grow up, finding work will probably be difficult for them.
	Consequently,	
	Because of this,	
	As a result (of this),	

V. Adverbial Phrases Expressing Causality

Malnutrition leads to illness and a reduced ability to work in adulthood,	*thus/ thereby*	perpetuating the poverty cycle.
Warm air rises above the surface of the sea,	*thus/ thereby*	creating an area of low pressure.

Other Examples:
- As a consequence of X, it appears that winds alone are not the causative factor of . . .
- Due to X and Y, inflowing surface water becomes more dense as it . . .
- X and Y are important driving factors of Z.
- The mixing of X and Y exerts a powerful effect on Z through . . .

VI. Possible Cause and Effect Relationships (expressed tentatively)

- This suggests that a weak link *may exist* between X and Y.
- The human papilloma virus is linked to most types of cervical cancer.
- In many cases, stomach cancer *may be associated with* certain bacterial infections.
- A high consumption of seafood *could be associated with* infertility.
- There is some evidence that X *may affect* Y.

Common Writing Errors and Their Corrections

The improper use of prepositions is one of the most common errors in non-native English academic writing. Errors in preposition usage can significantly change the meaning of a sentence because prepositions show how elements within a sentence relate to each other.

Using Prepositions

Prepositions can be confusing for learners of English because, at times, their usage does not seem logical. The following are some example of preposition rules:

1. **Time:** *about, after, around, at, before, by, during, for, from . . . to, in, on, since, until*
   - Fred arrived *in* Germany in August 1990.
   - He started school *on* September 6th.
   - His school day began *at* eight o'clock in the morning.
   - He works *from* sunup *to* sundown.
   - *By* March, the weather will be warmer.
   - The discount is available *until* this Saturday.

2. **Place:** *above, against, along, among, around, at, behind, below, beside, between, by close to, down, far from, from . . . to, in, in back of, in front of, inside, into, near, next to, off, on, out, out of, outside, over, under, up, upon, within*
   - Linda has lived *in* New York for 40 years.
   - She lives *on* West 63rd Street.
   - She lives *at* 598 West 63rd Street.
   - Linda takes the subway *to* work *at* six o'clock every morning.
   - Her friends often see her running *to* (*for*) the subway train.

3. **Reason:** *because of, due to, for*
   - Because *of* rain, the office canceled the tour.

- Parents often wish *for* a peaceful and quiet enviornment.
- *Due to* the storm, the officials canceled the marathon.
- *For* obvious reasons, the company did not raise salaries.

4. **Manner:** *by, in (for example, in a new way), through, with, without*
   - Students benefit from their degree *by* working in a related field.
   - Some people live *without* ever owning a car.
   - The paper was filled *with* redundancies.
   - *Through* friends, people often learn of new job opportunities.

5. **Quantity:** *of*
   - Tons *of* lava poured from the volcano.
   - Many (*of* the) states support gun control.

6. **Possession** (belonging to): *of*
   - Members *of* the Senate serve a six-year term, whereas members *of* the House of Representatives serve two-year terms.

> *"Your prepositions are misleading. You need to look up the rules on when to use 'at', 'on', 'in', and 'by.' Until those errors are fixed, I don't want to spend time reviewing the ideas in your paper."*
>
> — 2nd **Reviewer, Applied Physics Letters**

Original

Many other medications have an influence *in* cholesterol levels.

Modified

Many other medications have an influence *on* cholesterol levels.

Original

A consequence *from* vitamin A deficiency is blindness.

Modified

A consequence *of* vitamin A deficiency is blindness.

Original

By many cases, stomach cancer may be associated with certain bacterial infections.

Modified

In many cases, stomach cancer may be associated with certain bacterial infections.

Original

Physical activity is an important factor *by* maintaining fitness.

Modified

Physical activity is an important factor *in* maintaining fitness.

Punctuation Point

How to Use the Colon in Academic Writing

Let's start by looking at the *only* rule of colon use: a colon should only appear after a complete sentence. In other words, don't put a colon in the middle of a sentence:

- This study will examine: interest rates, financial structure, management issues, and systematic processes.

The writer has presumably used a colon here because what follows is a list. However, the decision about colon use actually needs to be made based on what precedes the colon. This example is no different, logically, than the following: "I went to 7-11 to buy: candy and noodles." In both cases, the colon is redundant because the items being listed are part of the sentence. Now consider a slight modification:

- This study will examine four major factors: interest rates, financial structure, management issues, and systematic processes.

In this case, we have a complete sentence before the colon. If we want to go on to say what those four major factors are, we need to provide that information separately. A colon allows us to indicate that what follows will provide the information necessary to complete the thought found in the first sentence. Note that what follows a colon need not be a full sentence; single words, phrases, and full sentences can all appear after a colon.

With one simple rule—a colon should appear after a complete sentence—we are ready to see the stylistic advantages of the colon. Here are the three possible versions of our example:

- This study will examine: interest rates, financial structure, management issues, and systematic processes.
- This study will examine four major factors: interest rates, financial structure, management issues, and systematic processes.
- This study will examine interest rates, financial structure, management issues, and systematic processes.

The final version seems to me to be the best. The first version, as we have seen, is incorrect, and the second version, while perfectly acceptable, is longer and seems more complex. In a sentence this simple, there is no need for a full sentence to introduce a list. If you find yourself putting a redundant colon in the midst of a simple list, you can just take it out and continue. If, however, you find such a colon in a more complex sentence, it may be trying to tell you something. Consider the following example:

- This study will examine: interest rates as set by the central bank, the financial structure of the XYZ company, management issues involving employees, and systematic processes used in the XYZ company supply chain.

In this case, the colon—while still technically redundant—is definitely there for a reason. The author used a colon because he thought the reader would need to know that a list is coming. So, in this case, try keeping the colon and adding the requisite words to create a full sentence before that colon.

- This study will examine four major factors: interest rates as set by the central bank; the financial structure of the XYZ company; management issues involving employees; and systematic processes used in the XYZ company supply chain.

You will see that I have also added semicolons in the place of commas between the list items; I have done so because one of the list items had internal commas, which will potentially inhibit the readers' ability to understand the list. I will address this issue in more detail in a future post on writing effective lists.

I will end by commenting on the way that colons can be an efficient and elegant way to convey the relationship that exists between parts of your writing. Here is a sentence that I used at the beginning of this post:

- Let's start by looking at the *only* rule of colon use: a colon should only appear after a complete sentence.

We don't have to say "Let's start by looking at the *only* rule of colon use, which is that a colon should only appear after a complete sentence."

The version with the colon is preferable because it uses fewer words while cleanly emphasizing our point.

The Writing Process
Making Time for Your Research

This is one of the biggest questions facing researchers anywhere, but especially academics with conflicting priorities and multiple competing demands on their time. Just about everyone in academia seems to be overcommitted, and being asked to do more with less. This post offers suggestions for ways of finding more time for your research; they're all things I've found to be effective and many other scholars I've spoken with use them as well.

I. Block Out Regular Time to Focus on Your Research

This is the foundation of any successful time management. Ideally, we're talking about a full day at least, or several half-days, to allow momentum to build. Trying to carve out an hour or so here or there isn't the most useful approach because doing serious research and writing requires a certain depth of immersion in the literature, data, and thinking space. Because of this:

- Consolidate teaching times/days. Try to organize your teaching, prep, and student hours to be across as few days of the week as possible.
- Only attend meetings that are constructive and where it is essential that you are there.
- If you work best from home, try not to have any reason to be on campus during research time. Similarly, do not do any housework/errands during your research time.

An important thing to remember is this: Your research days should never be considered "free time."

II. Engage with Extracurricular Stuff That Stimulates Thinking and Writing

A writing group can be extremely effective for regularly urging one's project or writing forward. It helps to defend against the depressing isolation that comes with writing up your research work. Other forums that might work for you include research lab meetings, monthly lunches with collaborators or mentors, your active school seminar series or public lectures, or academic association events. A regular shot of sociable productivity that keeps research in front of you is a healthy thing.

III. Be Careful About the Ways in Which You Waste Time

It is easy to waste time with the many technical devices, such as texting on a cell phone, checking email, updating facebook, and the hundreds of others things that keep us from doing real work. In saying this, though, I'm not opining that you must cut yourself off from social media or email; if these are tools that help you move a project ahead, or plan fieldwork, or collaborate on an article, use them as much as you want.

What needs to be separated out is time that is *wasted*, such as when you:
- Find domestic or administrative chores to do because you can't face the blank page of a grant application or article.
- Answer irrelevant-to-your-research emails just because they are in your inbox. Or leave your phone turned on when you're not expecting a call that's relevant to your research.
- Invite distraction with an open office door (just *shut it*; you are not "hiding" from your colleagues, you are prioritizing your research).
- Browse what conferences or locations you might get to in the next year or so.
- Get yourself caught up in academic or institutional politics that don't have constructive outcomes.

IV. Use Deadlines That Work

If you have discipline, self-set deadlines can work beautifully. If, like 99% of us, you tend not to have a consistently effective amount of discipline, you can use external triggers for finishing drafts, applications, or proposals. You can use a friend who won't let you get away with fudging a due date, or promise things to journal editors and senior colleagues; avoiding shame can be a constructive research endeavor. Working to deadlines can be very liberating when writing up your research. You can't endlessly wander around. You have an end date set, and your job is to get the piece of writing as good as it can be by a particular production timeline.

If possible, cultivate several items at once. For example, have one piece for which you are working on the literature review, one near finalization, and another going through peer review or submission. Knowing that you have pieces of work moving through all these phases of conceptualization, writing, and publication offers a gratifying momentum, one that also serves you well for completing the Track Record sections of grant applications.

The most effective element of planning your deadlines (self-set or externally triggered) is that they are *realistic*. There's no point setting yourself up to fail. Look at your weekly schedule with a pessimistic eye and work out how much time you'll get each week (at a conservative maximum) for your research once you've blocked it out. I'm always overly optimistic about how long writing an article will take, yet can be pleasantly surprised at being able to put together a conference presentation in half the time I've allocated. I plan for more time than I think I'll need. This is especially true for finishing journal articles for submission.

V. Beware of Time Wasters That Can Pretend to Be Research Work

There are some research-related tasks that can take over your world if you let them. They're harder to judge at times because they are related to your research. Sometimes, though, you can fall across the line between doing your research and wasting time. Make sure you're not:

- Playing endlessly with your referencing database, and thinking it'd be great to review it for the 1000th time.
- Building up spectacular piles (or files) of articles, books, and book chapters that you never read.
- Talking with peers about your research all the time but not actually doing any of it.

It's rare that a person can't find any time at all to set aside for their research. It's more often the case that there's a need to reprioritize your working week, and to have a consistent approach and clear plan as to how you will use precious research time.

Tips for Journal Submission

I. Submission of Query Letters

Submitting query letters is essential because doing so allows us to see if a journal is willing to publish our paper. Usually, we need to send two inquiries. The first inquiry is for the assistant editor, requesting information about the publication, such as how many submissions they receive a year or what their submission backlog is. The second inquiry is more important, where we ask the editor if our article and research are applicable to the journal. Using emails and query letters, we can learn from the information in the responses if the journal is likely or unlikely to publish our paper. The best-case scenario has the editor giving us a mini-review of our paper. The information from the assistant editor and the editor is imperative to know if we can publish in their journal and what possible changes we can make to our paper and/or research to increase the possibility of publication. Utilizing the sample query email and the sample query letters below, you can obtain this information.

II. When Asked to Revise, Resubmit Within Three Months

An invitation to revise indicates that your reviewers had good first impressions about your paper. Do not wait until their positive feelings disappear. However, do not resubmit the revised version within one month, even if you worked on it full time. If you do, the editor may think that you did not spend enough time revising.

III. Revision Letters

After you have revised your paper to meet the revision requests of the editor, you will need to submit a letter explaining how you made such changes, along with the new version of your paper. You can use the sample revision letters at the end of the chapter to help write your revision letter.

IV. If You Hate to Revise, Write One Paragraph a Day

If you think the reviewers or editors have asked you to do an impossible or terrible task, then just write one paragraph a day. As you write a little bit every day, you begin to get excited.

V. Listen to What the Editor Says

It is critical to catch the real message of the editor's letter. Do not try to fight with the editor. Share the editor's letter and reviewer reports with experienced colleagues. They may have different interpretations of what the editor is asking.

VI. Initial Cover Letters

Now that you have received responses from your query emails and query letters, you will need to write a formal cover letter. This letter is what you will use to formally submit your paper to the journal for publication. Utilizing the sample on P. 345 will make this vital letter easy for you.

Inappropriate Vocabulary and Improvements

for this reason
A better alternative would be:
because

for the reason that
A better alternative would be:
so

for the purpose of
A better alternative would be:
for/to

during the time that
A better alternative would be:
while

due to the fact that
A better alternative would be:
because

despite the fact that
A better alternative would be:
although

Academic Vocabulary

Headwords	Other Words in the Family
phenomenon	phenomena, phenomenal
philosophy	philosopher, philosophers, philosophical, philosophically, philosophies, philosophize, philosophized, philosophizes, philosophizing
physical	physically
plus	pluses
policy	policies
portion	portions
pose	posed, poses, posing
positive	positively
potential	potentially
practitioner	practitioners
precede	preceded, precedence, precedent, precedes, preceding, unprecedented
precise	imprecise, precisely, precision
predict	predictability, predictable, predictably, predicted, predicting, prediction, predictions, predicts, unpredictability, unpredictable
predominant	predominance, predominantly, predominate, predominated, predominates, predominating
preliminary	preliminaries
presume	presumably, presumed, presumes, presuming, presumption, presumptions, presumptuous
previous	previously
primary	primarily
prime	primacy
principal	principally
principle	principled, principles, unprincipled
priority	priorities, prioritization, prioritize, prioritized, prioritizes, prioritizing
proceed	procedural, procedure, procedures, proceeded, proceeding, proceedings, proceeds
process	processed, processes, processing

续表

Headwords	Other Words in the Family
professional	professionally, professionals, professionalism
prohibit	prohibited, prohibiting, prohibition, prohibitions, prohibitive, prohibits
project	projected, projecting, projection, projections, projects
promote	promoted, promoter, promoters, promotes, promoting, promotion, promotions
proportion	disproportion, disproportionate, disproportionately, proportional, proportionally, proportionate, proportionately, proportions
prospect	prospective, prospects
protocol	protocols
psychology	psychological, psychologically, psychologist, psychologists

Template Email to the Assistant Editor

Dear [First Name, Last Name]:

I would like to submit an article to your journal, and I am requesting some information. How many submissions do you receive a year? How long does it take you to respond to authors with a decision about their manuscript? What is the extent of your backlog? Do you have any special themes or topics coming up? Also, I was not able to find out your word limit: Do you have a maximum?

I know you are very busy, but this information would be very helpful to me.

Sincerely,

[Your first and last name]

[University, Department]

[City/Country]

[No need to mention student status.]

(Referral Belcher)

Sample Query Letter to an Editor

Dear Dr. [First Name, Last Name]:

I obtained your email address from Professor [name], and I hope you do not mind me emailing you. I am considering submitting my article titled [title] for possible publication in your journal, [name]. I notice that your journal has published articles on [your general topic] (I am thinking in particular of [title], published last year). Because there are few published studies on [your specific topic], my article may fill this gap and contribute to the understanding of [your argument].

My article argues that [abstract here].

My article is approximately [number] double-spaced pages long, including footnotes, references, and tables. I have never published this article, nor have I submitted it to any other journal. Grants from the [name of funders] funded the collection of data for this project.

Would such an article interest you? Please let me know if you feel that my broader focus on [your topic] would pose a problem for acceptance in your journal. As my section on [sub-topic] is quite strong, I could recast the article to focus entirely on this [sub-topic]. Thank you very much. I look forward to hearing from you.

[Name without any title]

[University, Department]

[City, State/Country]

(Referral Belcher)

Sample Revision Letter 1

Dear [Editor's Name]:

Enclosed is the revised version of my article titled [title]. I am grateful for the thorough reading of the reviewers and have addressed their concerns as follows.

Errors: I have added (*present perfect tense*) the missing . . . and have corrected the . . .

Significance: One of the reviewers suggested that I make my contribution clearer; therefore, I have . . .

Introduction: I have condensed the introduction but have also provided examples of . . . so that my subject is clearer and my main objective is . . .

Theoretical Framework: I have shortened the theoretical section but have added material on the work of (cited reference), as the second reviewer requested; therefore, the revised article is slightly longer. Following this recommendation allowed me to address the first reviewer's concern about . . . Hence, the increased length seems warranted.

Terms: I have abandoned the problematic classification of . . .

Section 1: In the section on . . . , I have incorporated the texts that the second reviewer recommended . . .

Section 2: For reasons of length, I have eliminated much of . . .

Section 3: I have developed the section as recommended . . .

Conclusion: I have focused on arguing more strongly from the rest of the article, providing more provocative conclusions from my analysis.

Length: By adding the recommended texts, defining my subject more clearly, expanding the readings with references to each other and the theoretical texts, and threading my argument throughout, the paper exceeded the word limit. To reduce the word total, I radically cut the notes, works cited, block quotes, and textual examples. This means that many careful notes had to be dropped. It also means that any secondary literature not directly related to the texts, had to be sacrificed, such as all the references in the introduction and theoretical section. The paper is now just under the word limit.

I believe these revisions have radically improved the article's argument and clarity. The thoughtful recommendations of the editors and reviewers are greatly appreciated. Please let me know if there is anything further I can do; in particular, I can return deleted material to the text for clarity.

Sincerely,
[Your Name]

(Referral Belcher)

Sample Revision Letter 2

Dear [Editor's Name]:

Thank you for considering my article [give title and journal number for the article] for publication in [journal title]. I appreciate the comments I received and am resubmitting this manuscript for your consideration. In this letter, I detail how I have addressed (*present perfect tense*) the reviewers' comments.

The first reviewer's comments and my revisions are as follows:

1. "I am curious to know if gender affected . . . "

My revisions:

- Because this reviewer noted the difficulty in determining a correlation because of the size of my sample (n = 9), I have revisited and reanalyzed the data. There appeared to be no significant differences in how men and women viewed . . .

- At the beginning of the "Results" section, I added a phrase that notes particular differences in responses across gender and socioeconomic status.

- To address the limitations of the study in the "Im plications" section, I have added a sentence suggesting that the small sample size limited my ability to determine differences between men and women in . . .

2. "I also wonder how [variable] may have changed over time . . ."

My Revisions:

- On page 24, I have added that the longitudinal study of [variable] changed over time, especially focusing on how . . . is necessary to further our understanding of this population.

- On page 26, I have highlighted a limitation of this study that it is not longitudinal.

Thank you very much for your time and consideration. If you have any questions about the manuscript or changes that I have made, please do not hesitate to contact me. I can be reached by email at . . .

Sincerely,
[Your Name]

(Referral Belcher)

V REVISING

Chapter 13
How Can You Use Examples?

How to Use Examples?

I. Giving Examples

Writers may give specific examples as supporting evidence for their general claims or arguments. Examples can also be used to help the reader understand and remember unfamiliar or difficult concepts.

Paragraphs in academic writing develop an idea from general statements to specific details or examples. In most paragraphs, examples usually come after a more general statement, as in the short extract below.

"Many words can often acquire a more narrow meaning over time, or may come to be mainly used in one special sense. An example of this is the word *doctor*. There were *doctors* (that is, learned men) in theology, law, and many other fields beside medicine, but nowadays when we send for the *doctor* we mean a member of only one profession."

II. Examples as the Main Information in a Sentence

- *For example*, the word doctor used to mean a learned man.
- *For instance*, Smith and Jones (2004) conducted a series of semi-structured interviews in . . .

- *By way of illustration*, Smith (2003) showed how the data for . . .
- *A classic example of this* is . . .
- *An example of this* is the study carried out by Smith (2004), who . . .
- X is a *well-known illustration of* . . .
- X *illustrates* this point clearly.
- This *can be illustrated briefly by* . . .
- Young people begin smoking for a variety of reasons. They may, *for example*, be influenced by their peers, or they may see their parents as role models.
- *Another example of* X is . . .
- Ailments that result at least in part from stress *include* arthritis, asthma, migraines, headaches, and ulcers.

III. Examples as Additional Information in a Sentence

- Young people begin smoking for a variety of reasons, *such as* pressure from peers and the example of parents.
- Pavlov found that if some other stimulus, *for example* the ringing of a bell, preceded the food, the dog would start salivating.
- In Paris, Gassendi kept in close contact with many other prominent scholars, *such as* Kepler, Galileo, Hobbes, and Descartes.
- The prices of resources, *such as* copper, iron ore, oil, coal, and aluminum, have declined in real terms over the past 20 years.
- Many ailments can result at least in part from stress, *including* arthritis, asthma, migraines, headaches, and ulcers.

Common Writing Errors and Their Corrections

Italics and Underlining

Italics and underlining are methods a writer can use to emphasize particular parts of a sentence. However, many writers do not understand what parts of their writing they can underline or italicize.

Original

Many ailments can result at least in part from stress, including *arthritis, asthma, migraines, headaches,* and *ulcers*.

Modified

Many diseases can result at least in part from stress, including arthritis, asthma, migraines, headaches, and ulcers.

Original

For example, the word doctor used to mean a learned man.

Modified

For example, the word *doctor* used to mean a learned man.

Punctuation Point

Italics and Underlining

Writers emphasize certain words and phrases by printing them in a slanted font called *italics* or by **underlining** the word or phrase. Italics and underlining are used exactly the same way. With today's different fonts, underlining a word is often easier for the reader to see. Here are some rules for using italics or underlining.

1. Use italics or underlining for the names of book titles, newspapers and magazines, and the names of movies, plays, television shows, radio programs, software, musical compositions, and works of art.

   Example *Microsoft Word 2000* / <u>Microsoft Word 2000</u> is a favorite word-processing program.

2. Consider using italics to highlight the names of commercial products, if highlighting helps remove confusion.

   Example Henry Ford introduced his first *Thunderbird* at approximately the same time as Chevrolet introduced the *Corvette*.

3. Use italics for words and phrases used as examples, or for words in other languages.

   Example Did you know that the word napkin means *diaper* in England? *Shukran* means *thanks* in Arabic.

4. Use italics or underlining for the names of spacecraft, aircraft, ships, and trains.

   Example *The Titanic* / The Titanic was thought to be unsinkable.

5. Do not use italics or underlining for the titles of legal documents, such as the Constitution.

6. Do not italicize or underline the title of your own theses or research papers.

7. Do not use italics or underlining to highlight quotations, footnotes, or notes under figures and tables. Using italics excessively makes your paper difficult to read.

8. Italicize Latin medical words and phrases (for example, *in vitro*, and *ex juvantibus*).

9. Do not use italics or underlining for the titles of articles, essays, or short published works.

The Writing Process

Avoid Trying to Write Everything at Once

Have you ever tried to write an entire paper in one weekend? How did that work out? This style of writing is called "binge writing." Binge writing is ineffective and unproductive because it involves writing for large blocks of time while expending great effort. Binge writing seldom produces high quality writing, and the process can be stressful and painful.

Binge writing often looks like this: You promise yourself, after not writing during the week, that you will write from 9 a.m. to 6 p.m. on Sunday. There is a lot of pressure to write well during this nine-hour period, resulting in high stress and writing that is of poor quality. If you are not writing regularly, at least 15 minutes every day, there is pressure to produce a large quantity of writing at one time.

Think about this: What one activity can you do well for nine hours straight? Binge writing increases the chances of poor productivity and frequent delays. In delaying your writing, you organize notes, read more, think about writing (instead of actually writing), or finish other projects that demand your attention. Nine hours later, you still have not written much. After weeks or months of this procrastination, imagine how much writing you could have produced if you had written *every day for only 15 minutes*, instead of failed attempts at a nine-hour writing day once a week.

Another problem with binge writing is that it takes a lot of time to focus your thinking. Writing *little but often* allows you to get into the flow of writing quickly and regularly with less stress. By focusing more on writing a little every day and less on the outcome, you will more easily accomplish what you desire.

Tips for Journal Submission

I. Discuss Real-World Examples

Prove that your paper is relevant by providing citations and statistics regarding real-world examples. If you do, your reviewers cannot say the paper is uninteresting, which is the most common reason for rejection. If the reviewers say it is uninteresting, no editors will publish it, and there is no way to argue with the decision because it is a personal opinion. One important purpose of the discussion section is to prevent your reviewers from making that remark. Without a connection to the real world, your paper will give readers a solution to a problem that does not exist.

II. Balance Theory and Application

A theoretical paper should say something about policies, applications, or empirical work. In turn, an empirical paper should say something about the theory that led to the empirical work. Check the preferences of the journals that you are considering. Do the journals prefer theoretical or empirical papers?

III. Summarize the Contribution of Your Paper in the Conclusion

A paper needs a concluding remark. Briefly mention the limitations of the results (without being negative). Discuss how the theory may be extended in certain areas. The reviewer may be interested in writing a related paper. Compare your results to those in the literature. If the literature does not have comparable results, discuss how your paper relates to previous studies.

IV. Stimulate Research with Your Continuing Research Questions

Encouraging a reader to continue your research could be a major contribution of your study. Every research answer should lead to two more questions. Make your continuing research questions interesting so that researchers will continue your topic, making your paper the basis for continuing research in your area. Subsequent researchers will then cite your paper, making it a high-impact paper.

V. Discuss Policy Implications

Explain how your theory applies to real-world examples. For example, common practice uses A, but you recommend B. Do not repeat what you already said in the main body of the paper. Never copy and paste sentences from other parts of the paper for a conclusion. If you do, the reviewers will know you have not been careful. Illustrate your main point for the real world. State what this means for policy makers, practitioners, or other researchers.

Inappropriate Vocabulary and Improvements

at such time as

A better alternative would be:
when

ascertain the location of

A better alternative would be:
find

along the lines of

A better alternative would be:
such as

a majority of

A better alternative would be:
most

Academic Vocabulary

Headwords	Other Words in the Family
publication	publications
publish	published, publisher, publishers, publishes, publishing, unpublished
purchase	purchased, purchaser, purchasers, purchases, purchasing
pursue	pursued, pursues, pursuing, pursuit, pursuits
qualitative	qualitatively
quote	quotation, quotations, quoted, quotes, quoting
radical	radically, radicals
random	randomly, randomness
range	ranged, ranges, ranging
ratio	ratios
rational	irrational, rationalization, rationalizations, rationalize, rationalized, rationalizes, rationalizing, rationalism, rationality, rationally
react	reacted, reacts, reacting, reaction, reactionaries, reactionary, reactions, reactive, reactivate, reactivation, reactor, reactors
recover	recoverable, recovered, recovering, recovers, recovery
refine	refined, refinement, refinements, refines, refining
regime	regimes
region	regional, regionally, regions
register	deregister, deregistered, deregistering, deregisters, deregistration, registered, registering, registers, registration
regulate	deregulated, deregulates, deregulating, deregulation, regulated, regulates, regulating, regulation, regulations, regulator, regulators, regulatory, unregulated
reinforce	reinforced, reinforcement, reinforcements, reinforces, reinforcing
reject	rejected, rejecting, rejection, rejects, rejections
relax	relaxation, relaxed, relaxes, relaxing

续表

Headwords	Other Words in the Family
release	released, releases, releasing
relevant	irrelevance, irrelevant, relevance
reluctance	reluctant, reluctantly
rely	reliability, reliable, reliably, reliance, reliant, relied, relies, relying, unreliable
remove	removable, removal, removals, removed, removes, removing
require	required, requirement, requirements, requires, requiring
research	researched, researcher, researchers, researches, researching
reside	resided, residence, resident, residential, residents, resides, residing
resolve	resolution, resolved, resolves, resolving, unresolved

VI WRITING THE ABSTRACT

Chapter 14
What Is the Report About in Short?

How to Write the Abstract

I. Key Questions We Must Answer
- **What** is your study about, in short and without specific details?
- **What** did you investigate? Why? State your objectives.
- **What** did you do? Describe your methods.
- **What** did you discover? Summarize the most important results.
- **What** do your results mean? Why are they important? State the biggest conclusions and significance.

II. The Importance of the Abstract
A well-written abstract will be widely published because many computerized databases and printed indexes reprint abstracts, so scholars can reference them. Associations and corporations often publish abstracts and mail them to researchers. Thus, if you want your research to have an impact, you should work hard to make it interesting.

III. Be Clear and Simple

Remove generalizations, extra words, and little known technical words. Use strong and specific language. Ask a friend or editor to read your abstract. If your reader cannot understand a sentence immediately, rewrite it. Conference organizers read hundreds of abstracts. Do not make them work hard to understand yours.

IV. Word Limit

Your abstract should be single-spaced in an easy-to-read 12-pt font, such as Times New Roman. Come as close as possible to the word limit, but do not go over. Stay within the recommended word count. If your abstract is too long, either it will be rejected or someone else will shorten it. Your paper will be better if you shorten it yourself. A typical abstract word limit is 150-200 words.

V. Technical Terms

Do not use company names, acronyms, abbreviations, or symbols in your abstract. You will have to explain these names and use valuable space.

VI. Tense

Unless predicting the relevance of findings, avoid using the future tense when writing the abstract. Reviewers may believe that your paper is a proposal for unfinished research, rather than a report of completed work. Use the *present tense* when explaining results, stating established facts, or drawing conclusions:

- The results of this research *correspond* with the findings of similar psychosocial studies of less diverse populations.
- Semiconductors *are always*, either intentionally or unintentionally, doped by impurities.
- This study *concludes* that both land use and nitrogen intensity must be thoroughly assessed when selecting bioenergy feedstocks.

Use the past tense to describe completed experiments and research:

- This study *discovered* that group performance is related to the amount and level of collaborative interaction in network-supported concept mapping.

Use the future tense to predict findings:
- Our findings *will provide* insight into the functions of isozymes and core proteins expressed in flies and worms.

VII. Style

Be precise and detailed in your argument and analysis. Never simply say "Results of the study will be discussed." Write what the results are and why they are important. Use your own words. Avoid long sentences, which use space and give no real information. For example, "Policy implications are discussed" or "It is concluded that." Emphasize your own ideas, not the ideas of others. Do not quote or paraphrase others in the abstract. Any major limitations in the results should be stated using conditional words such as "might," "could," "may," and "seem."

VIII. Avoid Using "I" or the Passive Voice

Do not use the first person "*I*" or "*we*." In addition, whenever possible, choose active verbs instead of those that are passive. Write "*The study discusses*" instead of "*It is discussed by the study*" or "*I discuss in the study*." Do not refer to figures or tables in the abstract.

IX. Search Phrases

Search engines use abstract keywords more frequently than they do index keywords. Think of phrases and keywords that people searching online might use to find your paper. Use those exact phrases in your abstract, so that your abstract is listed at the top of search results. Publications request "keywords" for two reasons. They are used to allow keyword index searches (which are not as important because online abstract text searching is used). They are also used to assign papers to reviewers or editors, which is highly crucial. Choose keywords that make you review the category clearly.

X. Title

Choose a clear, informative title that contains all of the essential parts of your presentation. These include: The key concept, the device or group studied, and your argument. Extremely short or long titles are not recommended. Using a title and a subtitle separated by a colon is often a

good way to maximize information in a short space. Compare the example titles below:
- Instructional behavior: decision-making in classrooms

This title is too short. The lack of specific information and key terms causes the main concept, focus of study, and central argument to be vague. Consider the next example title:
- Instructional behavior, practices, and norms: a study of the consequences of various decision-making processes while engaging in elementary school classroom management

This title is too long. Note the overabundance of unnecessary words and phrases, particularly "a study of", "while engaging", and "various." Assess the title of your paper carefully. If a word or phrase adds little or no meaning to your title, then omit it. Consider this final example title:
- Instructional behavior: decision-making processes in elementary classroom management

This title is neither too long nor too short. Each carefully chosen word has a purpose in stating specifically what type of study this paper reports.

How to Structure the Abstract

Abstracts are consistent in structure. Each section of the abstract may include one or more sentences.

I. Motivation

Why do we care about the problem and the results? If the problem is not clearly "interesting," it is better to begin with the motivation. If your research is continuing a problem that is recognized as important, then it is better to put the problem statement first to show which piece of the problem you are working on. This section should include the importance of your work, the impact it will have if successful, and the difficulties encountered in this area.

II. Problem Statement

What problem are you trying to solve? What is the *scope* of your work? Did you use a general approach or apply a specific method? Be careful not to use too many technical terms. State your research question clearly; the shorter the abstract, the sooner you need to let your audience know your main idea.

III. Approach

How did you solve the problem? Did you use a simulation, analytical model, prototype, or analysis of field data? What was the extent of your work? What important *variables* did you control, ignore, or measure? This should be written in the middle of the abstract. State here that your study offers a solution to the problem described in the problem statement. Briefly give details about the study. Where was it conducted, and with whom? Provide the number and background of participants and sources of data. How long did the study last and how much data were collected?

IV. Results

What is the answer? Conclude that something is faster, cheaper, smaller, or better than something else, by using a percentage to show the difference. Include the result, in numbers. Avoid general, unclear words when describing your results such as "very," "small," or "significant." Then summarize your research findings.

V. Conclusions

What are the implications of your answer? Is it going to change the world, be a noteworthy contribution, be a nice project, or warn other researchers that this area is a waste of time? Are your results general or specific to a particular case? You now need to return to the big picture: How do these findings answer the research question? What do they imply for the field? This discussion does not need to be long, but should show that your research has relevant implications.

Common Writing Errors and Their Corrections

How to Use A, An, and The in Scholarly Writing

What Are Articles?

Articles are special modifiers that appear before nouns or noun phrases. Like other adjectives, they help clarify the meaning of the noun in your sentence. There are only two articles in the English language: *the* and *a* (and its variant *an*, used before a word that starts with a vowel sound). A noun may also appear without an article in front of it. If you are a native speaker, you will probably know which article to place in front of a noun without having to think about it. If, however, English is your second language, knowing which article to use where can be difficult. Learning and consciously applying a few basic principles can help you improve your article use significantly. With time and a lot of practice, using articles correctly will become easy.

Where Do Articles Go?

Articles belong in front of all other modifiers preceding a noun:

- *a* comprehensive research project
- *the* first published researcher

There are other special modifiers called determiners that may appear in front of a noun phrase. Do not use an article if you also intend to use any of the following markers directly before the noun: *any, either, each, every, many, few, several, some, all, this, that, these, those, my, his, her, your, our, their, its.*

Useful Rules for Using Articles

You can determine which article to place in front of almost any noun by answering the following three questions: Is the noun countable or uncountable? Is it singular or plural? Is it definite or indefinite?

1. A noun is countable if you can have more than one instance of it. The word *hat* is countable because you can have four hats to choose from. The word *gold*, however, is uncountable, because it would not make sense to speak of having four *golds*, even though you will need a lot of *gold* to buy an airplane. Many words have both countable and uncountable meanings, depending on the sentence.

2. Knowing whether the particular use of a noun is singular or plural is easy. Ask the question: Am I referring to more than one of something?

3. A noun is definite when it is clear to your reader which specific instance or instances of an entity you are referring to; otherwise it is indefinite. Often the first use of a noun is indefinite and subsequent uses are definite.

"When I first started writing, I had *a fear* of English. I conquered *the fear* by continuing to write."

Here, the first sentence establishes for the reader the existence of the writer's former fear. By the second sentence, the reader knows exactly which fear the writer is talking about—the one about English just referred to in the previous sentence. The first use of a noun can be definite if the reader can figure out from context or some other clue just which instance of an entity the writer is referring to.

The reason we wrote the paper is to make sure we are acknowledged for *the research* we completed.

Note that the prepositional phrase following *reason* narrows down its meaning to something very specific, while the *research* can refer only to the research in this particular paper. Both nouns are therefore definite.

Once you have answered all three questions, you can use the following chart to help you choose the correct article (The symbol Ø means no article).

Countable:

	definite	indefinite
singular	the I need to finish *the paper* I am submitting to *Applied Mechanics*.	a, an I have *a paper* to write this summer.
plural	the *The papers* I wrote last year were all published.	Ø Writing papers are a necessity for academic survival.

Uncountable:

	definite	indefinite
singular	the The *importance* of publishing cannot be exaggerated.	Ø Do not attach *importance* to memorizing facts.

Observe the following: If the noun is definite, it always takes the article *the*; if the noun is indefinite it never takes the article *the*. If you don't have the chart in front of you, you can still often get the article right just by remembering that simple rule of thumb.

Using Articles to Refer to Classes of Objects

Nouns can refer to an entire group of similar objects, sometimes called a class. There are three ways to refer to a class: using (1) the definite singular, (2) the indefinite singular, or (3) the indefinite plural. Here is an example of each:

- *The researcher* is as important member of society.
- Being a *researcher* is a challenging job.

- *Researchers* help society progress.

All three sentences convey the same meaning with slightly different emphasis. The first sentence takes one researcher as a representative of all researchers and then talks about that representative. The second sentence says that you can take any researcher you like from the class of all researchers, and what you say about it will be true of all other researchers. The third sentence directly talks about all researchers. This third usage is probably the most common. Choose whichever usage sounds best in your sentence.

Using Articles in Front of Proper Nouns

The rules in the chart above do not work in all situations. In particular, they are not help much for proper nouns. Most proper nouns, however, are governed by simple rules. For example, do not place an article in front of the names of people.

Barak Obama is the president of the United States.

Most countries do not take article before them. But there are two noteworthy exceptions: *the United States*, and *the United Kingdom*. Rivers, mountain ranges, seas, and oceans should be preceded by the article the: *the Yangtze River, the Himalaya Mountains, the Indian Ocean*. Lakes, on the other hand, don't usually take an article: *Lake Superior, Lake Michigan*.

Is the Noun Indefinite (Unspecified) or Definite (Specific)?

The general rule states that the first mention of a noun is indefinite and all subsequent references to this noun are definite and take *the*.

- A man is standing beside a tree. There is a dog beside *the* man.

The second mention may be a synonym:

- Combine sugar, butter and eggs. Add flour to *the* mixture.

The first (indefinite) mention requires *a* or *an* for a singular count noun, no article for a plural or noncount noun. The second mention makes *the* correct for both count and noncount nouns:

- A growing plant must have water and minerals. *The* plant must also have sunlight. *The* minerals must include nitrates and *the* water must not be saline.

Three special groups of nouns are considered definite in reference even if they have not been mentioned in the preceding sentence or clause.

The **first group** consists of nouns that refer to shared knowledge of the situation or context. For example, in the United States you can say:

- *The* President will arrive tomorrow.

We say this because there is only one President in the United States, and so it is clear to whom you are referring. Similarly, if there is only one university in the town, you can say

- He's been working in *the* university for two years.

But you couldn't say this in New York, where there are many universities. You would have to name the particular university in your first reference to it:

- He's been working at New York University for two years. He says *the* University has beautiful trees.

The **second group** consists of nouns referring to unique objects:

- the sun/the earth/the Pope/the sky/the equator

The **third group** is formed of superlative adjectives and unique adjectives. Because there can be only one of these, only one can be the tallest or the best or the first so they take the definite article:

- He enjoyed *the* first part, but he was disappointed at *the* end.
- She is *the* first author on the paper.

Is the Noun Modified?

If the noun is preceded by one of the following: this, that, these, those, some, any, each, every, no, none, my, or mine, do not use the definite article.

- the blue books, some blue books, no blue book, his blue books, each blue book

If the noun is followed by a dependent clause (*who/which/that*) or a prepositional phrase (*of/in/to* . . .), it is made definite and takes the definite article.

- We take *the* library for granted.
- *The* trip to Tainan takes four hours by train.

EXCEPTION: collective nouns take the indefinite article:
- a box of candy/a deck of cards/a bar of soap/a flock of birds

Is the Noun Generic?

Generic reference is used when you refer to a whole group or class, to generalize about all possible members of a group. There are five patterns one can use:

1. No article PLUS plural count noun.
- It's amazing what *researchers* can do.

2. No article PLUS noncount noun.
- *Writing* can be a lot of trouble.

3. Indefinite article PLUS singular count noun.
- It's amazing what a *researcher* can do.

4. definite article PLUS singular count noun.
- It's astonishing what the *researcher* can do.

5. definite article PLUS plural nationality noun.
- *The Chinese* have an ancient culture.

Special Uses of Articles

I. Media and Communications

Use a noun PLUS definite article to refer to systems of communication and the mass media, in contrast to the actual machine of communications.
- *The* telephone is the system of communication; a telephone is the actual physical machine.
- *The* newspapers are all in agreement on the latest financial disaster.

II. Means of Transportation

Use the definite article to refer to the whole transport system, rather than to an individual vehicle:
- How long does it take on *the* bus?
- *The* train is quicker than the bus.

If you use the construction "*by* PLUS means of transport," there is no article: *I go by train.*

III. Forms of Entertainment

To refer to a form of entertainment in general, use the definite article:
- I enjoy seeing *the* movies.

To refer to a particular event, use the indefinite article:
- I saw *a* good show last night.

IV. Place/Object of Activity Nouns

Certain nouns refer to either a place/object or to an activity. When they refer to an activity, do **not** use the definite article:

activity	object
I go to *bed* at 11 o'clock.	Don't jump on *the bed*.
She went to *school* for many years.	*The room* was too small.
Many families eat *dinner* together.	*The meal* was delicious.
I shower before *breakfast*.	*The lunch* was delicious.
They are at *school*.	*The college* is very old.
She is in *class*.	*The class* is in building 105.

V. Directions

Nouns indicating direction do not take the definite article:
- Go two blocks *south* and turn *left*.

VI. Periods of Time

Names of decades, centuries and historic periods take the definite article, as they are a form of unique reference:
- The 1950s were a time of rapid technological progress.

The articles *the*, *a*, and *an* are often misunderstood by students. When wrongly used, the reviewers, editors, and readers may misunderstand your meaning. Below are some examples of incorrect article use with corrections.

Original

Liver is the largest solid organ in the human body.

Modified

The liver is the largest solid organ in the human body.

Original

Portions of the Sample A were reassessed for accuracy.

Modified

Portions of Sample A were reassessed for accuracy.

Original

The flow gauge and the servo motor are both necessary for optimal operation.

Modified

The flow gauge and servo motor are both necessary for optimal operation.

Original

No X-rays are used in a MRI scan.

Modified

No X-rays are used in an MRI scan.

Original

This study employed an UHF tuning circuit utilizing a varactor diode.

Modified

This study employed a UHF tuning circuit utilizing a varactor diode.

Punctuation Point

Good Linking Words and Phrases to Use in Academic Writing

You can use words or short phrases that guide your reader through your writing, and to link sentences, paragraphs and sections both forwards and backwards. Good use will make what you have written easy to follow; bad use might mean your style is disjointed, probably with too many short sentences, and consequently difficult to follow.

The best way to understand these words is through your reading. Most textbooks and articles are well written and will probably include a lot of these cohesive devices. Note how they are used and try to emulate what you have read. Do make sure though that you fully understand their meaning: incorrect use could change completely what you're trying to say. Try to use a variety of expressions, particularly in longer pieces of writing.

Don't forget "AND"! Two short sentences are often best connected together with this little word.

Here is a list of words and phrases that can be used. The list is not exhaustive, so BE CAREFUL: although grouped together, none are totally synonymous. Their position in the sentence can also vary; this is where your reading and dictionary come in.

Listing	Giving examples	Generalizing
first, second, third	for example	in general
first, furthermore, finally	for instance	generally
to begin, to conclude	as follows:	on the whole

续表

Listing	Giving examples	Generalizing
next	that is	as a rule
Reinforcement	in this case	for the most part
also	namely	in most cases
furthermore	in other words	usually
moreover	**Result/consequence**	**Highlighting**
what is more	so	in particular
in addition	therefore	particularly
besides	as a result/consequence	especially
above all	accordingly	mainly
as well (as)	consequently	**Reformulation**
in the same way	because of this/that	in other words
not only . . . but also	thus	rather
Similarity	hence	to put it more simply
equally	for this/that reason	**Expressing an alternative**
likewise	so that	alternatively
similarly	in that case	rather
correspondingly	under these circumstances	on the other hand
in the same way	Deduction	the alternative is
Listing	**Giving examples**	**Generalizing**
Transition to new point	then	another possibility would be
now	in other words	**Contrast**
as far as *x* is concerned	in that case	instead
with regard/ reference to	otherwise	conversely
as for . . .	this implies that . . .	on the contrary

Listing	Giving examples	Generalizing
it follows that	if so/not	in contrast
turning to	**Stating the obvious**	in comparison
Summary	obviously	**Concession**
in conclusion	clearly	however
to conclude	naturally	even though
in brief	of course	however much
to summarize	as can be expected	nevertheless
overall	surely	still
therefore	after all	yet

Here are just a few examples of some of the words in sentences:

REINFORCEMENT

- Driving a motorcycle is cheaper and more convenient than owning a car; ***furthermore***, motorcycles are easier to park.

CONTRAST

- Hsinchu often has the coldest weather in Taiwan in the winter. ***Conversely***, Kaohsiung frequently has the mildest winter temperatures.

RESULT/CONSEQUENCE

- Housing prices fell by more than 30% last year. ***As a result***, sales increased by 20%.

GENERALIZING

- On the whole, his class was well received by students, ***despite*** some complaints from new students about grading.

CONCESSION

- It was a very expensive city, the weather was bad and the people weren't very friendly. ***Nevertheless***, we will probably return.

The Writing Process

I. Delay Sending the Finished Paper for One Week

Do not submit your paper to a journal immediately after you finish writing it. The writing process is not yet complete. You will always find small errors in the text, notations, explanations, or references in your finished paper. Reread the introduction, conclusion, and abstract before submission. An English error on the first page of your introduction or abstract indicates that you were careless. English errors lead referees and editors to conclude that the paper should be rejected. They assume that if the author is careless in English, they are likely careless in content as well—and they might be right. If you fail to proofread your own introduction, why expect the referees to spot and correct all the errors?

II. Use but Do Not Completely Rely on Spell Checkers

You should always check the spelling before submitting your paper. However, there are no substitutes for reading your paper personally. Spell checkers do not check word meanings.

III. Diversify Your Research Portfolio

The average wait for an acceptance decision is three years, while the average wait for a rejection is only six to eight months. Surviving is the most important task when you are a PhD student. Sending your research to journals with a variety of decisive factors is critical during PhD study, when each publication counts heavily toward graduation. Diversify your research topics for a higher chance of publication. Publish in only one area, then focus on establishing yourself as an expert in that field before moving into another field. Writing several papers in a very small area is risky before getting published. It is like putting all your eggs in one basket.

IV. Concentrate on One or Two Fields

Normally, you should not select more than two fields of specialization. Long research durations may require your full attention in a single field. Choose, at most, two or three focused areas within your field of specialization. Then pursue those topics until you produce two publications. If you have published no papers in one area for three years, consider changing to another topic.

V. Approach Different Types of Journals

Sending all your papers to top journals is risky. Conversely, sending all papers to low-quality journals is unsatisfactory, and you may regret having the papers accepted. Your resume should contain some publications in top journals. The quantity of publications is also important. Having three papers in different journals is better than three in one journal, if the quality of the journals is the same.

VI. Understand Journal Biases

Journals, editors, or reviewers may have biases against you based on race, sex, nationality, or schooling. For instance, if a university journal has a reported acceptance rate of 10% but gives half the space to its own faculty and students, your acceptance rate will be 20% if you are from the university, but 5% or lower if you are not. You cannot remove biases, but you can avoid them by submitting your paper to a journal where you have a fair chance.

Tips for Journal Submission

I. Write an Interesting Abstract

Think of reading the abstract like watching a movie preview. Within 30 seconds you must convince the audience to watch your movie, or read your paper. If the 30-second preview does not catch the viewer, he will watch another movie. Reviewers will read the abstract more than any other paragraph in the paper. In 15 seconds, you must convince the reviewers and readers that they should continue with the rest of the paper. If the abstract is boring, your paper is dead.

II. Choose an Interesting Title

Give the paper a great title. If the title is boring, readers will avoid your paper even after it is published. As a result, your paper will not be cited. Never try to put all of the content of your paper in the title. The title should be short; one line is best. Never use more than two lines.

Inappropriate Vocabulary and Improvements

adoptive and adopted

Children are *adopted*, but parents are *adoptive*.

adverse and averse

Adverse means "unfavorable, bad," whereas *averse* means "strongly disliking or opposed to," as in "I am not *averse* to helping out."

affect and effect

Affect means "make a difference to," whereas *effect* means "a result" or "cause a result."

ambiguous and ambivalent

Ambiguous means "having more than one meaning, open to different interpretations," whereas *ambivalent* means "having mixed feelings."

amoral and immoral

Amoral means "not concerned with morality," whereas *immoral* means "not following accepted rules of morality."

> **appraise and apprise**
> *Appraise* means "assess," whereas *apprise* means "inform."

Academic Vocabulary

Headwords	Other Words in the Family
resource	resourced, resourceful, resources, resourcing, unresourceful, under-resourced
respond	responded, respondent, respondents, responding, responds, response, responses, responsive, responsiveness, unresponsive
restore	restoration, restored, restores, restoring
restrain	restrained, restraining, restrains, restraint, restraints, unrestrained
restrict	restricted, restricting, restriction, restrictions, restrictive, restrictively, restricts, unrestricted, unrestrictive
retain	retained, retaining, retainer, retainers, retains, retention, retentive
reveal	revealed, revealing, reveals, revelation, revelations
revenue	revenues
reverse	reversal, reversed, reverses, reversible, reversing, reversals, irreversible
revise	revised, revises, revising, revision, revisions
revolution	revolutionary, revolutionaries, revolutionize, revolutionized, revolutionizes, revolutionizing, revolutionist, revolutionists, revolutions
rigid	rigidities, rigidity, rigidly
role	roles
route	routed, routes, routing
scenario	scenarios
schedule	reschedule, rescheduled, reschedules, rescheduling, scheduled, schedules, scheduling, unscheduled
scheme	schematic, schematically, schemed, schemes, scheming
section	sectioned, sectioning, sections
sector	sectors
secure	insecure, insecurities, insecurity, secured, securely, secures, securing, securities, security

续表

Headwords	Other Words in the Family
seek	seeking, seeks, sought
select	selected, selecting, selection, selections, selective, selectively, selector, selectors, selects
sequence	sequenced, sequences, sequencing, sequential, sequentially
sex	sexes, sexism, sexual, sexuality, sexually
shift	shifted, shifting, shifts
significant	insignificant, insignificantly, significance, significantly, signified, signifies, signify, signifying
similar	dissimilar, similarities, similarity, similarly
simulate	simulated, simulates, simulating, simulation
site	sites
sole	solely

VII CITATIONS

Chapter 15
How Can We Write About Others Who Have Helped Us?

How to Write Your References Using Different Citation Styles

Whenever you quote, paraphrase, summarize, or reference a source, you must cite that source. Citations can be in a parenthetical note or a footnote, and be included in a bibliography, which may be called Works Cited or References.

Citations direct your readers to the sources from which your information was obtained and provides a means of critiquing your study. They also offer the opportunity to obtain additional information about the research problem under investigation. Citations are most importantly used to avoid plagiarism, to attribute prior or repeated work and ideas to their sources, to allow readers to determine whether the referenced material supports the study's argument in the claimed way, and to help readers gauge the strength and validity of the material used in the study.

There are several accepted styles of citations that are followed; however, in general, there are two important systems of citation. Below, we have elaborated on the two systems and covered the significant styles in the latter part of this chapter.

Harvard (author-date) System

This system follows a specific kind of referencing also known as parenthetical referencing. The Harvard referencing system involves a short author-date reference being inserted, wholly or partially, after the cited text within parentheses, e.g., (John, 2000), or John (2000) when citing it directly in the text. The full reference to the source is listed at the end of the article under a different section titled "References," or in some formats the footnote or endnote.

The Harvard system has two styles of parenthetical referencing, primarily, the *author-date* and *author-title* or *author-page*. The structure of a citation under the *author-date* style is the author's last name, year of publication, and page number or range, in parentheses. In the *author-date* style, the in-text citation is placed in parentheses after the sentence or part that the citation supports, and includes the author's name, year of publication, and/or page number(s) when a specific part of the source is referred, for example, (John 2000, p. 1) or (John, 2008:1). A full citation is given in the references section, for example, John (2000). Name of the Article, *Name of the Journal*, Volume and Issue number, Page Number(s).

The *author-title* or *author-page* style, primarily used in the arts and the humanities, requires the in-text citation to be placed in parentheses after the sentence or part thereof that the citation supports, and includes the author's name and title of the article or page number(s), if required. For example, (John, Economic drain in Europe 45–61) or (John 45–61). When you are citing the source directly in the text, include the citation as "John (45–61) . . . " or "John (Economic drain in Europe 45–61) . . . " A full citation is given in the reference section as:

Last name, First name. "Title of the Article. " *Name of the Journal* Volume and Issue number (Year): Page Number(s). Medium of Publication.

To clarify the citation and end-list referencing for the two styles, we have included the format elaborating the different sources that you would need to cite in your paper.

I. Author-Date

One Author	It was found that . . . (Woodrow 2011). Woodrow (2011) found that . . .
Two or Three Authors	It was found that . . . (Zimmer and Lim 2010). Jue, Marr, and Kassotakis (2010) reported that . . .
More than Three Authors	It was found that . . . (Loomis et al. 2009). The study by Loomis and others (2009) found that . . .
Corporate Authors	It was found that . . . (National Council of Social Service 2008) It was found that . . . (NCSS 2008).
Different Authors with Same Last Name	It was found that . . . (D. Lim 2008). The study found that . . . (W. Lim 2002)
Multiple References	It was found that . . . (Jordan 2010; Manzi et al. 2010; Mau 2010)
Multiple References by Same Author	It can be seen . . . (Obama 2004, 2006).
Multiple References by Same Author & Year	It was found that . . . (Brinkerhoff 2008a, 2008b)

• End-list references based on different sources

1. Books

• **Book with Single Author** (The format of first listing the last name and then the first name of the main author is followed for all references.)

Format: Last name, First name. YYYY. *Book Title: The Subtitle*. Place of Publication: Publisher.

• **Book with Multiple Authors** (List all authors following the format: Last name, First name (First Author), First name | Last name (Second Author), and so on.)

Format: First Author, Second Author, Third Author, and Last Author.

YYYY. *Book Title: The Subtitle*. Place of Publication: Publisher.

• **Book with Single Editor**
Format: Editor, ed. YYYY. *Book Title: The Subtitle*. Place of Publication: Publisher.

• **Book with Multiple Editors** (List all editors following the format: Last name, First name (First editor), First name | Last name (Second editor), and so on.)
Format: First Editor, Second Editor, and Third Editor, eds. YYYY. *Book Title: The Subtitle*. Place of Publication: Publisher.

• **Book with Edition Other than the First**
Author. YYYY. *Book Title: The Subtitle*. 2nd ed. Place of Publication: Publisher.

• **Book with Corporate Author**
Format: Organization Name. YYYY. *Book Title: The Subtitle*. Place of Publication: Publisher.

2. E-Book References
• **E-book from Library Subscription**
Format: Author. YYYY. *Book Title: The Subtitle*. Place of Publication: Publisher. Doi/url.

• **Freely Available E-book**
Format: Author. YYYY. *Book Title: The Subtitle*. Place of Publication: Publisher. URL.

3. Book Chapters
• **Book Chapter in Edited Book**
Format: Author. YYYY. "Chapter Title." In *Book Title: The Subtitle*, edited by Editor Name, xxx-yy. Place of Publication: Publisher.

• **Book Chapter in Single Author Book**
Format: Author. YYYY. "Chapter Title." In *Book Title*: *The Subtitle*, xxx-yy. Place of Publication: Publisher.

- **Book Chapter with Series**
Format: Author. YYYY. "Chapter Title." In *Book Title*, edited by Second Editor, xxx-yy. Series Title, vol. n. Place of Publication: Publisher. doi:www

4. Journal Articles

- **Journal Article with One Author**
Format: Author. YYYY. "Article Title: The Subtitle." *Journal Title* VX (IX):xxx-yy.

- **Journal Article with up to Three Authors** (List all editors following the format: Last name, First name (First editor), First name | Last name (Second editor), and so on.)
Format: First Author, Second Author, and Third Author. YYYY. "Article Title: The Subtitle." *Journal Title* VX (IX):xxx-yy.

- **Journal Article with Four or more Authors**
Format: First Author, Second Author, Third Author, Fourth Author, Fifth Author, and Sixth Author. YYYY. "Article Title." *Journal Title* VX (IX):xxx-yy.

- **Journal Article with Digital Object Identifier (DOI)**
Format: Author. YYYY. "Article Title." *Journal Title* VX (IX):xxx-yy. doi.

- **Journal Article on the Internet**
Format: Author. YYYY. "Article Title: The Subtitle." *Journal Title* VX (IX):xxx-yy. URL.

5. Magazine & Newspaper Articles

Newspaper and magazine articles are more commonly cited in the text, but if you need to include them in the reference list, use the example below:

- **Magazine Article**
Format: Author. YYYY. "Article Title." *Magazine Title*, Month dd, xxx-yy.

- **Magazine Article Without Author**
Format: "Article Title." YYYY. *Magazine Title*, Month dd, xx.

- **Magazine Article on the Internet**
Format: Author. YYYY. "Article Title." *Magazine Title*, Month dd. URL.

- **Newspaper Article**
Format: Author. YYYY. "Article Title." *Newspaper Title*, Month dd.

- **Newspaper Article Online**
Format: Author. YYYY. "Article Title." *Newspaper Title*, Month dd. URL.

- **Newspaper Article Without Author**
Format: "Article Title." YYYY. *Newspaper Title*. Month-date.

II. Author-Page
In-text citations

Author's name in text	Daven has expressed this concern (107-21).
Author's name in reference	This concern has been expressed (Daven 107-21).
Multiple authors of a work	This hypothesis (Bernard and Rendell 27) suggested this theory (Sorrel, Rhyne, and Welsh 43).
Two locations	Williamson alludes to this premise (146-49, 154).
Two works cited	(Berger 14; Thomason 127)
References to volumes and pages	(Williamson 7:1-10)
References to an entire volume	(Flanders, vol. 2)
In-text reference to an entire volume	In volume 3, Flanders suggests
Corporate authors	(United Nations, Economic Commission for Africa 71-73)

Works with no author When a work has no author, use the work's title or a shortened version of the title when citing it in text (if abbreviating a title, omit initial articles and begin with the word by which it is alphabetized in the Works Cited list):	as stated by the election commission (*Report* 4).
Online source with numbered paragraphs	(Cox, pars. 2-4)

- End-list references based on different sources

1. Book

- **Basic Format**

    Last name, First name. *Title of the Book*. Place of Publication: Publisher, Year of Publication. Medium of Publication.

- **One Author**

    Last name, First name. *Title of the Book*. Place of Publication: Publisher, Year of Publication. Medium of Publication.

- **Another Work, Same Author**

    ---. *Title of the Book*. Place of Publication: Publisher, Year of Publication. Medium of Publication.

- **Two Authors**

    Author, First and Second Author. *Title of the Book*. Place of Publication: Publisher, Year of Publication. Medium of Publication.

- **Three Authors**

    Author, First, Second Author, and Third Author. *Title of the Book*. Edition (if any). Place of Publication: Publisher, Year of Publication. Medium of Publication.

- **More than Three Authors**

    Author, First, et al. *Title of the Book*. Place of Publication: Publisher, Year of Publication. Medium of Publication.

- **Corporate Author**
    First name, Last name/Name of the Institute. *Title of the Book*. Place of Publication: Publisher, Year of Publication. Medium of Publication.

- **Multivolume Work**
    Author, First, Second Author, and Third Author. *Title of the Book*. Number of Volumes. Place of Publication: Publisher, Year of Publication. Medium of Publication.

- **No Author or Editor**
    Title of the Book. Place of Publication: Publisher, Year of Publication. Medium of Publication.
- **Editor (anthology or collection of essays)**
    Editor, First, and Second Editor, eds. *Title of the Book*. Place of Publication: Publisher, Year of Publication. Medium of Publication.

- **Essay or Chapter in Edited Books**
    Last name, First name. "Title of the Chapter." *Title of the Book*. Editors. Place of Publication: Publisher, Year of Publication. Page Number(s). Medium of Publication.

- **Reprinted Article**
    Last name, First name. "Title of the Article." *Title of the Book* (Year): Page number(s). Editors. Place of Publication: Publisher, Year of Publication. Page Number(s). Medium of Publication.

- **Article in Journals, Magazines, and Newspapers**
    Journal article, one author
    Last name, First name. "Title of the Article." *Journal Name* Vol. no. Issue no. (Year of Publication): Page Number(s). Medium of Publication.

- **Journal Article, Two Authors**
    Author, First, and Second Author. "Title of the Article." *Journal Name*. "Title of the Article." Journal Name Vol. no. Issue no. (Year of Publication): Page Number(s). Medium of Publication.

- **Magazine Article**
    Last name, First name. "Title of the Article." Magazine Name, Date, month, and year of publication: Page Number(s). Medium of Publication.

- **Newspaper Article, No Author**
  "Title of the Article." *Newspaper Name* Date, month, and year of publication, Language of publication: Page Number(s). Medium of Publication.

- **Newspaper Article, One Author, Discontinuous Pages**
  Last name, First name. "Title of the Article." *Newspaper Name* Date, month, and year of publication: Issue no. Medium of Publication.

2. Materials from Online Sources

- **Web Page**
  Name of the Institute. "*Title of the Article.*" Source Name, Year. Medium of Publication. Date Accessed <web link>.

- **Personal Website**
  If a work is untitled, you may use a general label such as Home page, Introduction, etc.
  Last name, First name. Name of the Page. Medium of Publication. Date Accessed.

- **Entry in an Online Encyclopedia**
  "Title of the Article." *Name of the Source.* Name of the Encyclopedia, Year. Medium of Publication. Date Accessed.

- **Article in an Online Periodical**
  If pagination is unavailable or is not continuous, use n. pag. in place of the page numbers.
  Last name, First name. "Title of the Article." *Name of the Periodical.* Date, month, year: n. pag. Medium of Publication. Date Accessed.

- **Article in a Full-text Journal Accessed from a Database**
  Last name, First name. "Title of the Article." *Name of the Journal* Vol. no. Issue no. (Year): Page Numbers. Name of the Website. Date Accessed.

- **Online Book with Print Information**
  Last name, First name. *Title of the Book.* Edition No. Place of Publication: Publisher, Year of Publication. Medium of Publication. Date Accessed.

Vancouver System

The Vancouver system uses sequential numbers in the text, either bracketed or superscript, or both. The numbers refer to complete references provided either in the footnotes (notes at the end of the page) or the endnotes (notes on a page at the end of the paper) that provide source detail.

In the humanities, many authors also use footnotes or endnotes to supply anecdotal information. Hence, it acts as a supplementary material or suggestions for further reading. In the table below, we have listed examples of the in-text citation and end-list reference for your paper.

Reference Type	In-text Example	Reference List xample
One author	The book, "Secrets from the black bag", by Butler[1] shows that ... OR Butler purported ' ... ' [1]	1. Butler SW. Secrets from the Black Bag. London: The Royal College of General Practitioners; 2005.
Two to six authors	'... needed to influence policy.'[2] OR Cheers, Darracott and Lonne have highlighted the fact that '...' [2]	2. Cheers B, Darracott R, Lonne B. Social care practice in rural communities. Sydney: The Federation Press; 2007.

Reference Type	In-text Example	Reference List xample
Six or more authors	Professionals in collaboration[3] or [3]	3. Hofmeyr GJ, Neilson JP, Alfirevic Z, Crowther CA, Gulmezoglu AM, Hodnett ED et al. A Cochrane pocketbook: Pregnancy and hildbirth. Chichester, West Sussex, England: John Wiley & Sons Ltd; 2008.
No author	'. . . do not die from the disease.'[4] or [4]	4. A guide for women with early breast cancer. Sydney: National Breast Cancer; 2003.
Multiple works by the same author	The main clinical and research interests of Dr Marilyn Campbell[5,6] are focused on . . . or [5, 6]	5. Campbell MA. A is for anxiety: A parent's guide to managing anxious children. Brisbane: Post Pressed; 2007. 6. Campbell MA. Anthony the shy alien. Brisbane: Post Pressed; 2006.
Journal Articles		
One author	As highlighted by Snowdon,[18] . . .	18. Snowdon J. Severe depression in old age. Medicine Today. 2002 Dec; 3(12):40-7.

Reference Type	In-text Example	Reference List xample
Two authors	McInnes & Bollen have developed a perspective which identifies . . . ,[19]	19. McInnes D, Bollen J. Learning on the job: metaphors of choreography and the practice of sex in sex-on-premises venues. Venereology 2000; 13(1):27-36.
Three to six authors	By using meta-analysis, Skalsky et al.[20] . . .	20. Skalsky K, Yahav D, Bishara J, Pitlik S, Leibovici L, Paul M. Treatment of human brucellosis: systematic review and meta-analysis of randomised controlled trials. BMJ. 2008 Mar 29; 336(7646):701-4.
More than six authors	Hanna et al.[21] report in this article that . . .	21. Hanna JN, McBride WJ, Brookes DL, Shield J, Taylor CT, Smith IL, Craig SB, Smith GA. Hendra virus infection in a veterinarian. Med J Aust. 2006 Nov 20; 185(10):562-4.

Reference Type	In-text Example	Reference List xample
In press	O'Leary[22] states that ...	22. O'Leary C. Vitamin C does little to prevent winter cold. The West Australian. Forthcoming 2005 June

Several style guides such as APA, MLA, and Chicago Manual of Style use the Harvard system of citation, whereas IEEE follows the Vancouver system of citation. The ACS style guide uses either the Harvard or the Vancouver system of citation. Hence, it is best to carefully follow the style guides to know the best citation system for your paper.

All citations share some basic elements: the title of the work being referred to, the name of the author(s), the publisher, and the date of publication. After these requirements, citation styles vary by discipline. In the humanities, the most common citation style is the *Modern Language Association* (MLA). Social sciences use the *American Psychological Association* (APA) style. Historians usually use the footnote style described in *The Chicago Manual of Style* (CMS). Each scientific discipline has its own format, usually available in a style manual produced by the discipline's scholarly organization. Many academic disciplines encourage using in-text citations rather than footnotes.

The examples that follow use four different citation styles. For the specifics of each style, you should consult an official style manual, because the rules for citation vary for different sources. For example, books are cited differently from articles, which are cited differently from email correspondence. You will need to consult a style manual to determine the proper format for each source.

Example 1: Literary Studies (MLA)

The MLA requires a parenthetical citation in the body of the text that corresponds to an entry in the Works Cited at the end of the paper. A citation for a quotation from a **book** in the MLA style is formatted this way:

As Frank Lentricchia argues, *The Waste Land* should not be understood as a logical sequence of events, but as "an intellectual and emotional complex grasped in an instant of time" (194).

The parenthetical citation "(194)" refers to a page number from a book by Frank Lentricchia. Publication information about the book would be found in the Works Cited section, where it would be formatted this way:

Lentricchia, Frank. *Modernist Quartet*. New York: Cambridge UP, 1994.

Example 2: Psychology (APA)

The APA also requires parenthetical citations in the body of the text, though these citations typically include the author and the date. A citation for a summary of an **article** in the APA style is formatted this way:

Studies that examine links between cardiovascular and mental activity must understand that cardiovascular activity itself comprises a suite of variables (Van Roon, Mulder, Althaus, & Mulder, 2004).

The parenthetical citation "(Van Roon, Mulder, Althaus, & Mulder, 2004)" refers to an **article** by the four listed co-authors. Publication information about the article would be found in the reference section, where it would be formatted this way:

Van Roon, A., Mulder, L., Althaus, M., & Mulder, G. (2004). Introducing a baroflex model for studying cardiovascular effects of mental workload. *Psychophysiology, 41*, 961–981.

Example 3: History (CMS)

CMS, or "Chicago," is a style in which citations are presented in footnotes. A citation for a quotation from a **book** in the Chicago style is formatted this way:

Nineteenth-century bohemians were more dependent on mainstream culture than might at first appear. As one scholar puts it, "Bohemia's self-designated types always existed in symbiotic relation to bourgeois culture rather than in opposition to it."[1]

The footnote[1] refers to a note at the bottom of the page containing full publication information and formatted as follows:

1. Christine Stansell, *American Moderns: Bohemian New York and the Creation of a New Century* (New York: Henry Holt and Co., 2000), 18.

Example 4: Biology

Citation styles in math, science, and engineering tend to vary from journal to journal. Immediately following a quotation or a reference to the text, the author might name the source or use a superscript number such as [13] or a parenthetical number such as (13) to indicate the number of the article in the final list of references. The journal *Nature Genetics* uses the following format for **articles**, and the references are listed numerically rather than alphabetically:

13. Herron, B.J. *et al.* Efficient generation and mapping of recessive developmental mutations using ENU mutagenesis. *Nat. Genet.* 30, 185–189 (2002).

Example 5: IEEE

All citation styles are established to give readers immediate information about sources cited and paraphrased in the text. In IEEE citations, the references should be numbered in the order they appear in the text. When referring to a reference in the text of the document, place the number of the reference in brackets.

The IEEE citation style has three main features:
1. The author's name is first name (or initial) and, then, last name.
2. The title of an article chapter, conference paper, or patent is in quotation marks.
3. The title of the journal, paper, or book is in italics.

G. Pevere. "Infrared Nation." *The International Journal of Infrared Design*, vol. 33, pp. 56-99, Jan. 1979.

Example 6: AMA
Text Citations

"Each reference should be cited in the text, tables, or figures in consecutive numerical order [as presented in the text] by means of superscript Arabic numerals."[1]

"Authors should always consult the primary source and should never cite a reference that they themselves have not read."[1]

Iverson C, Christiansen S, Flanagan A, et al. *American Medical Association Manual of Style*. 10th ed. New York, NY: Oxford University Press, 2007.

Iverson C, Flanagin A, Fontanarosa PB, et al., for the American Medical Association. *American Medical Association Manual of Style: A Guide for Authors and Editors*. 9th ed. Baltimore, MD: Lippincott Williams & Wilkins, 1997.

Electronic Sources

An electronic source is any source that is in electronic form and is accessed through electronic means. Websites, online periodicals, online books, emails and postings, and even CD-ROMs are all forms of electronic sources. Be careful: not all materials found through electronic means are necessarily electronic sources. For example, if a PDF of an article you found through a database on the library's website was originally published in a printed journal, then the article does not qualify as an electronic source. There is a difference between electronic sources and sources that are accessed electronically.

When citing an online source, your citation should contain the following elements:
- The author or editor (if available)
- The title of the text (if different from the name of the website)
- The name of the website
- The name of the site's sponsor or associated institution or organization
- The date you accessed the site
- The electronic address (URL)

For example, a short work posted on a website would be formatted in MLA style as follows:

> McCort, Dennis. "Kafka and the Coincidence of Opposites." *Romantic Circles Praxis Series: Romanticism and Buddhism.* Feb. 2007. Romantic Circles. 21 Apr. 2008 <*www.rc.umd.edu/praxis/ buddhism/mccort/mccort.html*>.

This citation includes not only the author's name and the work's title, but other important information such as the date of publication on the website (February 2007) and the date the website was accessed (21 April 2008).

Published guides of the MLA, APA, and Chicago styles include detailed descriptions of how to cite most electronic sources.

Recommended Style Manuals

For complete coverage of MLA, APA, and Chicago citation styles, you should obtain the most recent edition of each style's official manual: *MLA Handbook for Writers of Research Papers* (7th edition, 2009), the *Publication Manual of the American Psychological Association* (6th edition, 2009), and *The Chicago Manual of Style* (16th edition, 2010).

Acknowledgements

Acknowledgments are a simple expression of gratitude for the support, inspiration, and any assistance received by you throughout the research and writing process. It should include your professors, associates, guides, benefactors, universities, and/or anyone who helped you with the research. The acknowledgement is generally a short paragraph placed either in the beginning of the paper or towards the end of the paper, i.e., before the references.

Contributors who did not coauthor a research should also be listed in the acknowledgements. Hence, the people who may be acknowledged include people who provided technical help or assistance in writing. Apart from the people supporting the research, any form of financial and material support, including grants, should also be acknowledged in this section. Similarly, people who may have contributed material to the paper but whose contributions do not justify authorship may be listed and their function or contribution described.

The acknowledgements section forms a very small portion of the research paper. It consists of a single sentence to a short paragraph not exceeding 5–7 lines.

Five elements are seen in a research paper, although not always, and should be considered when writing this section.

1. **Introduction**: Introduce the acknowledgements section by thanking everyone who was directly related to your research or writing process, not coauthors. For example, "The authors would like to thank all colleagues and students who contributed to this study."
2. **Earlier versions and acknowledging copyrights** (*seen only in papers that are reprinted in other journals/books*): Include an acknowledgement for any previous publication or presentation of the paper.
3. **Thank people**: Begin by thanking all the people who
   - helped in data collection and analysis;
   - reviewed and commented on an early draft of the paper;
   - provided permissions to use and refer to materials;
   - contributed to the research;
   - collaborated, assisted, and provided constructive criticisms for an earlier version of the paper (during preliminary investigations and with recording and transcription);
   - provided helpful comments on the paper;
   - are professors who taught the subject and motivated the research in the field;
   - and, finally, those who suggested on ways to enhance the paper and the reviewers.
4. **Thank the beneficiaries**: Thank all those who supported the research financially, such as grants received. For example, "This paper was supported by the Psychological Science Research and Analysis Association, grant no. 6 R12 HL134952-13A2."
5. **Disclaimers (optional)**: This part of the section is optional and states any disclaimer that the author wishes to include, for example, "The errors idiocies and inconsistencies remain my own."

Common Writing Errors and Their Corrections

I. Using "et al." in Citations and Hyphenating Words

The abbreviation "et al." stands for "et alia," indicating "and others" in citations. If you cite one author in your text, it should be "Smith." Two authors: "Smith and Jones." Three or more authors: "Smith et al." For three authors you can also write, "Smith, Jones, and Thomson." Note that "et al." does not have a period after "et," but has one after "al."

Original

Smith, Jones, et al.

Modified

Smith et al.

II. Hyphenation

"*We built a high-performance system.*" "High-performance" is hyphenated because "high" modifies "performance" not "system." It is not a "high system." Here, "high-performance" is an adjective. In the statement, "*Our system has high performance*", "performance" is a noun modified by an adjective ("high"); therefore, no hyphen is necessary.

Original

This application is critical to the *high tech* industry.

Modified

This application is critical to the *high-tech* industry.

Punctuation Point

Adverbs

Most students use adverbs of frequency without difficulty. Adverbs of frequency include the following: *sometimes, often, never, seldom, rarely, occasionally,* and *always.* However, students rarely use adverbs of manner in their writing. Adverbs of manner describe *how* an action was performed, such as *rapidly, carefully, manually,* and *thoroughly.* Positioning the adverb of manner varies. However, the following two rules clarify when these adverbs should be used.

1. **Position the adverb in front of the verb or behind the object of the verb.**

    The President *reluctantly* signed the law that would lower taxes.

2. **Do not put the adverb in front of the verb if the object phrase is short.**

    The Minister of Education responded to the crisis *rapidly*.

    Most of the representatives signed the contract *enthusiastically*.

Instead of using these adverbs of manner, students often create unnecessarily wordy prepositional phrases. Here are some examples with revisions:

Example
The doctor performed the procedure in a thorough manner.

Revised
The doctor performed the procedure *thoroughly*.

Example

Parents who believe in home-schooling often teach their kids in an inadequate way.

Revised

Parents who believe in home-schooling often teach their kids *inadequately*.

Few students can perfect prepositional usage because it can be inconsistent at times. However, anything that can eliminate preposition problems should be used. Many papers do not include even one adverb of manner. Adverbs of manner are a writer's friends. Students should use them more often.

The Writing Process

Do you think of yourself as a writer? Or are you just a graduate student who must write to finish your degree, get published, get a job, keep your job, or get promoted in your job? It might help if you start to think and act like a writer.

Here is how:

It is simple. You must write all the time, every day. Or you can also think, worry, read, talk, take notes, cry, organize your materials, worry, buy a new desk, complain, sharpen your pencils, cry, wash your dishes, worry, eat a snack . . . but this is not writing. You must write every day.

You need to want to write—not to finish, or publish, or get a job, or receive approval or affection or recognition—but to write. You must think, "I really want to write today and will create opportunities to do it, rather than avoiding opportunities to write. I am writing today to write. I am writing today because I want to write." All you have to do is write. You do not have to finish, or meet a deadline or goal. You just have to write. It will make you feel better. Do not wait until you are ready. Do not wait until everything else is finished. Do not wait until you are well-rested. Do not wait until you have read every book or article on a topic. You will never be finished with these things. You will never do these things. If you wait, you will never write, or be a writer. Writers write every day.

Writing is difficult. Chances are that there is nothing wrong with you if you find writing a challenge. Even the very best writers say it is difficult. Many famous writers also find writing difficult. Therefore, do not stop writing when you find it challenging.

Write at least 15 minutes a day. Find what works best for you. Write in the morning or at night. Write on your laptop, on paper, or on your arm. Writing every day allows you to continually generate ideas you need to write. Your mind will function differently when you write every day. We all think about our writing every day, but the creative processes involved in writing are different from those involved in thinking. Your projects will move forward when you write, even for a small amount of time, every day.

Tips for Journal Submission

I. Cite Your Own Papers

A paper is considered "important" if it is cited 30 times or more by other scholars. Cite your own related papers if they were published in a high-level journal. Others may look up your other papers and cite them. However, do not cite yourself too much. If you have a good reputation, citing yourself can be useful because the reviewer may find out that it is your paper. However, do not cite your own unpublished papers or publications in low-level journals. The editor and reviewer may think that your current paper should also be published in those journals. Do not cite your thesis, as this will tell your reviewer that you are inexperienced. Do not cite someone else's thesis. The reviewer will conclude that you are referring to yourself or a close friend, both of whom are inexperienced.

II. Your Paper Should Not Exceed 25 Pages

As the length of the paper increases, the probability of acceptance decreases. Reviewers are more likely to find something wrong in a long paper. With longer papers, you are more likely to make mathematical errors, and the chance that a reviewer will think you made a mistake increases. You are also more likely to write something that will offend reviewers.

Inappropriate Vocabulary and Improvements

definite and definitive
Definite means "certain or sure," whereas *definitive* means "decisive and with authority."

discreet and discrete
Discreet means "careful not to attract attention or give offense," whereas *discrete* means "separate, distinct."

envelop and envelope
Envelop, without an "e" at the end, means "wrap up, cover, or surround completely," whereas an *envelope* (with an e) is a paper container used to enclose a letter or document.

exceptionable and exceptional
Exceptionable means "open to objection; causing disapproval or offense," whereas
exceptional means "not typical" or "unusually good."

forego and forgo
Forego means "precede," but is also a less common spelling for *forgo*, which means "go without."

imply and infer
Imply is used with a speaker as its subject, as in "He implied that the general was a liar," and indicates that the speaker is suggesting something though not making an explicit statement. *Infer* is used in sentences such as "We inferred from his words that the general was a liar," and indicates that something in the speaker's words allowed the listeners to determine that the man was a liar. The speaker *implies*, the listener *infers*.

Academic Vocabulary

Headwords	Other Words in the Family
source	sourced, sources, sourcing
specific	specifically, specification, specifications, specificity, specifics
specify	specifiable, specified, specifies, specifying, unspecified
sphere	spheres, spherical, spherically
stable	instability, stabilization, stabilize, stabilized, stabilizes, stabilizing, stability, unstable
statistic	statistician, statisticians, statistical, statistically, statistics
strategy	strategic, strategies, strategically, strategist, strategists
stress	stressed, stresses, stressful, stressing, unstressed
structure	restructure, restructured, restructures, restructuring, structural, structurally, structured, structures, structuring, unstructured
style	styled, styles, styling, stylish, stylize, stylized, stylizes, stylizing
submit	submission, submissions, submits, submitted, submitting
subordinate	subordinates, subordination
subsequent	subsequently
subsidy	subsidiary, subsidies, subsidize, subsidized, subsidizes, subsidizing
substitute	substituted, substitutes, substituting, substitution
successor	succession, successions, successive, successively, successors
sufficient	sufficiency, insufficient, insufficiently, sufficiently
sum	summation, summed, summing, sums
summary	summaries, summarize, summarized, summarizes, summarizing, summarization, summarizations
supplement	supplementary, supplemented, supplementing, supplements
survey	surveyed, surveying, surveys
survive	survival, survived, survives, surviving, survivor, survivors
suspend	suspended, suspending, suspends, suspension

续表

Headwords	Other Words in the Family
sustain	sustainable, sustainability, sustained, sustaining, sustains, sustenance, unsustainable
symbol	symbolic, symbolically, symbolize, symbolizes, symbolized, symbolizing, symbolism, symbols
task	tasks
team	teamed, teaming, teams
technique	techniques
technology	technological, technologically
temporary	temporarily
tense	tension, tensely, tenser, tensest, tensions

VIII WRITING THE COVER LETTER TO THE EDITOR

Chapter 16
How Can We Write a Cover Letter to the Editor?

How to Write the Cover Letter to the Editor of an Academic Journal

Completing an article for an academic journal is an impressive accomplishment, but it is not the last. You still have to write a cover letter to accompany it. Your cover letter should be what your journal article is about. Convince the editor that his or her readers will benefit from reading it, and demonstrate your professional expertise on the topic. This may sound like a lot of ground to cover in one letter, but you can do it effectively by following a sensible plan of action that includes a call to action for your article. To simplify this process further, we have listed the steps that should be considered when writing a cover letter.

Step 1

Direct your cover letter to the proper editor. Even a name on a website can be obsolete, so call the journal to confirm the person's name and title so that you can address the person in your letter accordingly.

Step 2

Begin the cover letter with your name and contact information at the top of your letter, either aligned to the left or center. You may or may not wish to include your residential address, but be sure to include either your email address, phone number, or both so that the editor can contact you.

Step 3

Open your letter with a statement or question that represents the essential point or finding of your journal article. In addition, you need to address the uniqueness of your paper and the difference it would make in your field of study. When doing this, strive for a balance between enthusiasm and professionalism.

Step 4

Reveal other key elements of the journal article in the second paragraph. You would want to include, for scientific research, the number of participants included in your research, the name of the institute, and crucially, what your findings would contribute for academia. Include important information about your article in this paragraph, including its title. But refrain from making this paragraph too long.

Step 5

Proceed to explain why your article would be of interest to readers of the academic journal. This is where you should demonstrate that you have read on the journal's readership and interests. This is done to not only to impress the editor of the journal, but also to prove that your article is suitable for the publication. Here, you can refer to the predominant readers of the journal and how your findings might help them improve the quality of their instruction for students.

Step 6

Cite your credentials with confidence. They might include your educational background, teaching experience, and any previous publication credits. Be specific and include the exact names of the courses you have taught and at which institutions. Similarly, include the titles of your previous works, the names of the journals in which they were published and the dates of publication, if any.

Step 7

Reveal your enthusiasm for your article and your conviction in its worth. You can also display confidence of your article's influence on the readers of the journal, and reinforce its effectiveness and contribution.

Step 8

Close your letter by offering to answer any questions the editor might have. Do not forget to thank the editor for his or her time and consideration.

Step 9

Proofread your letter to ensure that there are no spelling and editing errors. These nine steps will help you arrange a short yet effective cover letter, which will help you take one step closer to getting your article published. To add to these steps, there are a few points that need to be considered when writing a cover letter.

Determine Your Target Journal's Requirements

Before you begin, check your target journal's author instructions for any cover letter requirements, such as certain specifically worded statements. No matter what else you decide to include, always make sure that your cover letter contains any required information and statements described in your target journal's author instructions.

Develop an Outline for the Cover Letter

In addition to any information and statements required by your target journal, every cover letter should contain the following elements:

1. An introduction stating the title of the manuscript and the journal to which you are submitting.
2. The reason why your study is important and relevant to the journal's readership or field.
3. The question your research answers.
4. Your major experimental results and overall findings.
5. The most important conclusions that can be drawn from your research.
6. A statement that the manuscript has not been published and is not under consideration for publication in any other journal.
7. A statement that all authors approved the manuscript and its submission to the journal.
8. Any other details that will encourage the editor to send your manuscript for review.

Write one or more sentences to address each of these points. You will revise and polish these sentences to complete your cover letter.

Revise the Cover Letter

Read through your cover letter to proofread and revise the text for clarity. Remove any vague sentences that do not directly relate to the purpose, major results, and most important findings and conclusions of your study. Rewrite any sentences that are very long or are cluttered with lots of details.

Cover letters should not exceed one page unless absolutely necessary. If you write a cover letter that is longer than one page, think about how it can be made concise. As you revise the cover letter, proofread for the same basic grammar and construction issues you would look for when revising your manuscript.

- Eliminate unnecessary or redundant phrases like "in order to" and "may have the potential to."
- Make sure the letter is written in plain English. Remove any

jargon and define all abbreviations at first use.
- Proofread for spelling and grammar errors.

During your review, read the cover letter at least once to ensure you avoid the following:

- Statements that exaggerate or overstate results.
- Conclusions that are not supported by the data reported in the manuscript.
- Sentences repeated word-for-word from the manuscript text.
- Too many technical details.

Always complete a final check to confirm that your cover letter includes all elements required by your target journal.

Sample Cover Letter

Dear Dr. [Editor],

Thank you for encouraging me, at the [conference name], to submit the enclosed article, [article title], for possible publication in [journal name]. I believe this paper reflects the type of research that would interest your readers, because you regularly publish relevant scholarship on [your topic].

I am the sole author of this 8,000-word article, which has not been published before in any form and is not under submission to any other journal or publisher.

In this article, I argue that . . . (*objective*). While investigating . . . (*method*), I found that . . . (*results*). Based on . . . (*findings*), I identified . . . (*results*). After discussing these issues . . . (*implications*), I suggest how . . . (*applications*).

I have included a photocopy of a potential illustration, which is the only material for which I would need permission. I look forward to hearing from you.

Sincerely,

[Your Name]

(Referral Belcher)

Example Cover Letter

Dear Dr. Eisenstein:

Thank you for encouraging me, at the Murinae Conference this year, to submit the enclosed article, "White rats of Taiwan," for possible publication in *White Rat Journal*. I believe this type of research would interest your readers because you regularly publish influential scholarship on white rats. I am the sole author of this 7,200-word article, which has not been published before in any form and is not under submission to any other journal or publisher.

In this article, I argue that *(objective)* Taiwanese white rats are useful to the environment. While investigating *(methods)* the impact of the white rat on Taiwan's environment, I found that *(results)* these rats were instrumental in other types of pest control. Based on this finding, I identified several ways that these white rats can be used to address other pest control concerns.

After discussing *(implications)* these issues, I suggest *(applications)* how other environments could use these rats for greater pest control purposes.

I have included three copies of my paper for submission. I look forward to hearing from you.

Sincerely,

Stanley Wong
Associate Professor
Kenting University
swong@gmail.com

Common Writing Errors and Their Corrections

The comma tells the reader to pause, just like a yellow traffic light. Below are four general ways to use commas.

I. Between Items in a List

When you are listing three or more items in a sentence, simply place a comma between each item of the list. Here are two examples:

> Mr. Chen used the money that he won from the sweepstakes to buy a house, a car, and a small yacht.

> We will purchase the stock if the price falls to $30 per share, if we are allowed to buy a block of over 10,000 shares, and if we receive a guarantee that no new shares will be created in the next fiscal year.

The commas above show where one item of the list finishes and the next one begins. A conjunction (*and*, *but*, *or*) does the same thing as a comma: it marks the place between two items in the set.

II. Between Two Sentences

You can connect two sentences with a comma and conjunction (such as *and* or *but*). Here are the examples:

> The Thomson Corporation has just acquired the Johnson company, *and* it has agreed to sell Johnson's oil-drilling rights in Texas as soon as possible.

The above sentence is made up of two sentences joined with a comma and conjunction.

| The Thomson Corporation has just acquired the Johnson company. | and | It has agreed to sell Johnson's oil-drilling rights in Texas as soon as possible. |

More examples:

I knew that the price of IBM stock would increase after it entered the home computer market, *but* I had no idea that the price would skyrocket.

I first conducted a thorough audit of the company, *and* I then interviewed the manager to try to determine how much money was missing.

You may also use a conjunction without complete sentences on either side. In this case, you do *not* need a comma. For example, you could easily rewrite the above sentences so that one part of each sentence is not a full sentence:

The Thomson Corporation has just acquired the Johnson company *and* has agreed to sell Johnson's oil-drilling rights in Texas as soon as possible.

I knew the price of IBM stock would increase after it entered the home computer market *but* had no idea that the price would skyrocket.

I first conducted a thorough audit of the company *and* then interviewed the manager to try to determine how much money was missing.

Because the above examples do not have full sentences on both sides of the conjunction, there is no need to include a comma.

III. To Attach Words to the Front or Back of Your Sentence

Most sentences consist of a short core sentence accompanied by additional details. Frequently, we add information to sentences by attaching one or more words to the front or back of the core sentence. Here are three examples:

> Curiously, the second experiment yielded an identical result.

> Regardless of supposed biases, comparative statements can be credible and informative.

> Weight variability has been proven to increase cardiovascular mortality rates, despite inconsistencies in relevant literature.

If you examine the sentences above, you will see where the writer has attached words to the front or back of each core sentence. When you add one word, such as "curiously" in the first example, you show your reader where the core sentence begins.

IV. On Both Sides of a Nonessential Component

When writing, you will often insert a group of words into the middle of a sentence. This group of words may or may not need to be separated by commas from the rest of the sentence. To determine whether you need commas, you must determine if the added words are *necessary* to the meaning of the sentence or whether they provide extra detail. If a component group of words is added to a sentence but does not affect the *meaning* of the sentence when it is removed, then that component is not necessary.

To inform a reader that a group of words is a nonessential component, place commas in front of and behind the group of words. However, if deleting the group of words would largely change the meaning of the sentence, then those words are *not* a component, but are *essential* to the meaning of the sentence. In that case, you would not want to put commas on either side of the component so that the reader knows that those words are important to the meaning of the sentence. For example, look at the following sentences:

> Ms. Johnson, who is the company president, will present the award at our annual dinner.

> Banks that hold over a billion dollars in assets are uncommon.

In the first sentence, the information about Johnson being the company president has no connection to the main idea of the sentence: She will present the awards at the annual dinner. Because this information is added or *extra*, let the reader know it is a component by placing commas on either side of it. By contrast, the second sentence contains information that is absolutely essentialto the meaning of the sentence: "that hold over a billion dollars in assets." If you were to place commas around these words, you would be telling the reader that the words are a nonessential component. For example, look at this sentence:

Banks, that hold over a billion dollars in assets, are uncommon.

This sentence tells the reader that the main idea is that "banks are uncommon." Certainly, banks are not uncommon, but by incorrectly using commas, you have stated that they are.

When proofreading, remember to check your sentences for essential and nonessential components.

Commas are one of the most commonly used elements in writing. Understanding their use is critical to being an effective writer.

Original

However far too little attention has been paid to balancing X and Y.

Modified

However, far too little attention has been paid to balancing X and Y.

Original

In addition no research has been found that surveyed X's effect on Y.

Modified

In addition, no research has been found that surveyed X's effect on Y.

Original

The experimental data are rather controversial and there is no general agreement about interpretation.

Modified

The experimental data are rather controversial, and there is no general agreement about interpretation.

Punctuation Point

How to Use Affect and Effect in Scholarly Writing

Affect and *effect* are very frequently misused, even by native speakers of English. This is understandable because they each have a noun and verb form with unrelated meanings; there is only a one letter difference between the two, and they even sound alike when spoken. Although they appear highly similar and are thus easily confused, using one in place of the other radically changes the meaning of a sentence, or, more often, renders it nonsensical.

Outlining a general rule is an appropriate place to start when learning to differentiate between the two: *affect* is more often used as a verb, and *effect* is more often used as a noun. *Affect* as a verb means to influence something or cause it to change.

- Tooth movement is *affected* by chewing.
- The materials used in geopolymers *affect* the microstructure of the gel.
- Antidepressants did not *affect* the risk of epilepsy.
- The stock price is *affected* by local factors.

Effect as a noun means the consequence or result of something.

- We investigated the *effects* of deposition potential.
- Treatment to overcome the toxic *effect* is critical.
- The release of carbon dioxide causes the greenhouse *effect*.
- We examined the mediating *effect* of corporate governance.

These are the most typical uses of these two words. A simple mnemonic device to help recall which is which is RAVEN: "Remember! Affect = Verb, Effect = Noun." Of course, it is imperative to keep in mind that this is only a general guide to the most common usage; *affect* does have a less common noun form, and *effect* has a less common verb form, and these are vital to academic writing in particular.

Affect as a noun is a psychological term meaning the appearance of a feeling or emotion in a person. This term is used to acknowledge the fact that it is impossible to know how another person feels. If you are writing in a psychological or psychiatric domain, or if your writing involves emotions in general, *affect* as a noun may be required. Typical examples of this usage would be "Affect is crucial in theatrical performances" or "The psychologist observed the patient's affect."

Effect as a verb means to produce a result or to cause something to occur. Common synonyms for *effect* as a verb are "to implement" and "to bring about"; if it is possible to substitute these words without changing the meaning of a sentence, *effect* as a verb is appropriate. Examples of this usage would be "Firing staff was intended to *effect* savings" or "The strategy *effected* wide distribution of information."

The most common and confusing misuses of *affect* and *effect* occur in sentences where both can make grammatical sense. The most frequently appearing instance of such confusion is perhaps best represented by the following phrases:

(a) *Affect* a change
(b) *Effect* a change

Whereas both make grammatical sense, the meaning of (a) is unlikely to be intended; to alter the manner in which a change is occurring. Much more probable is (b), which simply means to cause a change to occur.

The Writing Process

Prepare a Perfect Title Page and Abstract

The title page should contain complete contact information about the author and paper:

- Title of the article
- Author's name
- Academic degrees
- Address of university or institute
- Name of the person for correspondence
- Postal address
- Telephone and fax numbers
- Email address
- Word count

If you move, give your new address to the editorial office. If updating a paper, give the current date. Do *not* mention when a paper was first written and when it was revised. If the editor knows how often the paper has been rejected, he may conclude that it should be rejected again. If the reviewer finds out that the paper has been rejected more than once, he is more likely to recommend rejection again. Also, include the word count of the paper on the title page.

The abstract and the paper should be prepared together. The abstract should appear on the second page of the paper. This way, if the editor removes the title page, the abstract will still reach the reviewer.

Eliminate English errors in the title page and the abstract. If there is an error, it is a sign of carelessness. Of course, you have to check the spelling for the entire paper, and you should do that every time you revise the paper.

Tips for Journal Submission

I. Do Not Get Angry When You Are ejected

Do not think about ways to get even with the reviewers or editors if you are rejected. Your energy would be focused on a useless and painful goal. Writing a letter to argue with the editor rarely changes his or her decision. The editor already has many complaints. One more complaint is not likely to change the editor's decision. The reviewers will also defend their opinions, even if they made mistakes. When a reviewer successfully defends the report to the editor, you lose respect for future papers. Write only if it is a simple issue. For example, argue that there is no mathematical error, contrary to the report. Instead of trying to prove that the reviewer is wrong on several points, explain why you might deserve a second or third opinion.

II. Do Not Attack Reviewers

Generally, it is not a good idea to attack reviewers. Avoid saying bad things about them. Although they may not have a favorable opinion of your paper, they took the time to read it. Do not say: "The reviewer's idea is bad, but mine is good." It would be better to say, "the reviewer has an interesting idea, but the proposed idea is also good, particularly because of this fact." If the reviewer makes a good point, and you can almost always find conditions under which the reviewer's points are true, explain why you are not using his approach in your paper.

III. Follow Up by Email if Your Paper Is Being Reviewed Late

Most journals will respond to your submission within three to six months. Some journals specify their average time for submission review on the website. If you have not heard back and you are curious about the status of your submission, sending a brief email is appropriate. Be sure to include your name, the title of your paper, and the date it was sent.

If you follow these tips, you will increase your chances of success with busy editors. Your cover letter is your first impression: be sure it is professional, accurate, convincing, and brief.

IV. A Few Basics About Letters to the Reviewer

The process of submitting a paper to an academic journal can be complicated, involving multiple revisions and various interactions with journal editors and reviewers. After the effort exerted to complete your research and draft a paper in a foreign language, responding to reviewers can become particularly daunting. We receive numerous such response letters every day and would like to share a few tips for formulating effective responses.

Responding to reviewers often involves composing a formal cover letter; if this is not required, make sure that you include a basic introductory paragraph that states how you have responded to the reviewer feedback. For example, "we have addressed your concerns point-by-point in the attached document" or "our responses to your comments are italicized below." Make sure that you consistently apply whatever guidelines are established here. We often receive response letters in which the author states specific comments are in bold or highlighted, but no such formatting is applied.

The introductory section is the perfect place to thank reviewers, stating how grateful you are for their time, effort, and expertise; however, many (if not most) authors tend to over-thank reviewers. If you convey your thanks at the beginning of the paper, it does not need to be restated after each reviewer comment. "Thank you for the comment" becomes redundant when applied 20 times in a document, particularly in response to superficial suggestions. For example, responding to "please correct the spelling of 'equation' on p. 6" with "Thank you for this valuable comment" is silly at best, but could be construed as unnecessary flattery.

Personal pronouns can be used when responding to reviewers and the present perfect tense is typically applied: "we have revised this sentence as follows," "we have corrected the typo," or "we have included an additional citation on p. 2." In this case, the present perfect tense indicates that an action was completed in the past, but continues to affect the present, indicating that the revision is a work in progress. When addressing minor problems, inserting a simple "please see the revised version of the manuscript" is often appropriate.

Font effects can be prudently applied to organize your response. The difference between the reviewer comment and your relevant response should be explicit and you may wish apply bold, italics, or a non-black text color to the reviewer section. Avoid organizing your response as a single large block of text that merges with the reviewer comments. We sometimes receive letters in which it is difficult to distinguish whose comments are whose. Although this is clear to you as the author, journal reviewers read numerous papers and may forget their own suggestions over time; your primary goal should be to ensure that no excessive effort is required on their part.

Although your data and revisions ultimately determine whether your paper is accepted, the response letter can be used to impress. If a clean, concise, and organized response is drafted, reviewers and editors will assume that the same effort has been exerted on the work. Showing your professionalism can only improve your chances of getting your work published.

Inappropriate Vocabulary and Improvements

censure and censor
To *censure* means "to express strong disapproval of," whereas *to censor* means "to suppress unacceptable parts of such media as a book or film."

climactic and climatic
Climactic describes the "forming of a climax," whereas *climatic* means "relating to climate."

complacent and complaisant
Complacent means "self-satisfied," whereas *complaisant* means "willing to please."

complement and compliment
To complement means "to enhance something by contributing extra features," whereas *to compliment* means "to express praise" or "politely congratulate."

continuous and continual
Continuous primarily means "without interruption," and can refer to space as well as time, as in "The cliffs form a continuous line along the coast." *Continual*, by contrast, typically means "happening frequently, with intervals between," as in "The bus service has been disrupted by continual breakdowns."

council and counsel
A *council* is an administrative or advisory group, whereas *to counsel* means to offer advice or guidance.

Academic Vocabulary

Headwords	Other Words in the Family
terminate	terminal, terminals, terminated, terminates, terminating, termination, terminations
text	texts, textual
theme	themes, thematic, thematically
theory	theoretical, theoretically, theories, theorist, theorists
thesis	theses
topic	topical, topics
trace	traceable, traced, traces, tracing
tradition	nontraditional, traditional, traditionalist, traditionally, traditions
transfer	transferable, transference, transferred, transferring, transfers
transform	transformation, transformations, transformed, transforming, transforms
transit	transited, transiting, transition, transitional, transitions, transitory, transits
transmit	transmission, transmissions, transmitted, transmitting, transmits
transport	transportation, transported, transporter, transporters, transporting, transports
trend	trends
trigger	triggered, triggering, triggers
ultimate	ultimately
undergo	undergoes, undergoing, undergone, underwent
underlie	underlay, underlies, underlying
undertake	undertaken, undertakes, undertaking, undertook
uniform	uniformity, uniformly
unify	unification, unified, unifies, unifying
unique	uniquely, uniqueness
utilize	utilization, utilized, utilizes, utilizing, utilizer, utilizers, utility, utilities
valid	invalidate, invalidity, validate, validated, validating, validation, validity, validly
vary	invariable, invariably, variability, variable, variables, variably, variance, variant, variants, variation, variations, varied, varies, varying
vehicle	vehicles

续表

Headwords	Other Words in the Family
version	versions
violate	violated, violates, violating, violation, violations
virtual	virtually
visible	visibility, visibly, invisible, invisibility
vision	visions
visual	visualize, visualized, visualizing, visualization, visually
volume	volumes, vol.
voluntary	voluntarily, volunteer, volunteering, volunteered, volunteers

References

I want to thank the authors of the following resources for providing information that was helpful writing this book.

BOOKS

On Writing Well, 30th Anniversary Edition: The Classic Guide to Writing Nonfiction by William Zinsser, Collins; 30th Anv edition, 2006.

Technical Writing by John M. Lannon; 6th edition

How to Write and Illustrate a Scientific Paper by Bjorn Gustavii, Cambridge University Press; 2nd edition, 2008.

How to Write a Lot: A Practical Guide to Productive Academic Writing by Paul J. Silva, American Psychological Association; 1st edition, 2007.

How to Write and Publish Engineering Papers and Reports by Herbert B. Michaelson; 2nd edition

The Scientist's Handbook for Writing Papers and Dissertations by Antoinette M. Wilkinson

From Research to Manuscript: A Guide to Scientific Writing by Michael Jay Katz. Springer; 2nd ed., 2009.

The Elements of Style by William Strunk Jr, E.B White, Longman; 4th edition (August 2, 1999).

Advanced Copyediting Practice for Chinese Technical Writers by Ted Knoy

Technical Writing and Professional Communication for Nonnative Speakers of English by Thomas N. Huckin and Leslie A. Olsen; International edition

How to Write and Publish a Scientific Paper by Robert A. Day, 4th edition

Writing Up Research: Experimental Research Report Writing for Students of English by Robert Weissberg and Suzanne Buker

A Handbook for Technical Communication by Jacqueline K. Neufeld

Writing Your Journal Article in Twelve Weeks by Wendy Laura Belcher

Highest-Impact Journal in 1987, Eos Trans. AGU, 70, 658, 1989 by Dagan, G.

Garfield, E., Citation Comments, Current Contents, 25, 3-8, June 20, 1994.

Institute for Scientific Information, Journal Citation Reports, Institute for Science Information, Philadelphia, Pa., 1991-1996.

McDonnell, J. Comparing the Hydrology Journals, Eos, Trans. AGU, 78 (20), p. 210, 1997.

WEBSITES

Explorations of Style
A Blog about Academic Writing
http://explorationsofstyle.com/

About Writing an Academic Paper
http://www.utoronto.ca/writing/advise.html

Practical Academic Writing Resources
Central European University – Great general resources for writing
http://web.ceu.hu/writing/sfaccess.html

How to Publish a Paper
http://www.csee.wvu.edu/~mvalenti/HowToPublishPaper.html

How to Publish Your Journal Paper
http://www.apa.org/monitor/sep02/publish.html

Purdue's Online Writing Lab
http://owl.english.purdue.edu/owl/

Punctuation Made Simple
http://lilt.ilstu.edu/golson/punctuation/

Academic Writing Tips
http://homepages.inf.ed.ac.uk/jbednar/writingtips.html

Great Academic Writing Reference for Students
http://www.dartmouth.edu/~writing/materials/student

Academic Sentence Structures
http://www.phrasebank.manchester.ac.uk/

Review of International Economics
http://www.roie.org/

Citation and Style Manuals
www.lib.vt.edu/find/citation/index.html

A Guide to Writing Different Parts of a Paper
http://writing.colostate.edu/guides/documents/abstract/index.cfm

How to Write in an Academic Style
http://abacus.bates.edu/~ganderso/biology/resources/writing/HTWtoc.html

IEEE Author Guidelines
http://www.ieee.org/web/publications/authors/transjnl/index.html

IEEE Guide to Journal Preparation
www.ieee.org/portal/cms_docs/transactions/TRANS-JOUR.pdf

List of all IEEE Journals and Publications
www.ieee.org/publications_standards/publications/periodicals/new_titles.html

Which IEEE Journal Would Be Right for My Research?
www.ieee.org/web/publications/journmag/newperiodicals.html

北京大学出版社教育出版中心

部分重点图书

一、北大高等教育文库·大学之道丛书

大学的理念	［英］亨利·纽曼 著
德国古典大学观及其对中国的影响（第三版）	陈洪捷 著
哈佛，谁说了算	［美］理查德·布瑞德利 著
美国大学之魂（第二版）	［美］乔治·M. 马斯登 著
大学理念重审：与纽曼对话	［美］雅罗斯拉夫·帕利坎 著
什么是博雅教育	［美］布鲁斯·金博尔 著
美国文理学院的兴衰——凯尼恩学院纪实	［美］P. E. 克鲁格
营利性大学的崛起	［美］理查德·鲁克 著
学术部落及其领地：当代学术界生态揭秘（第二版）	［英］托尼·比彻等 著
大学如何应对市场化压力	［美］埃里克·古尔德 著
美国现代大学的崛起（第二版）	［美］劳伦斯·维赛 著
大学的逻辑（第三版）	张维迎 著
我的科大十年（续集）	孔宪铎 著
教育的终结——大学何以放弃了对人生意义的追求	［美］安东尼·克龙曼 著
欧洲大学的历史	［美］威利斯·鲁迪 著
美国高等教育简史	［美］约翰·赛林 著
哈佛通识教育红皮书	［美］哈佛委员会 著
知识社会中的大学	［美］杰勒德·德兰迪 著
高等教育理念	［美］罗纳德·巴尼特 著
知识与金钱——研究型大学与市场的悖论	［美］理查德·布瑞德雷 著
美国大学时代的学术自由	［美］罗杰·盖格 著
高等教育何以为"高"——牛津导师制教学反思	［英］大卫·帕尔菲曼 主编
美国高等教育通史	［美］亚瑟·科恩 著
现代大学及其图新	［英］谢尔顿·罗斯布莱特 著
印度理工学院的精英们	［印度］桑迪潘·德布 著
麻省理工学院如何追求卓越	［美］查尔斯·韦斯特 著
后现代大学来临？	［英］安东尼·史密斯 弗兰克·韦伯斯特 主编
高等教育的未来	［美］弗兰克·纽曼 著
学术资本主义	［美］希拉·斯劳特等 著
美国公立大学的未来	［美］詹姆斯·杜德斯达等 著
21世纪的大学	［美］詹姆斯·杜德斯达 著
理性捍卫大学	眭依凡 著
美国高等教育质量认证与评估	［美］美国中部州高等教育委员会 编
大学之用（第五版）	［美］克拉克·克尔 著

废墟中的大学	[加拿大] 比尔·雷丁斯 著
高等教育市场化的底线	[美] 大卫·L. 科伯 著
世界一流大学的管理之道——大学管理决策与高等教育研究	程星 著
美国的大学治理	[美] 罗纳德·G. 艾伦伯格 编

二、21世纪高校教师职业发展读本

美国大学如何培养研究生	[美] 唐纳德·吴尔夫 著
给大学新教员的建议（第二版）	[美] 罗伯特·博伊斯 著
学术界的生存智慧	[美] 约翰·达利等 著
如何成为卓越的大学教师	[美] 肯·贝恩 著
给研究生导师的建议	[英] 萨拉·德兰蒙特等 著
如何提高学生学习质量	[英] 迈克尔·普洛瑟等 著

三、高等教育与全球化丛书

激流中的高等教育：国际化变革与发展	[加拿大] 简·奈特 著
全球化与大学的回应	[美] 简·柯里 著
高等教育变革的国际趋势	[美] 菲利普·阿特巴赫 著
高等教育全球化：理论与政策	[英] 皮特·斯科特 著
发展中国家的高等教育：环境变迁与大学的回应	[美] 戴维·查普曼
	安·奥斯汀 主编

四、北京大学研究生学术规范与创新能力建设丛书

法律实证研究方法（第二版）	白建军
学位论文撰写与参考文献著录规范	段明莲
传播学定性研究方法	李琨
生命科学论文写作指南	白青云
学位论文写作与学术规范	肖东发、李武
学术训练与学术规范——中国古代史研究入门	荣新江

五、其他好书

向史上最伟大的导师学习	[美] 罗纳德·格罗斯 著
未来的学校：变革的目标与路径	[英] 路易斯·斯托尔等 著
美国大学的通识教育：美国心灵的攀登	黄坤锦 著
中国博士质量报告	中国博士质量分析课题组 著
博士质量：概念、评价与趋势	陈洪捷等 著
中国博士发展状况	蔡学军 范巍等 著
教学的魅力：北大名师谈教学（第一辑）	郭九苓 编著
科研道德：倡导负责行为	美国医学科学院、
	美国科学三院国家科研委员会 撰
国立西南联合大学校史（修订版）	西南联合大学北京校友会 编
我读天下无字书	丁学良 著
大学与学术	韩水法 著
大学何为	陈平原 著
科学的旅程	[美] 雷·斯潘根贝格
	[美] 黛安娜·莫泽 著